UPGRADING
AND
REPAIRING PCs
FIELD GUIDE

Scott Mueller and Mark Soper

Upgrading and Repairing PCs Field Guide

Copyright © 2002 by Que

International Standard Book Number: 0-7897-2694-7

Library of Congress Catalog Card Number: 2001096307

Printed in the United States of America

First Printing: October 2001

04   03   02   4   3   2

Trademarks

Warning and Disclaimer

Associate Publisher
Greg Wiegand

Executive Editor
Rick Kughen

Acquisitions Editor
Rick Kughen

Managing Editor
Thomas F. Hayes

Project Editor
Tricia S. Liebig

Copy Editor
Krista Hansing

Technical Editor
Mark Reddin

Proofreader
Kelly Ramsey

Indexer
Ginny Bess

Interior Designer
Kevin Spear

Cover Designer
Ann Jones

Page Layout
Ayanna Lacey

Contents

About the Authors

Scott Mueller is president of Mueller Technical Research, an international research and corporate training firm. Since 1982, MTR has specialized in the industry's most in-depth, accurate, and effective corporate PC hardware and technical training seminars, maintaining a client list that includes Fortune 500 companies, the U.S. government and foreign governments, major software and hardware corporations, as well as PC enthusiasts and entrepreneurs. His seminars have been presented to several thousands of PC support professionals throughout the world.

Scott has developed and presented training courses in all areas of PC hardware and software. He is an expert in PC hardware, operating systems, and data-recovery techniques. He currently spends about 20–25 weeks per year on the road teaching his seminars at several corporate clients. For more information about a custom PC hardware or data-recovery training seminar for your organization, contact Lynn at

>   Mueller Technical Research
>
>   21 Spring Lane
>
>   Barrington Hills, IL 60010-9009
>
>   (847) 854-6794
>
>   (847) 854-6795 Fax
>
>   Internet: scottmueller@compuserve.com
>
>   Web: http://www.upgradingandrepairingpcs.com
>
>   http://www.m-tr.com

Scott has many popular books, articles, and course materials to his credit, including *Upgrading and Repairing PCs*, which has sold more than two million copies, making it by far the most popular PC hardware book on the market today.

If you have suggestions for the next version of the book, or any comments about the book in general, send them to Scott via email at scottmueller@compuserve.com, or visit www. upgradingandrepairingpcs.com and click the Ask Scott button.

When he is not working on PC-related books or on the road teaching seminars, Scott can usually be found in the garage working on several projects. This year he continues to work on his customized '99 Harley FLHRCI Road King Classic with a 95ci Twin-Cam motor (see you in Sturgis <g>), as well as a modified 1998 5.9L Grand Cherokee (imagine a hotrod SUV).

Mark Edward Soper is president of Select Systems and Associates, Inc., a technical writing and training organization.

Mark has taught computer troubleshooting and other technical subjects to thousands of students from Maine to Hawaii since 1992. He is an A+ Certified hardware technician and a Microsoft Certified Professional. He has been writing technical documents since the mid-1980s and has contributed to many other Que books, including *Upgrading and Repairing PCs, 11th, 12th*, and *13th Editions; Upgrading and Repairing Networks, Second Edition; Special Edition Using Microsoft Windows Millennium Edition; Special Edition Using Microsoft Windows XP Home Edition;* and *Special Edition Using Microsoft Windows XP Professional Edition.* Mark coauthored both the first and second editions of *Upgrading and Repairing PCs, Technician's Portable Reference* and *Upgrading and Repairing PCs: A+ Study Certification Guide, Second Edition.* He is the author of *The Complete Idiot's Guide to High-Speed Internet Connections* and coauthor of *TechTV's Upgrading Your PC.*

Mark has been writing for major computer magazines since 1990, with more than 140 articles in publications such as *SmartComputing, PCNovice, PCNovice Guides,* and the *PCNovice Learning Series.* His early work was published in *WordPerfect Magazine, The WordPerfectionist,* and *PCToday.* Many of Mark's articles are available in back issues or electronically via the World Wide Web at www.smartcomputing.com. Select Systems maintains a subject index of all Mark's articles at http://www.selectsystems.com.

Mark welcomes comments at mesoper@selectsystems.com.

About the Technical Editor

Mark Reddin is president of Trinity Microsystems, Inc., a computer reseller and repair center in Indiana. He is a Microsoft Certified Systems Engineer (MCSE) and A+ Certified PC technician who has enjoyed using computers, as well as breaking and fixing them, since the days of the early Commodore and Atari machines. Mark still enjoys being involved with computers and networks at a hands-on level and can often be found in the trenches, configuring hardware and running cables. He has been involved with several Que publications, providing technical verification as well as development. You can reach him through the contacts page at www.trinitymicrosystems.com.

Dedication

For Edward, Ian, and Jeremy—who love to see what's inside the box.—Mark Soper

Acknowledgments

Mark wants to thank Scott Mueller, whose *Upgrading and Repairing PCs* series has made an amazing difference in his knowledge of PCs and in his work life; Rick Kughen and the rest of the gang at Que; whose support, guidance, and encouragement have been terrific; Mark Reddin, for his expert technical comments; and Cheryl, for reminding him what's most important in life and eternity.

Tell Us What You Think!

As the reader of this book, *you* are our most important critic and commentator. We value your opinion and want to know what we're doing right, what we could do better, what areas you'd like to see us publish in, and any other words of wisdom you're willing to pass our way.

As an associate publisher for Que, I welcome your comments. You can fax, e-mail, or write me directly to let me know what you did or didn't like about this book—as well as what we can do to make our books stronger.

Please note that I cannot help you with technical problems related to the topic of this book, and that due to the high volume of mail I receive, I might not be able to reply to every message.

When you write, please be sure to include this book's title and author as well as your name and phone or fax number. I will carefully review your comments and share them with the author and editors who worked on the book.

Fax: 317-581-4666

E-mail: feedback@quepublishing.com

Mail: Greg Wiegand
                Que
                201 West 103rd Street
                Indianapolis, IN 46290 USA

Introduction

If you're a computer repair technician or student, you know just how crucial it is to have concise, yet detailed technical specifications at your fingertips. It can mean the success or failure of your job.

Unfortunately, most detailed hardware books are far too large to tote around in a briefcase, in a book bag, or in your back pocket—where you need them.

Upgrading and Repairing PCs: Field Guide is the exception. This concise book provides just the information you need to upgrade or repair your PC, without weighing you down. And it contains more hands-on, from-the-trenches information than you will find in most heavy-duty PC hardware tomes.

Although you should consider this book to be a companion to Scott Mueller's best-selling opus, *Upgrading and Repairing PCs*, you'll also find that it stands quite well on its own. While much of the information is in the mother book, much of what is found here is presented in a boiled-down, easy-to-digest reference that will help you get the job done quickly and efficiently. You'll also find that this portable reference contains some information not found in the main book—information that is specially geared to help the technician in the field.

I recommend that you keep *Upgrading and Repairing PCs, 13th Edition* (ISBN: 0-7897-2542-8) on your desk or workbench and *Upgrading and Repairing PCs: Field Guide* with your toolkit so that it's ready to go with you anytime—whether it's to a customer job site or a class.

Chapter 1

General Technical Reference

PC Subsystem Components Quick Reference

Table 1.1 lists the major PC subsystems and how they are configured. Use this table as a shortcut to the most likely place(s) to look for problems with these subsystems. Then go to the appropriate chapter for more information.

Table 1.1   Major PC Subsystems

Subsystem	Components	How Controlled and Configured	Where Located or How Attached	See Chapters for Details
Motherboard	CPU, RAM, BIOS, expansion slots, RTC/NVRAM, battery	Jumper or BIOS configuration (CPU), BIOS configuration (all others)	Inside case	2, 3
Standard I/O ports	Serial (COM)	BIOS and operating system	Rear of motherboard or add-on card	3, 6
	Parallel (LPT)	BIOS and operating system	Rear of motherboard or add-on card	3, 6
	USB	BIOS and OS drivers	Rear of motherboard, front of case or add-on card	3, 7
	PS/2 mouse	MB jumper blocks, BIOS and OS drivers	Rear of motherboard	3, 8
	Keyboard	BIOS and OS drivers	Rear of motherboard	3, 8
Optional I/O ports	IEEE-1394	Mfr. drivers, OS drivers, and BIOS	Add-on card or rear of motherboard	3, 7
	Analog (dial-up) modem	Mfr. drivers, OS drivers, jumper blocks on add-on card, BIOS	Add-on card or AMR/CMR riser card or connected to external COM or USB ports	6
	Sound	OS drivers, BIOS, jumper blocks on add-on card	Motherboard based or add-on card, or AMR/CMR riser card	10
	SCSI	OS drivers, add-on card BIOS, add-on card switches, BIOS	Add-on card or motherboard connectors	4
Input devices	Mouse, trackball, touchpad, keyboard	Mfr. drivers, OS drivers, BIOS	Connected to USB, PS/2, or COM ports	8
		OS drivers, BIOS	Connected to USB or PS/2 ports	8
Standard mass storage	Floppy	OS drivers, BIOS	Motherboard floppy interface	5
	IDE	OS drivers, BIOS	Motherboard IDE interface	4

Table 1.1 Major PC Subsystems Continued

Subsystem	Components	How Controlled and Configured	Where Located or How Attached	See Chapters for Details
Removable media mass storage	CD-ROM, DVD-ROM	OS drivers, BIOS	Motherboard IDE interface, SCSI, IEEE-1394, or USB ports	4
	CD-RW, writeable DVD drives	OS drivers, BIOS, application drivers	Motherboard IDE interface, SCSI, IEEE-1394, or USB ports	4
	SuperDisk, Jaz, Zip, Orb, Peerless	Mfr. drivers, OS drivers, BIOS	IDE, SCSI, USB, IEEE-1394, LPT port (varies with device)	4
	Tape backup	Mfr. drivers, OS drivers, application drivers	IDE, SCSI, USB, IEEE-1394, LPT port (varies with device)	4
Display	Video card or integrated video	Mfr. drivers, (advanced features), BIOS (basic features)	AGP or PCI slot	9
	Monitor	Mfr. drivers, OS drivers	VGA or DVI port on rear of motherboard, or add-on video card	9
Power supply	Power supply	Autoselects voltage or uses sliding switch on rear of unit; some BIOS might display voltage levels	Rear of case or top rear of case	2

The Motherboard and Its Components

Figure 1.1 shows a typical motherboard, with its major components labeled as it would appear before installation in a system.

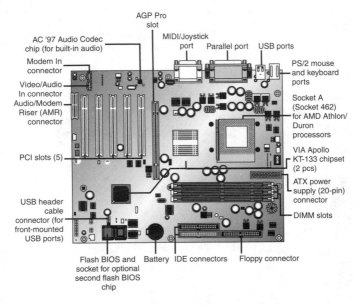

Figure 1.1   A typical ATX motherboard (overhead view).

Figure 1.2 shows the ports on a typical ATX motherboard as they would be seen from the rear of the system. Motherboards without integrated video often have a second serial port in place of VGA, and motherboards without integrated Ethernet or audio omit those ports.

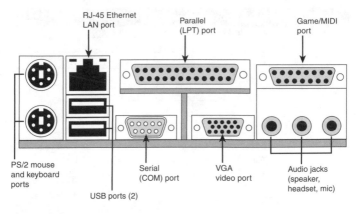

Figure 1.2   Ports on the rear of a typical ATX motherboard, with integrated audio and LAN ports.

Understanding Bits and Bytes

The foundation of all memory and disk size calculations is the *byte*. When storing plain-text data, a byte equals one character.

Data also can be stored or transmitted in portions of a byte. A *bit* equals 1/8 of a byte—or, in other words, a byte equals 8 bits. Keep the difference between bits and bytes in mind as you review the table of standard capacity abbreviations and meanings.

When bits and bytes are used as part of some other measurement, the difference between bits and bytes is often distinguished by the use of a lower- or uppercase *B*. For example, megabits are typically abbreviated with a lowercase *b*, resulting in the abbreviation Mbps for megabits per second, whereas MBps indicates megabytes per second.

Standard Capacity Abbreviations and Meanings

Use the following table to translate megabytes, gigabytes, and the other abbreviations used to refer to memory and disk space into their decimal or binary values.

The industry-standard abbreviations for the units used to measure the capacity of magnetic (and other) drives are shown in Table 1.2.

Table 1.2	Standard Abbreviations and Meanings		
Abbreviation	**Description**	**Power**	**Value**
K	Kilo	10^3	1000
Ki*	Kibi	2^{10}	1024
M	Mega	10^6	1,000,000
Mi*	Mebi	2^{20}	1,048,576
G	Giga	10^9	1,000,000,000
Gi*	Gibi	2^{30}	1,073,741,824
T	Tera	10^{12}	1,000,000,000,000
Ti*	Tebi	2^{40}	1,099,511,627,776
P	Peta	10^{15}	1,000,000,000,000,000
Pi*	Pebi	2^{50}	1,125,899,906,842,624

Table Note: These prefixes and meanings were standardized by the International Electrotechnical Commission (IEC) in December 1998 but are not yet widespread.

According to the new prefix standard, 1 mebibyte (1MiB = 2^{20}B = 1,048,576B). This is the same value formerly referred to by some as a binary megabyte. One megabyte (1MB = 10^6B = 1,000,000B); this value was previously called by some a decimal megabyte. However, M or MB may refer to either decimal millions or binary mebibytes. Similarly, G or GB may refer to either decimal billions or binary gibibytes.

In general, memory values are expressed by using the binary values, although disk capacities can go either way. This often leads to confusion in reporting disk capacities because many manufacturers tend to use whichever value makes their products look better. For example, drive capacities are often rated in decimal billions (G—Giga), while most BIOS chips and operating system utilities such as Windows' Fdisk rate the same drive in binary gigabytes (Gi—Gibi).

Glossary of Essential Terms

Table 1.3	Terms and Their Definitions
Term	**Definition**
ACPI	Advanced configuration and power interface. Power management for all types of computer devices.
AGP	Accelerated graphics port developed by Intel. A fast dedicated slot interface between the video adapter or chipset and the motherboard chipset North Bridge. AGP is 32 bits wide, runs at 66MHz, and can transfer 1, 2, or 4 bits per cycle (1*x*, 2*x*, and 4*x* modes).
APM	Advanced power management. Power management for hard drives and monitors.
ATA	AT attachment (also called IDE). A storage interface used on PCs since the late 1980s. The 40-pin interface used on most hard drives, CD-ROMs, and other internal storage devices.

Table 1.3 Terms and Their Definitions Continued	
Term	**Definition**
ATAPI	AT attachment-packet interface. Modified version of IDE that supports removable media and optical drives that use software drivers. Can coexist on the same cable with ATA hard drives.
Beep code	A series of one or more beeps used by the system BIOS to report errors. Beep codes vary by BIOS brand and version.
BIOS	Basic input/output system. A collection of drivers used to interface the operating system to the hardware.
Cluster	The minimum disk space actually used by a file when it is stored. Also called an *allocation unit*. This size increases with larger drives due to the limitations of the FAT size.
Color depth	How many colors a video card can display at a given resolution. The higher the resolution is, the more RAM is required to display a given color depth.
COM	Communication port. Also called *serial* port.
Combo slot	A pair of slots that share a single card bracket. Also called a *shared slot*. Only one of the two slots can be used at a time.
Compact flash	A type of flash memory device.
CPU	Central processing unit. The "brains" of a computer.
CRT	Cathode-ray tube. Conventional TV-like picture tube display technology used on most desktop monitors.
Data bus	The connection that transmits data between the processor and the rest of the system. The width of the data bus defines the number of data bits that can be moved in to or out of the processor in one cycle.
DCC	Direct cable connection. Windows 9*x*/Me/2000 program that enables computers to link up through parallel or serial ports. Windows NT 4.0 supports serial port linkups only.
Device Manager	Part of the System Properties sheet for Windows 9*x*/2000/Me/XP that enables you to view, change the configuration of, and remove system and add-on devices and drivers.
DFP	Digital flat panel. An early digital monitor standard replaced by DVI.
DIMM	Dual inline memory module. Leading type of memory device from late 1990s to present. Current versions have 168 edge connectors.
DMA	Direct memory access. Data transfer method used by some devices to bypass the CPU and go directly to and from memory. Some ISA devices require the use of a specific DMA channel.
DNS	Domain name system. Matches IP addresses to Web site and Web server names.
DPMS	Display Power Management Standard. The original power management standard for monitors.

Table 1.3   Terms and Their Definitions Continued

Term	Definition
Drive geometry	Combination of heads, sectors per track, and cylinders used to define an IDE drive in the system BIOS CMOS setup program. When a drive is moved to another system, the same drive geometry and translation settings must be used to enable the new system to read data from the drive.
DVD	Digital versatile disc. The emerging standard for home video and also a popular add-on for computers.
DVI	Digital video interface. The current digital monitor standard.
ECC	Error-correcting code. A method of error correction. A type of system memory or cache that is capable of detecting and correcting some types of memory errors without interrupting processing. ECC requires parity-checked memory plus an ECC-compatible motherboard with ECC enabled.
EISA	Enhanced Industry Standard Architecture. A 32-bit version of ISA developed in 1989 and found primarily in older servers. It is obsolete but can be used for ISA cards.
FAT	File allocation table. On-disk directory that lists filenames, sizes, and locations of all clusters in a file. The size of the FAT limits the size of the drive.
FAT-16	16-bit FAT supported by MS-DOS and Windows 95/95 OSR 1.*x*. The drive letter is limited to 2.1GB.
FAT-32	32-bit FAT supported by Windows 95 OSR 2.*x*/98/Me. The drive letter is limited to 2.1TB.
FCC ID	Identification number placed on all computer hardware to certify approval by the Federal Communications Commission. Use this number to locate drivers for some boards.
Firmware	"Software on a chip." General term for BIOS code on motherboards and in devices such as modems, printers, and others.
Flash BIOS	BIOS/firmware on systems or devices that can be updated through software.
Flash memory	Memory device whose contents can be changed electrically but which doesn't require electrical power to retain its contents. Used in digital cameras and portable music players.
HomePNA	Home Phoneline Networking Alliance. A trade group that develops standards for networking over telephone lines within a home or small office.
Host-based	A type of printer in which the computer processes the image data. These printers are cheaper but less versatile than those containing a page-description or printer command language.
Hub	Device that accepts multiple connections, such as USB, 10BASE-T, and 10/100 or Fast Ethernet hubs.
I/O port	Input/output port. Used to communicate to and from motherboard or add-on devices. All devices require one or more I/O port address ranges, which must be unique to each device.

Table 1.3   Terms and Their Definitions Continued

Term	Definition
ICS	Internet connection sharing. A feature on Windows 98SE, Windows 2000, and Windows Me that enables one computer to share its Internet connection with other Windows computers, including Win95 and Win98 original versions.
IDE	Integrated Drive Electronics. More properly called the *AT Attachment* interface. See the earlier "ATA" entry.
IEEE-1284	A series of parallel-port standards that include EPP and ECP high-speed bidirectional modes.
IEEE-1394	Also called *i.Link* and *FireWire*. A high-speed, direct-connect interface for high-performance digital video, storage, and scanning devices.
IPX/SPX	Standard protocols used on NetWare 3.*x*/4.*x* networks.
IRQ	Interrupt request line. Used by devices to request attention from the CPU.
ISA	Industry Standard Architecture, also called the AT-bus. A slot standard developed by IBM in 1981 for 8-bit cards and enhanced by IBM in 1984 for 16-bit cards. It is now obsolete, although some systems still have one or two on board.
KDE	K Desktop Environment, a popular GUI for Linux.
LAN	Local area network.
LBA	Logical block addressing; a BIOS-based method of addressing sectors on a hard drive to overcome the 8.4GB limit imposed by cylinder head sector (CHS) addressing. Can also be implemented by add-on cards or software drivers (not recommended).
LCD	Liquid crystal display. Flat-panel display technology used on notebook and advanced desktop computers.
Legacy	Non–plug-and-play (PnP) card. Also can refer to serial and parallel ports.
Local bus	A series of high-speed slot standards (VL-Bus, PCI, and AGP) for video that bypass the slow ISA bus.
Loopback	A method of testing ports that involves sending data out and receiving data back through the same port. It is implemented with loopback plugs that loop send lines back to receive lines.
LPT	Line printer port. Also called *parallel* port.
LS-120	A 3.5-inch drive and disk made by Imation (originally 3M) with 120MB capacity. Also called *SuperDisk*. The drive also can read/write/format standard 1.44MB 3.5-inch media.
MCA	Micro Channel Architecture. A 16/32-bit slot standard developed by IBM in 1987 for its PS/2 models. It never became popular outside IBM circles and now is obsolete and incompatible with any other standard.
Memory bank	Amount of memory (in bits) equal to the system bus of a specific CPU. The number of memory modules to achieve a memory bank on a given system varies with the CPU and the memory types that the system can use.

Table 1.3   Terms and Their Definitions Continued

Term	Definition
Memory stick	A type of flash memory device developed by Sony for use in its camera and electronic products.
Mwave	A series of IBM-made digital signal processor chips that combine sound and modem functions.
NetBEUI	Microsoft version of NetBIOS network protocol. Can be used for small, nonroutable workgroup networks.
NIC	Network interface card. Connects the computer to a local area network (LAN).
Parity	A method of error checking in which an extra bit is sent to the receiving device to indicate whether an even or an odd number of binary 1 bits was transmitted. The receiving unit compares the received information with this bit and can obtain a reasonable judgment about the validity of the character. Parity checking was used with many early memory chips and SIMMs, but it is now used primarily in modem and serial port configuration.
Parity error	An error displayed when a parity check of memory reveals that incorrect values were stored.
PC Card	Current term for former PCMCIA Card standard used in notebook computers.
PC/AT	Systems using an 80286 or better CPU. These have a 16-bit or wider data bus.
PC/XT	Systems using an 8088 or 8086 CPU. These have an 8-bit data bus.
PCI	Peripheral Component Interconnect. A 32/64-bit slot standard developed by Intel in 1992. The 32-bit version is used in all PCs from mid-1990s onward for most add-on cards. The 64-bit version is found in some servers.
PCL	Printer Control Language. A series of printer control commands and routines used by Hewlett-Packard on its LaserJet printers.
PCMCIA	Personal Computer Memory Card International Association, original term for what are now called *PC Cards*. These primarily are used in notebook computers. Some use the term "PCMCIA/PC Card" to avoid confusion with regular add-on cards for desktop computers.
PDL	Page Description Language. General term for any set of printer commands, such as PCL or PostScript.
Peer server	Computer that can be used as a client and that also shares printers, folders, and drives with other users.
PIO	Programmed input/output. A series of IDE data-transfer rates that enable faster data throughput. Both the drive and the interface must support the same PIO mode for safety.
PnP	Plug-and-play. The combination of add-on device, BIOS, and operating system (OS) that enables the OS to detect, install software for, and configure the device. PnP is supported by Windows 9x/Me/2000/XP.

Term	Definition
Table 1.3	**Terms and Their Definitions Continued**
POST	Power-on self-test. A test performed by the system BIOS during system startup.
PostScript	Adobe's sophisticated printer language used in laser and inkjet printers designed for graphic arts professionals.
QIC	Quarter-Inch Committee. The standards body responsible for tape drive standards used by many PC clients and small network servers.
QIC-EX	Extra-capacity cartridges developed for some QIC, QIC-Wide, and Travan drives by Verbatim.
Register size	Number of bits of data that the CPU can process in a single operation.
Resolution	Combination of horizontal and vertical pixels in an image. Larger monitors support higher resolutions.
ROM BIOS	Read-only memory BIOS. A chip or chips on the motherboard or adapter cards containing BIOS drivers and code needed to start or boot the system.
RS-232	Diverse serial port standard with many different device-specific pinouts. Supports both 9-pin and 25-pin ports.
Scan codes	Hexadecimal codes transmitted by the keyboard when keys are struck. Must be converted to ASCII for display onscreen.
SCSI	Small computer system interface. A family of high-performance interfaces used on high-speed hard drives, optical drives, scanners, and other internal and external devices. Each device must have a unique ID number.
SIMM	Single Inline Memory Module. Common type of memory device from late 1980s to mid-1990s. Can have 30 or 72 edge connectors.
SmartMedia	A type of flash memory device.
SoundBlaster	Creative Labs' longtime family of sound cards. The *de facto* standard for DOS-based audio.
TCP/IP	Transmission Control Protocol/Internet Protocol. The protocol of the World Wide Web and the Internet.
Travan	A family of tape drives and media developed from QIC and QIC-Wide standards by Imation (originally 3M).
UART	Universal Asynchronous Receive/Transmit chip. The heart of a serial port or hardware-based modem.
UDMA	Ultra DMA. A series of IDE data transfer rates that use DMA for even faster performance. Most effective when combined with bus-mastering hard disk host adapter driver software.
USB	Universal Serial Bus. A high-speed, hub-based interface for pointing, printing, and scanning devices.
UTP	Unshielded twisted-pair cable, such as Category 5 used with 10/100 Ethernet.
V.90	Current 56Kbps high-speed, dial-up modem standard. Replaced x2 and K56flex.

Table 1.3 Terms and Their Definitions Continued

Term	Definition
V.92	New version of V.90. Supports call waiting and faster uploading.
VESA	Video Electronic Standards Association. Trade group of monitor and video card makers that develops various display and power management standards.
VGA	Video graphics array. A family of analog display standards that support 16 or more colors and 640 × 480 or higher resolutions.
VL-Bus	VESA Local-Bus. A slot standard based on ISA that added a 32-bit connector to ISA slots in some 486 and early Pentium models. It is obsolete but can be used for ISA cards.
Windows keys	Keys beyond the normal keyboard's 101 keys that perform special tasks in Windows 9x/NT4/2000/Me/XP.
WINS	Windows Internet Naming Service. Matches IP addresses to computers on a Windows network.
x86	All processors that are compatible with Intel CPUs from the original 8088 through the newest Pentium 4s and Celerons. Can refer to both Intel and non-Intel (AMD, VIA/Cyrix) CPUs that run x86 instructions.

Hexadecimal/ASCII Conversions

Use Table 1.4 to look up the various representations for any character that you see onscreen or that you want to insert into a document. You can use the Alt+keypad numbers to insert any character into an ASCII document that you create with a program such as Windows Notepad or MS-DOS's Edit.

Table 1.4 Hexadecimal/ASCII Conversions

Dec	Hex	Octal	Binary	Name	Character
0	00	000	0000 0000	blank	
1	01	001	0000 0001	happy face	☺
2	02	002	0000 0010	inverse happy face	☻
3	03	003	0000 0011	heart	♥
4	04	004	0000 0100	diamond	♦
5	05	005	0000 0101	club	♣
6	06	006	0000 0110	spade	♠
7	07	007	0000 0111	bullet	•
8	08	010	0000 1000	inverse bullet	◘
9	09	011	0000 1001	circle	o
10	0A	012	0000 1010	inverse circle	○
11	0B	013	0000 1011	male sign	♂

Dec	Hex	Octal	Binary	Name	Character
12	0C	014	0000 1100	female sign	♀
13	0D	015	0000 1101	single note	♪
14	0E	016	0000 1110	double note	♫
15	0F	017	0000 1111	sun	☼
16	10	020	0001 0000	right triangle	►
17	11	021	0001 0001	left triangle	◄
18	12	022	0001 0010	up/down arrow	↕
19	13	023	0001 0011	double exclamation	‼
20	14	024	0001 0100	paragraph sign	¶
21	15	025	0001 0101	section sign	§
22	16	026	0001 0110	rectangular bullet	■
23	17	027	0001 0111	up/down to line	↨
24	18	030	0001 1000	up arrow	↑
25	19	031	0001 1001	down arrow	↓
26	1A	032	0001 1010	right arrow	→
27	1B	033	0001 1011	left arrow	←
28	1C	034	0001 1100	lower left box	∟
29	1D	035	0001 1101	left/right arrow	↔
30	1E	036	0001 1110	up triangle	▲
31	1F	037	0001 1111	down triangle	▼
32	20	040	0010 0000	space	Space
33	21	041	0010 0001	exclamation point	!
34	22	042	0010 0010	quotation mark	"
35	23	043	0010 0011	number sign	#
36	24	044	0010 0100	dollar sign	$
37	25	045	0010 0101	percent sign	%
38	26	046	0010 0110	ampersand	&
39	27	047	0010 0111	apostrophe	'
40	28	050	0010 1000	opening parenthesis	(
41	29	051	0010 1001	closing parenthesis	)
42	2A	052	0010 1010	asterisk	*
43	2B	053	0010 1011	plus sign	+
44	2C	054	0010 1100	comma	,
45	2D	055	0010 1101	hyphen or minus sign	-
46	2E	056	0010 1110	period	.
47	2F	057	0010 1111	slash	/
48	30	060	0011 0000	zero	0

Table 1.4   Hexadecimal/ASCII Conversions Continued

Table 1.4	Hexadecimal/ASCII Conversions Continued				
Dec	Hex	Octal	Binary	Name	Character
49	31	061	0011 0001	one	1
50	32	062	0011 0010	two	2
51	33	063	0011 0011	three	3
52	34	064	0011 0100	four	4
53	35	065	0011 0101	five	5
54	36	066	0011 0110	six	6
55	37	067	0011 0111	seven	7
56	38	070	0011 1000	eight	8
57	39	071	0011 1001	nine	9
58	3A	072	0011 1010	colon	:
59	3B	073	0011 1011	semicolon	;
60	3C	074	0011 1100	less-than sign	<
61	3D	075	0011 1101	equal sign	=
62	3E	076	0011 1110	greater-than sign	>
63	3F	077	0011 1111	question mark	?
64	40	100	0100 0000	at sign	@
65	41	101	0100 0001	capital A	A
66	42	102	0100 0010	capital B	B
67	43	103	0100 0011	capital C	C
68	44	104	0100 0100	capital D	D
69	45	105	0100 0101	capital E	E
70	46	106	0100 0110	capital F	F
71	47	107	0100 0111	capital G	G
72	48	110	0100 1000	capital H	H
73	49	111	0100 1001	capital I	I
74	4A	112	0100 1010	capital J	J
75	4B	113	0100 1011	capital K	K
76	4C	114	0100 1100	capital L	L
77	4D	115	0100 1101	capital M	M
78	4E	116	0100 1110	capital N	N
79	4F	117	0100 1111	capital O	O
80	50	120	0101 0000	capital P	P
81	51	121	0101 0001	capital Q	Q
82	52	122	0101 0010	capital R	R
83	53	123	0101 0011	capital S	S
84	54	124	0101 0100	capital T	T
85	55	125	0101 0101	capital U	U

Table 1.4	Hexadecimal/ASCII Conversions Continued				
Dec	**Hex**	**Octal**	**Binary**	**Name**	**Character**
86	56	126	0101 0110	capital V	V
87	57	127	0101 0111	capital W	W
88	58	130	0101 1000	capital X	X
89	59	131	0101 1001	capital Y	Y
90	5A	132	0101 1010	capital Z	Z
91	5B	133	0101 1011	opening bracket	[
92	5C	134	0101 1100	backward slash	\
93	5D	135	0101 1101	closing bracket	]
94	5E	136	0101 1110	caret	^
95	5F	137	0101 1111	underscore	_
96	60	140	0110 0000	grave	`
97	61	141	0110 0001	lowercase A	a
98	62	142	0110 0010	lowercase B	b
99	63	143	0110 0011	lowercase C	c
100	64	144	0110 0100	lowercase D	d
101	65	145	0110 0101	lowercase E	e
102	66	146	0110 0110	lowercase F	f
103	67	147	0110 0111	lowercase G	g
104	68	150	0110 1000	lowercase H	h
105	69	151	0110 1001	lowercase I	i
106	6A	152	0110 1010	lowercase J	j
107	6B	153	0110 1011	lowercase K	k
108	6C	154	0110 1100	lowercase L	l
109	6D	155	0110 1101	lowercase M	m
110	6E	156	0110 1110	lowercase N	n
111	6F	157	0110 1111	lowercase O	o
112	70	160	0111 0000	lowercase P	p
113	71	161	0111 0001	lowercase Q	q
114	72	162	0111 0010	lowercase R	r
115	73	163	0111 0011	lowercase S	s
116	74	164	0111 0100	lowercase T	t
117	75	165	0111 0101	lowercase U	u
118	76	166	0111 0110	lowercase V	v
119	77	167	0111 0111	lowercase W	w
120	78	170	0111 1000	lowercase X	x
121	79	171	0111 1001	lowercase Y	y
122	7A	172	0111 1010	lowercase Z	z

Table 1.4		Hexadecimal/ASCII Conversions Continued			
Dec	Hex	Octal	Binary	Name	Character
123	7B	173	0111 1011	opening brace	{
124	7C	174	0111 1100	vertical line	|
125	7D	175	0111 1101	closing brace	}
126	7E	176	0111 1110	tilde	~
127	7F	177	0111 1111	small house	⌂
128	80	200	1000 0000	C cedilla	Ç
129	81	201	1000 0001	u umlaut	ü
130	82	202	1000 0010	e acute	é
131	83	203	1000 0011	a circumflex	â
132	84	204	1000 0100	a umlaut	ä
133	85	205	1000 0101	a grave	à
134	86	206	1000 0110	a ring	å
135	87	207	1000 0111	c cedilla	ç
136	88	210	1000 1000	e circumflex	ê
137	89	211	1000 1001	e umlaut	ë
138	8A	212	1000 1010	e grave	è
139	8B	213	1000 1011	I umlaut	ï
140	8C	214	1000 1100	I circumflex	î
141	8D	215	1000 1101	I grave	ì
142	8E	216	1000 1110	A umlaut	Ä
143	8F	217	1000 1111	A ring	Å
144	90	220	1001 0000	E acute	É
145	91	221	1001 0001	ae ligature	æ
146	92	222	1001 0010	AE ligature	Æ
147	93	223	1001 0011	o circumflex	ô
148	94	224	1001 0100	o umlaut	ö
149	95	225	1001 0101	o grave	ò
150	96	226	1001 0110	u circumflex	û
151	97	227	1001 0111	u grave	ù
152	98	230	1001 1000	y umlaut	ÿ
153	99	231	1001 1001	O umlaut	Ö
154	9A	232	1001 1010	U umlaut	Ü
155	9B	233	1001 1011	cent sign	¢
156	9C	234	1001 1100	pound sign	£
157	9D	235	1001 1101	yen sign	¥
158	9E	236	1001 1110	Pt	₧
159	9F	237	1001 1111	function	ƒ

Table 1.4   Hexadecimal/ASCII Conversions Continued

Dec	Hex	Octal	Binary	Name	Character
160	A0	240	1010 0000	a acute	á
161	A1	241	1010 0001	I acute	í
162	A2	242	1010 0010	o acute	ó
163	A3	243	1010 0011	u acute	ú
164	A4	244	1010 0100	n tilde	ñ
165	A5	245	1010 0101	N tilde	Ñ
166	A6	246	1010 0110	a macron	ā
167	A7	247	1010 0111	o macron	ō
168	A8	250	1010 1000	opening question mark	¿
169	A9	251	1010 1001	upper-left box	⌐
170	AA	252	1010 1010	upper-right box	¬
171	AB	253	1010 1011	1/2	$^1/_2$
172	AC	254	1010 1100	1/4	$^1/_4$
173	AD	255	1010 1101	opening exclamation	¡
174	AE	256	1010 1110	opening guillemets	«
175	AF	257	1010 1111	closing guillemets	»
176	B0	260	1011 0000	light block	░
177	B1	261	1011 0001	medium block	▒
178	B2	262	1011 0010	dark block	▓
179	B3	263	1011 0011	single vertical	│
180	B4	264	1011 0100	single right junction	┤
181	B5	265	1011 0101	2 to 1 right junction	╡
182	B6	266	1011 0110	1 to 2 right junction	╢
183	B7	267	1011 0111	1 to 2 upper-right	╖
184	B8	270	1011 1000	2 to 1 upper-right	╕
185	B9	271	1011 1001	double right junction	╣
186	BA	272	1011 1010	double vertical	║
187	BB	273	1011 1011	double upper-right	╗
188	BC	274	1011 1100	double lower-right	╝
189	BD	275	1011 1101	1 to 2 lower-right	╜
190	BE	276	1011 1110	2 to 1 lower-right	╛
191	BF	277	1011 1111	single upper-right	┐
192	C0	300	1100 0000	single lower-left	└
193	C1	301	1100 0001	single lower junction	┴
194	C2	302	1100 0010	single upper junction	┬
195	C3	303	1100 0011	single left junction	├
196	C4	304	1100 0100	single horizontal	─

Table 1.4 Hexadecimal/ASCII Conversions Continued

Dec	Hex	Octal	Binary	Name	Character
197	C5	305	1100 0101	single intersection	┼
198	C6	306	1100 0110	2 to 1 left junction	╞
199	C7	307	1100 0111	1 to 2 left junction	╟
200	C8	310	1100 1000	double lower-left	╚
201	C9	311	1100 1001	double upper-left	╔
202	CA	312	1100 1010	double lower junction	╩
203	CB	313	1100 1011	double upper junction	╦
204	CC	314	1100 1100	double left junction	╠
205	CD	315	1100 1101	double horizontal	═
206	CE	316	1100 1110	double intersection	╬
207	CF	317	1100 1111	1 to 2 lower junction	╧
208	D0	320	1101 0000	2 to 1 lower junction	╨
209	D1	321	1101 0001	1 to 2 upper junction	╤
210	D2	322	1101 0010	2 to 1 upper junction	╥
211	D3	323	1101 0011	1 to 2 lower-left	╙
212	D4	324	1101 0100	2 to 1 lower-left	╘
213	D5	325	1101 0101	2 to 1 upper-left	╒
214	D6	326	1101 0110	1 to 2 upper-left	╓
215	D7	327	1101 0111	2 to 1 intersection	╫
216	D8	330	1101 1000	1 to 2 intersection	╪
217	D9	331	1101 1001	single lower-right	┘
218	DA	332	1101 1010	single upper-right	┐
219	DB	333	1101 1011	inverse space	■
220	DC	334	1101 1100	lower inverse	▬
221	DD	335	1101 1101	left inverse	▌
222	DE	336	1101 1110	right inverse	▐
223	DF	337	1101 1111	upper inverse	▀
224	E0	340	1110 0000	alpha	α
225	E1	341	1110 0001	beta	β
226	E2	342	1110 0010	Gamma	Γ
227	E3	343	1110 0011	pi	π
228	E4	344	1110 0100	Sigma	Σ
229	E5	345	1110 0101	sigma	σ
230	E6	346	1110 0110	mu	μ
231	E7	347	1110 0111	tau	τ
232	E8	350	1110 1000	Phi	Φ
233	E9	351	1110 1001	theta	θ

Table 1.4	Hexadecimal/ASCII Conversions Continued				
Dec	**Hex**	**Octal**	**Binary**	**Name**	**Character**
234	EA	352	1110 1010	Omega	Ω
235	EB	353	1110 1011	delta	δ
236	EC	354	1110 1100	infinity	∞
237	ED	355	1110 1101	phi	φ
238	EE	356	1110 1110	epsilon	ε
239	EF	357	1110 1111	intersection of sets	∩
240	F0	360	1111 0000	is identical to	≡
241	F1	361	1111 0001	plus/minus sign	±
242	F2	362	1111 0010	greater/equal sign	≥
243	F3	363	1111 0011	less/equal sign	≤
244	F4	364	1111 0100	top half integral	⌠
245	F5	365	1111 0101	lower half integral	⌡
246	F6	366	1111 0110	division sign	÷
247	F7	367	1111 0111	approximately	≈
248	F8	370	1111 1000	degree	°
249	F9	371	1111 1001	filled-in degree	•
250	FA	372	1111 1010	small bullet	·
251	FB	373	1111 1011	square root	√
252	FC	374	1111 1100	superscript n	ⁿ
253	FD	375	1111 1101	superscript 2	²
254	FE	376	1111 1110	box	▪
255	FF	377	1111 1111	phantom space	˘

Windows Release/Version Numbers

The capabilities of any system are affected in large measure by the version of Windows that it is running. Table 1.5 lists the release numbers for Windows 95, Windows 98, and Windows Me.

Table 1.5	Windows 9x/Me Release/Version Numbers	
Windows Version Number	**Revision**	**Features**
Windows 95 4.00.950	Original release of Windows 95	2.1GB limit per drive letter, FAT16 file system only
Windows 95 4.00.950a	Windows 95 OSR 1 or original after installing Service Pack 1	Bug fixes to original Windows 95
Windows 95 4.00.950B	Windows 95 OSR 2 (a.k.a. Win95B); not available for download	Introduced FAT32 file system with 2TB (theoretical) limit per drive letter and IRQ steering

Table 1.5   Windows 9x/Me Release/Version Numbers Continued

Windows Version Number	Revision	Features
Windows 95 4.00.950C	Windows 95 OSR 2.1 (a.k.a. Win95C)	Introduced USB and AGP support
Windows 98 4.10.1691	Windows 98 beta	All Windows 95 OSR 2.x features, plus capability to use hard drives over 32GB in size
Windows 98 4.10.1998	Windows 98 original release	Service Pack 1 installation doesn't change release number
Windows 98 4.10.2222A	Windows 98 Second Edition	Introduced Internet Connection Sharing (ICS) and IE 5.0
Windows Me 4.90.3000	Windows Me original release	Improved ICS, Home Networking Wizard, IE 5.5, imaging and DV camcorder wizards, System Restore

Note

Windows XP versions numbers were not available at the time this book was being produced.

Chapter 2

System Components and Configuration

Processors and Their Data Bus Widths

Table 2.1 Processors and Their Data Bus Widths	
Processor	**Data Bus Width**
Intel 8088	8-bit
Intel 8086	16-bit
Intel 286	16-bit
Intel 386SX	16-bit
Intel 386DX	32-bit
IBM 486SLC	16-bit[1]
Intel 486 (all SX/DXseries)	32-bit
Intel Pentium	64-bit
AMD K5	64-bit[2]
Intel Pentium MMX	64-bit
AMD K6	64-bit[2]
Cyrix 6×86	64-bit[2]
Cyrix 6×86MX	64-bit[2]
Cyrix MII	64-bit[2]
Cyrix III	64-bit[3]
Intel Pentium Pro	64-bit
Intel Pentium II	64-bit
Intel Celeron	64-bit
Intel Pentium III	64-bit
Pentium II Xeon	64-bit
Intel Pentium III Xeon	64-bit
Intel Pentium 4	64-bit
Intel Xeon	64-bit
AMD Athlon	64-bit
AMD Duron	64-bit
Intel Itanium	64-bit[4]

1. Designed and produced by IBM, under license from Intel. Despite the name, the 486SLC was based on the 386SX.

2. Pin-compatible with Pentium.

3. Pin-compatible with Intel Celeron.

4. Runs new 64-bit instructions as well as existing 32-bit instructions; previously code-named "Merced."

Differences Between PC/XT and AT Systems

Systems that feature an 8-bit memory bus are called *PC/XT* systems after the pioneering IBM PC and IBM PC/XT. As you can see in Table 2.2, the differences between these systems and descendents of the IBM AT (16-bit memory bus and above) are significant. All modern systems fall into the AT category.

Table 2.2   Differences Between PC/XT and AT Systems

System Attributes PC/XT Type	8-Bit	16-, 32-, 64-Bit AT Type
Supported processors	All x86 or x88	286 or higher
Processor modes	Real	Real, Protected, Virtual Real[2]
Software supported	16-bit only	16- or 32-bit[2]
Bus slot width	8-bit	16-, 32-[1], and 64-bit[4]
Slot type	ISA only	ISA, EISA[1], MCA, PC Card, Cardbus[3], VL-Bus[3], PCI[3], AGP[4]
Hardware interrupts	8 (6 usable)	16 (11 usable)
DMA channels	4 (3 usable)	8 (7 usable)
Maximum RAM	1MB	16MB/4GB[1] or more
Floppy controller speed	250Kbps	250, 300, 500, and 1000Kbps
Standard boot drive	360KB or 720KB	1.2M, 1.44MB, and 2.88MB
Keyboard interface	Unidirectional	Bidirectional

Table 2.3   Intel Processor Specifications

Processor	CPU Clock	Voltage	Internal Register Size	Data Bus Width
8088	1x	5V	16-bit	8-bit
8086	1x	5V	16-bit	16-bit
286	1x	5V	16-bit	16-bit
386SX	1x	5V	32-bit	16-bit
386SL	1x	3.3V	32-bit	16-bit
386DX	1x	5V	32-bit	32-bit
486SX	1x	5V	32-bit	32-bit
486SX2	2x	5V	32-bit	32-bit
487SX	1x	5V	32-bit	32-bit
486DX	1x	5V	32-bit	32-bit
486SL	1x	3.3V	32-bit	32-bit
486DX2	2x	5V	32-bit	32-bit
486DX4	2–3x	3.3V	32-bit	32-bit
486 Pentium OD	2.5x	5V	32-bit	32-bit

Table 2.2 Differences Between PC/XT and AT Systems Continued		
System Attributes **PC/XT Type**	**8-Bit**	**16-, 32-, 64-Bit** **AT Type**
CMOS memory/clock	None standard	MC146818-compatible
Serial-port UART	8250B	16450/16550A or better

1. Requires 386DX-based system or above.

2. Requires 386SX-based system or above.

3. Requires 486SX-based system or above.

4. Requires Pentium-based system or above.

Intel and Compatible Processor Specifications

See Tables 2.3 and 2.4 to help determine the features of any CPU that you encounter. It might be necessary to remove the heat sink or fan to see the processor markings on an older system, but many recent systems display CPU identification and speeds at startup.

Table 2.4 shows the major Pentium-class CPUs made by companies other than Intel. The newest versions of these processors often can be used to upgrade an older Pentium—as long as proper voltage and system configuration information can be provided, either through adjusting the motherboard/BIOS settings or by purchasing an upgrade-type processor with third-party support.

Max. Memory	Level 1 Cache	L1 Cache Type	L2 Cache	L2 Cache Speed	Special Features
1MB	—	—	—	—	—
1MB	—	—	—	—	—
16MB	—	—	—	—	—
16MB	—	—	—	Bus	—
16MB	0KB[1]	WT	—	Bus	—
4GB	—	—	—	Bus	—
4GB	8KB	WT	—	Bus	—
4GB	8KB	WT	—	Bus	—
4GB	8KB	WT	—	Bus	FPU
4GB	8KB	WT	—	Bus	FPU
4GB	8KB	WT	—	Bus	FPU Opt.
4GB	8KB	WT	—	Bus	FPU
4GB	16KB	WT	—	Bus	FPU
4GB	2×16KB	WB	—	Bus	FPU

Table 2.3   Intel Processor Specifications Continued

Processor	CPU Clock	Voltage	Internal Register Size	Data Bus Width
Pentium 60/66	1x	5V	32-bit	64-bit
Pentium 75-200	1.5–3x	3.3–3.5V	32-bit	64-bit
Pentium MMX	1.5– 4.5x	1.8–2.8V	32-bit	64-bit
Pentium Pro	2–3x	3.3V	32-bit	64-bit
Pentium II	3.5– 4.5x	1.8–2.8V	32-bit	64-bit
Celeron	3.5– 4.5x	1.8–2.8V	32-bit	64-bit
Celeron A	3.5–8x	1.8–2.8V	32-bit	64-bit
Pentium II PE[3]	3.5–6x	1.6V	32-bit	64-bit
Pentium II Xeon	4–4.5x	1.8–2.8V	32-bit	64-bit
Celeron III	4.5–9x	1.3–1.6V	32-bit	64-bit
Pentium III Slot1	4–6x	1.8–2V	32-bit	64-bit
Pentium IIIE	4–9x	1.8–2V	32-bit	64-bit
Pentium III Xeon	5–6x	1.8–2.8V	32-bit	64-bit
Pentium IIIE Xeon	4.5– 6.5x	1.65V	32-bit	64-bit
Pentium 4	3–5x	1.7V	32-bit	64-bit
(Pentium 4) Xeon	3–5x	1.7V	32-bit	64-bit
Itanium	3–5x	1.6V	64-bit	64-bit

Table 2.4   Intel-Compatible Pentium-Class Processors

Processor	CPU Clock	Voltage	Internal Register Size	Data Bus Width	Max. Memory
AMD K5	1.5– 1.75x	3.5V	32-bit	64-bit	4GB
AMD K6	2.5– 4.5x	2.2– 3.2V	32-bit	64-bit	4GB
AMD K6-2	2.5–6x	1.9–	32-bit	64-bit	4GB

Max. Memory	Level 1 Cache	L1 Cache Type	L2 Cache	L2 Cache Speed	Special Features
4GB	2×8KB	WB	—	Bus	FPU
4GB	2×8KB	WB	—	Bus	FPU
4GB	2×16KB	WB	—	Bus	FPU, MMX
64GB	2×8KB	WB	256KB, 512KB, 1MB	Core	FPU
64GB	2×16KB	WB	512KB	1/2 Core	FPU, MMX
64GB	2×16KB	WB	0KB	—	FPU, MMX
64GB	2×16KB	WB	128KB	Core	FPU, MMX
64GB	2×16KB	WB	256KB	Core	FPU, MMX
64GB	2×16KB	WB512KB,	Core 1MB 2MB	FPU, MMX	
64GB	2×16KB	WB	128KB	Core	FPU, SSE
64GB	2×16KB	WB	512KB	1/2 Core	FPU, SSE
64GB	2×16KB	WB	256KB	Core	FPU, SSE
64GB	2×16KB	WB	512KB, 1MB, 2MB	Core	FPU, SSE
64GB	2×16KB	WB	256KB, 1MB, 2MB	Core	FPU, SSE
64GB	8KB+12KB	WB	256KB	Core	FPU, SSE2
64GB	8KB+12KB	WB	256KB	Core	FPU, SSE2
16TB	2×16KB	WB 2MB	96KB+	Core	FPU, MMX

Level 1 Cache	L1 Cache Type	Level 2 Cache	L2 Cache Speed	Special Features	Similar to [4]
16+8KB	WB	—	Bus	FPU	Pentium
2×32KB	WB	—	Bus	FPU, MMX	Pentium MMX
2×32KB	WB	—	Bus	FPU, 3DNow	Pentium MMX

Table 2.4	Intel-Compatible Pentium-Class Processors Continued				
Processor	CPU Clock	Voltage	Internal Register Size	Data Bus Width	Max. Memory
		2.4V			
AMD K6-3	3.5–4.5x	1.8–2.4V	32-bit	64-bit	4GB
AMD Athlon	5–10x[10]	1.6–	32-bit	64-bit	8TB
		1.8V			
AMD Duron	5–10x[10]	1.5–1.8V	32-bit	64-bit	8TB
AMD Athlon 4	5–10x[10]	1.5–1.8V	32-bit	64-bit	8TB
AMD Athlon MP	5–10x[10] 10x1.8V	1.75V	32-bit	64-bit	8TB
Cyrix 6×86	2x	2.5–3.5V	32-bit	64-bit	4GB
Cyrix 6x86MX/MII	2–3.5x	2.2–2.9V	32-bit	64-bit	4GB
VIA Cyrix III	2.5–7x	2.2V	32-bit	64-bit	4GB
Nexgen Nx586	2x	4V	32-bit	64-bit	4GB
IDT Winchip	3–4x	3.3–3.5V	32-bit	64-bit	4GB
IDT Winchip2/2A	2.33–4x	3.3–3.5V	32-bit	64-bit	4GB
Rise mP6	2–3.5x	2.8V	32-bit	64-bit	4GB

FPU = Floating-point unit (internal math coprocessor)

WT = Write-through cache (cache reads only)

WB = Write-back cache (cache both reads and writes)

Bus = Processor external bus speed (motherboard speed)

Core = Processor internal core speed (CPU speed)

MMX = Multimedia extensions, 57 additional instructions for graphics and sound processing

3DNow = MMX plus 21 additional instructions for graphics and sound processing

SSE = Streaming SIMD (Single Instruction Multiple Data) extensions, MMX plus 70 additional instructions for graphics and sound processing

1. The 386SL contains an integral-cache controller, but the cache memory must be provided outside the chip.

2. Intel later marketed SL Enhanced versions of the SX, DX, and DX2 processors. These processors were available in both 5V and 3.3V versions and included power-management capabilities.

Level 1 Cache	L1 Cache Type	Level 2 Cache	L2 Cache Speed	Features	Similar to[4]
2×32KB	WB	256KB	Core	FPU, 3DNow	Pentium MMX
2×64KB	WB	512KB[6]	1/3[7] Core	FPU, 3DNow	Pentium III[8]
2×64KB	WB	64KB	Core	FPU, 3DNow	Celeron III
2×64KB	WB	256KB	Core	FPU, 3DNow	Pentium III
2×64KB	WB	256KB	Core	FPU, 3DnowPro	Pentium III Xeon
16KB	WB	—	Bus	FPU	Pentium
64KB	WB	—	Bus	FPU, MMX	Pentium MMX
64KB	WB	256KB	Core		
2×16KB	WB	—	Bus	FPU	Pentium[5]
2×32KB	WB	—	Bus	FPU, MMX	Pentium MMX
2×32KB	WB	—	Bus	FPU, 3DNow	AMD K6-2
2×8KB	WB	—	Bus	FPU, MMX	Pentium MMX

3. The Enhanced mobile PII has an on-die L2 cache similar to the Celeron.

4. These processors physically fit into the same Socket 7 used by Intel Pentium 75MHz and above models except as noted, but they might require special chipsets or BIOS settings for best operation. Check with the motherboard and chip manufacturer before installing them in place of your existing Pentium-class chip.

5. Pentium-class performance, but unique, nonstandard pinout.

6. Cache size for initial shipments (3rd Q 1999). Athlon designed it to allow cache sizes up to 8MB.

7. Athlon's cache interface is designed to handle variable speed ratios, so later versions can run L2 cache more quickly.

8. Athlon uses the new AMD Slot A, physically similar to Slot 1 but with a different electrical pinout.

9. Duron and "Thunderbird" versions of Athlon use new Socket A.

10. Clock multipliers listed based on 100MHz system bus (FSB) speeds; although Athlon and Duron use 200MHz bus, memory for these systems runs at PC100 or PC133 speeds, depending on the processor model.

Use Tables 2.5 and 2.6 to help determine which processors *might* fit in place of your existing CPU. Note that a replacement CPU must have the same pinout and the same electrical requirements, and must be compatible with your motherboard. Many vendors sell upgrade-compatible processor versions, which have been modified from their original forms by adding a voltage regulator and other support options.

Table 2.5   Intel and Compatibles 486/Pentium-Class/Itanium CPU Socket Types and Specifications

Socket Number	Pins	Pin Layout	Voltage	Supported Processors
Socket 1	169	17×17 PGA	5V	486 SX/SX2, DX/DX2[1], DX4 OverDrive
Socket 2	238	19×19 PGA	5V	486 SX/SX2, DX/DX2[1], DX4 OverDrive, 486 Pentium OverDrive
Socket 3	237	19×19 PGA	5/3.3V	486 SX/SX2, DX/DX2, DX4, 486 Pentium OverDrive, AMD 5×86, Cyrix 5×86
Socket 4	273	21×21 PGA	5V	Pentium 60/66, OverDrive
Socket 5	320	37×37 SPGA	3.3/3.5V	Pentium 75-133, OverDrive
Socket 6[2]	235	19×19 PGA	3.3V	486 DX4, 486 Pentium OverDrive
Socket 7	321	37×37 SPGA	VRM	Pentium 75-233+, MMX, OverDrive, AMD K5/K6, Cyrix M1, VIA Cyrix MII
Socket 8	387	Dual pattern SPGA	Auto VRM	Pentium Pro
Socket 370	370	37×37 SPGA	Auto VRM	Celeron/Pentium III PPGA/FC-PGA, VIA C3
Socket PAC418	418	38×22 split SPGA	Auto VRM	Itanium
Socket 423	423	39×39 SPGA	Auto VRM	Pentium 4
Socket 603	603	31×25 SPGA	Auto VRM	Xeon (P4 version)
Slot 1 (SC 242)	242	Slot	Auto VRM	Pentium II/III, Celeron
Slot 2 (SC 330)	330	Slot	Auto VRM	Pentium II Xeon/Pentium III Xeon
Slot A	242	Slot	Auto VRM	AMD Athlon (K7) SECC
Socket A	462	SPGA	Auto VRM	AMD Duron, AMD Athlon 4 PGA, AMD Athlon MP

1. *Nonoverdrive DX4 or AMD 5×86 also can be supported with the addition of an aftermarket 3.3V voltage-regulator adapter.*

2. *Socket 6 was a paper standard only and was never actually implemented in any systems.*

PGA = Pin grid array

SPGA = Staggered pin grid array

VRM = Voltage regulator module

Table 2.6 lists the fastest processors that you can install according to the socket type in your system. Note that newer socket designs allow faster processors, but the bus speed and clock multiplier settings of your motherboard are also limiting factors for some CPU types.

Table 2.6	Maximum Processor Speeds by Socket
Socket Type	**Fastest Processor Supported**
Socket 1	5×86 133MHz with 3.3V adapter
Socket 2	5×86 133MHz with 3.3V adapter
Socket 3	5×86 133MHz
Socket 4	Pentium OverDrive 133MHz
Socket 5	Pentium MMX 233MHz or AMD K6 with 2.8v adapter
Socket 7	AMD K6-2 up to 550MHz, K6-III up to 500MHz
Socket 8	Pentium Pro OverDrive (333MHz Pentium II performance)
Slot 1	Celeron 433MHz (66MHz bus)
Slot 1	Pentium III 1.0GHz(100MHz bus)
Slot 1	Pentium III 1.13GHz (133MHz bus)
Slot 2	Pentium III Xeon 550MHz (100MHz bus)
Slot 2	Pentium III Xeon 866MHz (133MHz bus)
Socket 370	Celeron 700MHz (66MHz bus)
Socket 370	Pentium III 933MHz (100MHz bus), Pentium III 1GH (133MHz bus)
Socket 426	Pentium 4 1.7GHz (400MHz bus using RDRAM)
Socket 603	Xeon (P4) 1.7GHz (400MHz bus using RDRAM)
Slot A	1GHz AMD Athlon, 1GHz AMD Athlon Thunderbird
Socket A	950MHz AMD Duron and 1.3GHz AMD Athlon (200MHz FSB), 1.4GHz Athlon (266MHz FSB)

Troubleshooting Processor Problems

Table 2.7 provides a general troubleshooting checklist for processor-related PC problems.

Table 2.7	Troubleshooting Processor-Related Problems	
Problem Identification	**Possible Cause**	**Resolution**
System is dead; no cursor, no beeps, or no fan.	Power cord failure.	Plug in or replace power cord. Power cords can fail even though they look fine.
	Power supply failure.	Replace the power supply. Use a known, good spare for testing.
	Motherboard failure.	Replace motherboard. Use a known, good spare for testing.

Table 2.7   Troubleshooting Processor-Related Problems

Problem Identification	Possible Cause	Resolution
	Memory failure.	Remove all memory except one bank, and retest. If the system still won't boot, replace bank 1.
System is dead; no beeps, or locks up before POST begins.	All components either not installed or incorrectly installed.	Check all peripherals, especially memory, processor, and graphics adapter.
		Reseat all boards and socketed components, such as CPUs and memory modules.
System beeps on startup; fan is running, but no cursor onscreen.	Improperly seated or failing graphics adapter.	Reseat or replace graphics adapter. Use known, good spare for testing.
Locks up during or shortly after POST.	Poor heat dissipation.	Check CPU heat sink/fan; replace, if necessary, using one with a higher capacity.
		Use thermal paste between fan/heatsink and CPU, as directed by heatsink and CPU vendors.
	Improper voltage settings.	Set motherboard for proper core processor voltage.
	Wrong motherboard bus speed.	Set motherboard for proper speed.
	Wrong CPU clock multiplier.	Jumper motherboard for proper clock multiplier.
Improper CPU identification during POST.	Old BIOS.	Update BIOS from manufacturer.
	Board not configured properly.	Check manual and jumper board according to proper bus and multiplier settings.
		If board is jumperless, adjust bus and multiplier in BIOS.
Operating system will not boot.	Poor heat dissipation.	Check CPU fan; replace, if necessary. May need higher-capacity heatsink and thermal paste.
	Improper voltage settings.	Jumper motherboard for proper core voltage.
	Wrong motherboard bus speed.	Jumper motherboard, or adjust BIOS settings to correct speed.
	Wrong CPU clock to multiplier.	Jumper motherboard, or adjust BIOS settings correct multiplier.
	Applications will not install or run.	Improper drivers or incompatible hardware. Update drivers and check for compatibility issues.
System appears to work, but no video is displayed	Monitor turned off or failed.	Check monitor and power to monitor. Replace with known good spare for testing.

If during POST the processor is not identified correctly, your motherboard settings might be incorrect or your BIOS might need to be updated. Check that the motherboard is jumpered or configured correctly for the processor that you have, and make sure that you have the latest BIOS for your motherboard.

If the system seems to run erratically after it warms up, try setting the processor to a lower speed. If the problem goes away, the processor might be defective or overclocked.

Many hardware problems are really software problems in disguise. Be sure that you have the latest BIOS for your motherboard and the latest drivers for your peripherals. Also, it helps to use the latest version of your given operating system because, normally, fewer problems will occur.

Note
For more information about processors, see Chapter 3 of *Upgrading and Repairing PCs, 13th Edition*, also published by Que.

Motherboard Form Factors

Although many PC users have extended the life span of their systems by changing the CPU, any system that will be kept for a long time could be a candidate for a motherboard replacement. Use the following charts to determine whether your system uses one of these standard form factors, which will give you the choice of many vendors for a replacement. A replacement motherboard provides you with these benefits:

- Access to faster, more advanced CPUs

- "Free" updated BIOS with support for large hard drives, Y2K, and boot from LS-120, Zip, and CD-ROM drives

- Newer I/O features, such as USB ports, UDMA-66 hard-disk interfacing, and AGP video

Baby-AT Motherboard

Until mid-1996, this descendent of the original IBM/XT motherboard was the dominant design. Even though limited numbers of these motherboards are still available for use with both Pentium-class and Pentium II/III/Celeron processors, the lack of built-in ports and cooling problems make this an obsolete design. If you are trying to upgrade a system that uses this motherboard design, consider purchasing a new ATX-style case, power supply, and motherboard. In addition, you should consider moving the CPU, RAM, drives, and cards from your existing system to the new box (see Figure 2.1).

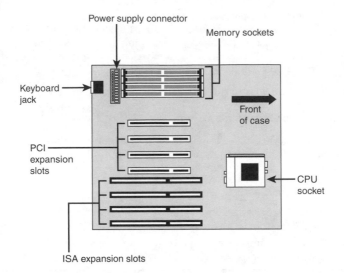

Power supply connector

Memory sockets

Keyboard jack

Front of case

PCI expansion slots

CPU socket

ISA expansion slots

Figure 2.1   Baby-AT motherboard layout with major components.

LPX Motherboard

Since 1987, many low-cost systems have used variations on this layout, which features a single slot used for a riser card. The expansion cards for video, audio, and so forth are connected to the riser card, not the motherboard. Most LPX systems use riser cards that mount the expansion slots parallel to the motherboard; some use a T-shape riser card that keeps the expansion slots at their normal upright position. Additionally, most LPX systems have built-in video, audio, and other I/O ports. Unfortunately, because its details were never standardized, it is virtually impossible to upgrade. Systems with this motherboard are essentially disposable (see Figure 2.2).

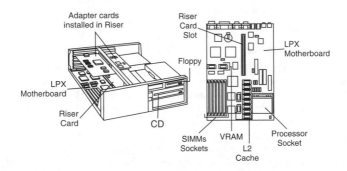

Adapter cards installed in Riser

Riser Card Slot

LPX Motherboard

Floppy

LPX Motherboard

Riser Card

CD

SIMMs Sockets

VRAM

L2 Cache

Processor Socket

Figure 2.2   Typical LPX system chassis and motherboard.

ATX Motherboard

Since mid-1996, the ATX motherboard has become the standard for most systems using nonproprietary motherboards (see Figure 2.3). Similar to Baby-AT, it's also an industry standard, and, similar to LPX, it features built-in ports. Compared to both, though, it offers much greater ease of upgrading and servicing. ATX motherboards are rotated 90° when compared to Baby-ATs and also use a different power supply for advanced power-management features. Because of their built-in ports and differences in layout, ATX motherboards require an ATX case. Some ATX cases also can be used for Baby-AT motherboards, though (depends on case design). Figure 2.3 shows a full-size ATX layout; however, several smaller versions now exist, including micro-ATX and flex-ATX.

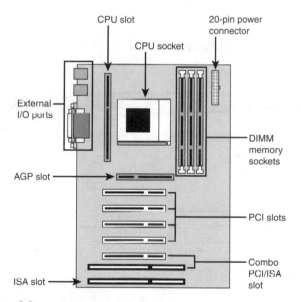

Figure 2.3 ATX motherboard layout and its major components. Very few motherboards have both a CPU socket and a CPU slot, as shown here.

NLX Motherboard

The replacement for the old LPX low-profile motherboard is the NLX motherboard (see Figure 2.4). NLX also features built-in ports and a riser card, but its standard design means that replacement motherboards can be purchased from some suppliers, (unlike LPX systems, which are not standardized). A major advantage of NLX systems is that the motherboard is easy to remove for servicing through a side panel, a feature that makes NLX-based systems popular as corporate network client PCs.

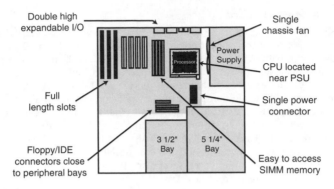

Figure 2.4   NLX motherboard and riser combination.

Which Motherboard Is Which?

Use Table 2.8 to help determine whether a system is a Baby-AT, an LPX, an ATX, or an NLX-based system.

Table 2.8 Comparison of Major Motherboard Form Factors				
	Baby-AT	**LPX**	**ATX/Micro ATX[1]**	**NLX**
Ports built into board	No	Yes	Yes	Yes
Riser card	No	Yes	No	Yes
Single row of ports at rear below expansion slots	—	Yes	No	No
Two rows of ports to left of expansion slots	—	No	Yes	Yes
Two rows of ports to right of expansion slots	—	No	—	Yes
Slots on both sides of riser card	—	Opt	—	No
Riser card near location of MB power supply	—	Middle	—	

1. MicroATX motherboards can fit into ATX cases but have fewer slots and are designed for sock-eted rather than slot-based processors. They also mostly feature onboard audio and video, both of which are usually optional on ATX motherboards.

PC99 Color-Coding for Ports

Microsoft and Intel have developed the following standardized color-coding of connectors for computers compliant with the PC99 design standards. Use Table 2.9 to help you match non–color-coded peripherals with the correct external ports.

> **Note**
>
> Some systems, especially those built before 1999, might use a proprietary color scheme for ports.

See Chapter 12, "Connector Quick Reference," for pictures of these ports. For color samples, see the Web site http://www. pcdesguide.com/documents/pc99icons.htm.

Table 2.9   PC99 Color-Coding Standards for Ports

Port Type	Color
Analog VGA (DB15)	Blue
Audio line in	Light blue
Audio line out	Lime green
Digital monitor	White
IEEE-1394 (iLink, FireWire)	Gray
Microphone	Pink
MIDI/Gameport	Gold
Parallel port	Burgundy
Serial port	Teal or turquoise
Speaker out (subwoofer)	Orange
Right-to-left speaker	Brown
USB	Black
Video out	Yellow
SCSI, network, telephone, modem, and so on	None

Power Supplies

Power supplies actually convert high-voltage alternating current (AC) into low-voltage direct current (DC) for use by PCs. Power supplies come in several form factors and also feature various motherboard connectors to correspond with the newer motherboard designs on the market. Table 2.10 illustrates which power supplies are most likely to be used with various motherboards.

Table 2.10   Matching Power Supplies and Motherboards

Motherboard Form Factor	Most Common PS Form Factor Used	Other PS Form Factors Used
Baby-AT	LPX style	Baby-AT, AT/Tower, or AT/Desk
LPX	LPX style	None
ATX	ATX style	SFX style

Table 2.10	Matching Power Supplies and Motherboards Continued	
Motherboard Form Factor	Most Common PS Form Factor Used	Other PS Form Factors Used
MicroATX	ATX style	SFX style
NLX	ATX style	SFX style

LPX Versus ATX Power Supplies

Some motherboards are designed to handle either LPX or ATX power supplies. The ATX is the preferred design because it provides the lower voltage needed by today's circuits, offers foolproof installation, and also provides better cooling than older designs.

Table 2.11 compares two of the more common power supply form factors used in computers today, and Figure 2.5 shows an LPX power supply.

Table 2.11	Comparing ATX and LPX Power Supplies		
Power Supply Type	Voltage Output	Motherboard Power Connectors	Other Features/ Notes
LPX	5V, 12V	2–6 pins each (P8/P9)	Easy to reverse the plug due to poor keying
ATX	3.3V, 5V, 12V	1–20 pins	Keyed to go in only one way; allows hibernation via operating system or keyboard command

Table 2.12 breaks down the typical LPX power supply connector.

Caution

To get the cables oriented correctly, keep the ground wires (black) next to each other. Although most connectors are keyed to prevent you from improperly plugging them in, some connectors can easily be inserted incorrectly. This will destroy your motherboard the first time you switch on the power and could cause a fire.

Table 2.12	Typical LPX Power Supply Connections	
Connector	Voltage	Standard Color/Notes
P8-1	Power_Good (+5V)	Orange
P8-2	+5V	Red
P8-3	+12V	Yellow
P8-4	−12V	Blue

Table 2.12 Typical LPX Power Supply Connections Continued		
Connector	**Voltage**	**Standard Color/Notes**
P8-5	Ground (0)	Black
P8-6	Ground (0)	Black
---------------	---------------	---------------
P9-1	Ground (0)	Black
P9-2	Ground (0)	Black
P9-3	−5V	White
P9-4	+5V	Red
P9-5	+5V	Red
P9-6	+5V	Red

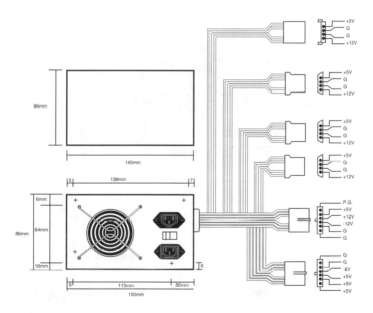

Figure 2.5   LPX form factor power supply.

Power Connectors for the Drive(s)

The connectors shown in Table 2.13 might not be labeled, but they easily can be distinguished by the four-wire cable and color-coding. The same colors are used for drive power connectors on ATX power supplies. Figure 2.6 shows an ATX power supply.

Table 2.13   ATX/LPX Drive Power Supply Color Coding

Connector	Voltage	Standard Color/Notes
P10-1	+12V	Yellow
P10-2	Ground (0)	Black
P10-3	Ground (0)	Black
P10-4	+5V	Red

ATX Power Supply Connectors

The ATX power supply uses a 20-pin connector (see Figure 2.6) that is keyed to connect in only one way to the motherboard. The additional power leads provide 3.3V power to the motherboard and enables the motherboard to turn the power supply on and off.

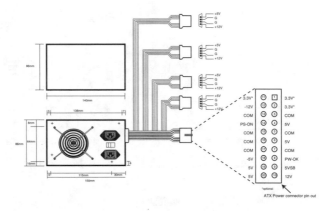

Figure 2.6   ATX form factor power supply used with both ATX and NLX systems. The pinout for the motherboard power is shown at lower right. Note the single square pin used for keying.

Table 2.14 shows the pinout for the ATX motherboard power connector.

Table 2.14   ATX Motherboard Power Supply Connections

Color	Signal	Pin	Pin	Signal	Color
Orange	+3.3V	11	1	+3.3v	Orange
Blue	−12V	12	2	+3.3v	Orange
Black	GND	13	3	GND	Black
Green	PS_On	14	4	+5v	Red
Black	GND	15	5	GND	Black

Color	Signal	Pin	Pin	Signal	Color
Table 2.14	**ATX Motherboard Power Supply Connections Continued**				
Black	GND	16	6	+5v	Red
Black	GND	17	7	GND	Black
White	–5V	18	8	Power_Good	Gray
Red	+5V	19	9	+5VSB (Standby)	Purple
Red	+5V	20	10	+12v	Yellow

ATX Auxiliary Connector

Many ATX power supplies also feature a six-pin auxiliary connector, which provides additional levels of 3.3V and 5V power to motherboards that require it. Generally, systems that need 250 watts or more use these connectors.

The Aux. Connector (shown in Figure 2.7) is a six-pin Molex-type connector, similar to one of the motherboard power connectors used on AT/LPX supplies. It is keyed to prevent misconnection.

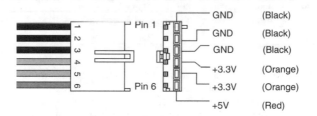

ATX Auxiliary Power Connector

Figure 2.7   ATX auxiliary power connector.

The pinouts of the auxiliary connector are shown in Table 2.15.

Pin	Signal	Color
Table 2.15	**ATX Auxiliary Power Connector Pinout**	
1	Gnd	Black
2	Gnd	Black
3	Gnd	Black
4	+3.3V	Orange
5	+3.3V	Orange
6	+5V	Red

ATX12V Power Connector

To augment the supply of +12V power to the motherboard, Intel created a new ATX12V power supply specification. This adds a third power connector, called the ATX12V connector, specifically to supply additional +12V power to the board. This connector is shown in Figure 2.8.

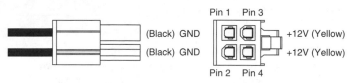

ATX12V Power Connector

Figure 2.8   An ATX12V power connector.

The pinout of the +12V power connector is shown in Table 2.16.

Table 2.16 ATX +12V Power Connector Pinout (Wire Side View)					
Color	Signal	Pin	Pin	Signal	Color
Yellow	+12V	3	1	Gnd	Black
Yellow	+12V	4	2	Gnd	Black

If your new motherboard requires the ATX12V connector (new Pentium 4 motherboards are some that do) and your current power supply lacks this ATX12V connector, contact PC Power and Cooling (http://www.pcpowerandcooling.com) for an adapter.

Dell Proprietary ATX Main and Auxiliary Power Connectors

Starting in September 1998, Dell computers switched to a proprietary version of the ATX main and power connectors. Unfortunately, the Dell power supply and motherboard, which uses completely different voltages than standard ATX, still use the same physical connectors. Thus, you can *destroy* your power supply, your motherboard, or both by using a Dell power supply with a standard motherboard, or by using a standard power supply with a Dell motherboard. If you are servicing a Dell system, compare the pinouts in Tables 2.17 and 2.18 with the standard ATX pinouts in Tables 2.15 and 2.16 to determine whether the system is using a proprietary power supply.

Table 2.17   Dell Proprietary (Nonstandard) ATX Main Power Connector Pinout (Wire Side View)

Color	Signal	Pin	Pin	Signal	Color
Gray	PS_On	11	1	+5V	Red
Black	GND	12	2	GND	Black
Black	GND	13	3	+5V	Red
Black	GND	14	4	GND	Black
White	–5V	15	5	Power_Good	Orange
Red	+5V	16	6	+5VSB (standby)	Purple
Red	+5V	17	7	+12V	Yellow
Red	+5V	18	8	–12V	Blue
KEY (blank)	—	19	9	GND	Black
Red	+5V	20	10	GND	Black

Table 2.18   Dell Proprietary (Nonstandard) ATX Auxiliary Power Connector Pinout

Pin	Signal	Color
1	Gnd	Black
2	Gnd	Black
3	Gnd	Black
4	+3.3V	Blue/White
5	+3.3V	Blue/White
6	+3.3V	Blue/White

Some 3rd-party vendors sell Dell-compatible power supplies, or you could replace both the motherboard and the power supply with standard units if you decide to upgrade a Dell unit that uses a proprietary power supply.

See Chapter 21 in *Upgrading and Repairing PCs, 13th Edition*, for more information about Dell proprietary power supplies.

Quick-Reference Chart for Troubleshooting Power Supplies

Table 2.19   Troubleshooting Power Supplies

Symptom	Cause(s)	Tests and Solution(s)
System is overheating.	Inadequate system cooling	Check ventilation around system. Clean system internally. Check for missing slot covers.
	Higher load on system in watts than power supply rating	Replace power supply with higher-rated unit.

Table 2.19	Troubleshooting Power Supplies *Continued*	
Symptom	**Cause(s)**	**Tests and Solution(s)**
System reboots itself.	Incorrect power level on Power_Good; can indicate overloaded power supply or otherwise bad unit	Use DC-voltage digital multimeter (DMM) to test P8-1 (orange wire) on LPX and older power supplies, or Pin 8 (gray wire) on ATX and newer power supplies. Rated voltage is +5V; acceptable range is +3.0V to +6.0V.
		Replace failed power supply with higher-rated unit.
Fan turns for only a moment and then stops.	Wrong voltage (PS set to 220/230V in U.S.)	Turn off system; reset PS to correct voltage (110/115V in U.S.), and restart. Using 220/230V power on a PS set for 110/115V will destroy it!
	Dead short in system	Short can be caused by loose screws, failed hard drives, or add-on cards.
		Turn off and unplug system; disconnect the hard drive and see whether the system starts. If the system still fails, plug in the drive and remove the add-on card; repeat until each card and drive has been checked. Also check Y-adapter cables because bad cables can cause shorts.
		Replace faulty component(s).

Note

For more information on power supplies, wattage ratings, and testing, see Chapter 21 of *Upgrading and Repairing PCs, 13th Edition*, published by Que.

Memory Types

Random access memory (RAM) provides the work area that processors use to create and modify data. RAM was sometimes found on expansion boards on old XT-class and early AT-class systems, but now all standard 486-based and Pentium-class systems have their memory modules attached to the motherboard.

Memory modules come in three major forms: SIMMs, DIMMs, and RIMMs. *SIMM* stands for single-sided inline memory module, and *DIMM* stands for dual-sided inline memory module. These terms refer to the pin configurations used on the module rather than the location of the memory chips on the module. *RIMM* stands for Rambus inline memory module, referring to the Rambus DRAM chips used in RIMM modules.

> **Note**
>
> The 30-pin and 72-pin SIMMs have not been used in new sys-
> tems for several years and are obsolete. For more information
> about SIMMs, see *Upgrading and Repairing PCs, 13th Edition*.

DIMMs

The 168-pin DIMMs became popular with the rise of the Pentium
II/III/Celeron family of processors—AMD's Athlon series—and also can
be found on many late-model Pentium and "Super Socket 7" motherboards used with AMD K6-series and Cyrix 6×86MX/MII processors
(see Figure 2.9). DIMMs are the most popular and fastest type of memory module in widespread use. Most DIMMs are Synchronous DRAM
(SDRAM). On motherboards with both SIMM and DIMM sockets,
SDRAMs cannot be used in conjunction with SIMMs, but the relatively
rare EDO DIMMs can be used along with EDO SIMMs.

The following features are common to all DIMMs:

- Three edge connectors of varying widths for positive keying
- Different pinouts on each side of the DIMM

Figure 2.9 compares 30-pin and 72-pin SIMMs with a 168-pin
DIMM module.

SDRAM DIMMs are available in different speeds, and most motherboards are capable of using memory faster than they were originally designed to use without ill effects. Table 2.20 lists the timing
and speed values for standard SDRAM memory modules.

Table 2.20 SDRAM Timing, Actual Speed, and Rated Speed		
Timing	**Actual Speed**	**Rated Speed**
15ns	66MHz	PC66
10ns	100MHz	PC66
8ns	125MHz	PC100
7.5ns	133MHz	PC133

RDRAM

The *RDRAM*, or *Rambus DRAM*, is a radical new memory design
that is slowly appearing in high-end PC systems that use Intel
chipsets. RDRAM differs from previous memory devices in that it
provides multiple high-speed (800MHz), narrow-channel (16-
bit–wide) data transfers to and from a 128-bit memory bus instead
of the slower (100MHz or 66MHz) 32-bit or 64-bit data transfers of
SDRAM and previous memory types.

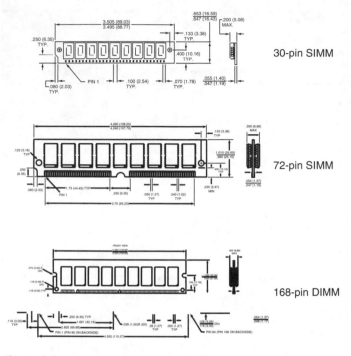

Figure 2.9 Comparing 168-pin DIMM memory to 72-pin and 30-pin SIMM memory.

RDRAM modules are called *RIMMs*, and any unused RIMM slots on a motherboard must be filled with a continuity module to permit a continuous high-speed data pathway through the RIMMs. Each RIMM represents multiple memory banks, and thus a single RIMM at a time can be added to a system—much the way installation of DIMMs works, although the memory types are not interchangeable.

DDR SDRAM

Double Data Rate (*DDR*) SDRAM memory is an improved version of standard SDRAM in which data is transferred twice as fast. Instead of doubling the actual clock rate, DDR memory achieves the doubling in performance by transferring twice per transfer cycle—once at the leading (falling) and once at the trailing (rising) edge of the cycle. This is similar to the way RDRAM operates and effectively doubles the transfer rate, even though the same overall clock and timing signals are used.

DDR SDRAM is supported by many of the newest server chipsets, and it provides a design alternative to the more radical RDRAM. The DDR Consortium—an industry panel consisting of Fujitsu, Ltd.; Hitachi, Ltd.; Hyundai Electronics Industries Co.; Mitsubishi Electric Corp.; NEC Corp.; Samsung Electronics Co.; Texas Instruments, Inc.; and Toshiba Corp.—undertook official standardization of DDR.

DDR SDRAM uses a new DIMM module design with 184 pins. Figure 2.10 shows the DDR SDRAM DIMM.

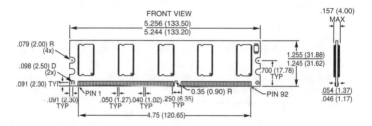

Figure 2.10 A 184-pin DDR SDRAM DIMM module; it has only two connectors, compared to the three connectors used on conventional 168-pin SDRAM DIMM modules.

DDR DIMMs are rated for either PC1600 (200MHz × 8, or 1,600MBps) or PC2100 (133MHz × 8 or 2,100MBps) operation, and they normally run on 2.5 volts. They are basically an extension of the PC100 and PC133 DIMMs redesigned to support double clocking, where data is sent on each clock transition (twice per cycle) rather than once per cycle, as is standard with SDRAM.

Parity Versus Nonparity Memory

Parity-checked RAM uses units of 8 memory bits plus 1 parity bit, for a total of 9 bits. In addition, parity checking uses both the data bits and the parity bit to ensure that memory contents are accurate with each memory access.

Virtually all 386-based and older systems, and most 486-based systems, require parity-checked memory, which can detect but not correct memory errors. On the other hand, most Pentium-class and higher systems don't require parity-checked RAM, but they will ignore the parity bit(s) if present.

Parity-checked memory *must* be used on systems that require it and *should* be used on systems that can be configured to use the parity bits, *especially* if the systems support Error Correction Code (ECC) operation, which uses the parity bit as a means of *correcting* a faulty memory bit.

Requirements for ECC Memory Use

ECC requires the following:

- Parity-checked or ECC-compatible memory modules

- A motherboard chipset that offers ECC support

- ECC support enabled in the BIOS system configuration

ECC operation is recommended for servers and other systems that are performing mission-critical tasks because ECC operation can correct single-bit memory errors. Larger memory errors will cause the system to display an error message and halt.

However, systems using ECC will cost more because of the higher cost of parity-checked RAM. Additionally, system performance is slightly slower because of the extra time involved in ECC operation. Check your motherboard or system documentation to determine whether ECC is an option for your system.

To determine whether a memory module supports parity-checking or ECC, use the following tips.

Table 2.22   Memory Bank Widths on Various Systems

Processor	Data Bus	Memory Bank Size (No Parity)	Memory Bank Size (Parity)	
8088	8-bit	8 bits	9 bits	
8086	16-bit	16 bits	18 bits	

Using the "Divide by 9" Rule to Determine Parity Support

The "divide by 9" rule can be used to determine parity checking if you know the number of memory bits in the module. Note in Table 2.21 that the number of bits in parity-checked modules can be divided by 9, but the number of bits in nonparity modules can be divided only by 8.

Table 2.21   DIMM and RIMM Capacities

168- or 184-Pin DIMM Capacities		
Capacity	**Parity DIMM**	**Nonparity DIMM**
8MB	1MB × 72	1MB × 64
16MB	2MB × 72	2MB × 64
32MB	4MB × 72	4MB – 64
64MB	8MB × 72	8MB × 64
128MB	16MB × 72	16MB × 64
256MB	32MB × 72	32MB × 64

RIMM Capacities		
	ECC RIMM	**Non-ECC RIMM**
64MB	32MB × 18	32MB × 16
128MB	64MB × 18	64MB × 16
256MB	128MB × 18	128MB × 16

Expanding Memory on a System

Memory must be added to a system in banks when conventional memory chips, SIMMs, or DIMMs are used. Simply put, a *bank* of memory is the amount of RAM in bits equal to the data bus width of the computer's CPU (see Table 2.22). Thus, a Pentium's data bus is 64 bits, and a memory module(s) used with a Pentium must have a total width of 64 bits for nonparity memory and 72 bits for parity-checked or ECC memory.

RIMM modules must be added in channels. Some systems using RIMMs use a single channel (single RIMM), while others feature dual channels, requiring two matched RIMMs.

30-Pin SIMMs per Bank	72-Pin SIMMs per Bank	168-Pin DIMMs per Bank	184-Pin DIMMs per Bank
1	—	—	n/a
2	—	—	n/a

Table 2.22   Memory Bank Widths on Various Systems Continued

Processor	Data Bus	Memory Bank Size (No Parity)	Memory Bank Size (Parity)	
286	16-bit	16 bits	18 bits	
386SX, SL, SLC	16-bit	16 bits	18 bits	
386DX	32-bit	32 bits	36 bits	
486SLC, SLC2	16-bit	16 bits	18 bits	
486SX, DX, DX2, DX4, 5×86	32-bit	32 bits	36 bits	
Pentium, K5, K6 6×86, 6×86MX, MII	64-bit	64 bits	72 bits	
Pentium Pro, PII, PIII, Celeron, Xeon, AMD Athlon, Duron, Intel Itanium	64-bit	64 bits	72 bits	

1. Very few motherboards for these processors actually use this type of memory.

The number of bits for each bank can be made up of single chips, SIMMs, or DIMMs. Modern systems don't use individual chips; instead, they use only SIMMs or DIMMs. If the system has a

Memory Troubleshooting

Figure 2.11 provides basic steps that enable you to effectively test and troubleshoot your system RAM. First, let's cover the memory testing and troubleshooting procedures.

After you've determined that the system's memory is defective, you need to determine which memory module is at fault. Follow the procedure in Figure 2.12 to isolate the module for replacement.

Memory Usage Within the System

The original PC had a total of 1MB of addressable memory, and the top 384KB of that was reserved for use by the system. Placing this reserved space at the top (between 640KB and 1024KB, instead of at the bottom, between 0KB and 640KB) led to what is often called the *conventional memory barrier*. Systems with more than 1MB of RAM treat the additional RAM as extended memory, beginning at 1MB.

Thus, there is a "hole" in memory usage between 640KB and 1MB. Some standard add-on cards and motherboard devices use part of this memory area for RAM and ROM addresses, leaving the remainder of this space free for additional card usage.

30-Pin SIMMs per Bank	72-Pin SIMMs per Bank	168-Pin DIMMs per Bank	184-Pin DIMMs per Bank
2	—	—	n/a
2	—	—	n/a
4	1	—	n/a
2	—	—	n/a
4	1	—	n/a
8[1]	2	1	1
8[1]	2	1	1

16-bit processor, such as a 386SX, it probably uses 30-pin SIMMs and has two SIMMs per bank. All the SIMMs in a single bank must be the same size and type.

The 30-pin SIMMs have 8 bits per module; 72-pin SIMMs have 32 bits per module; 168-pin SDRAM and 184-pin DDR SDRAM have 64 bits per module.

Hardware and Firmware Devices That Use Memory Addresses

The listing of hardware and firmware devices that use memory addresses is relatively short when compared to IRQ, DMA, and I/O port address usage, but it is no less important. No two devices can share a memory address. Table 2.23 shows memory usage in the 640KB–1MB memory range for standard devices.

Table 2.23   Memory Usage in the 640KB–1MB Range

Device	Address Range	Notes
Graphics Mode Video RAM	0A0000–0AFFFF	
Monochrome Text Mode Video RAM	0B0000–0B7FFF	
Color Text Mode Video RAM	0B8000–0BFFFF	
Video ROM for VGA, Super VGA	0C0000–0C7FFF	
Unassigned	0C8000–0DFFFF	Available for use by BIOS or RAM chips on add-on cards or by memory managers, such as QEMM or EMM386

Table 2.23 Memory Usage in the 640KB–1MB Range Continued		
Device	**Address Range**	**Notes**
Motherboard ROM BIOS extension (IBM PS/2s, most Pentium-class and newer systems)	0E0000–0EFFFF	If not used by BIOS extensions, can be treated as additional unassigned space
Motherboard ROM BIOS (all systems)	0F0000–0FFFFF	

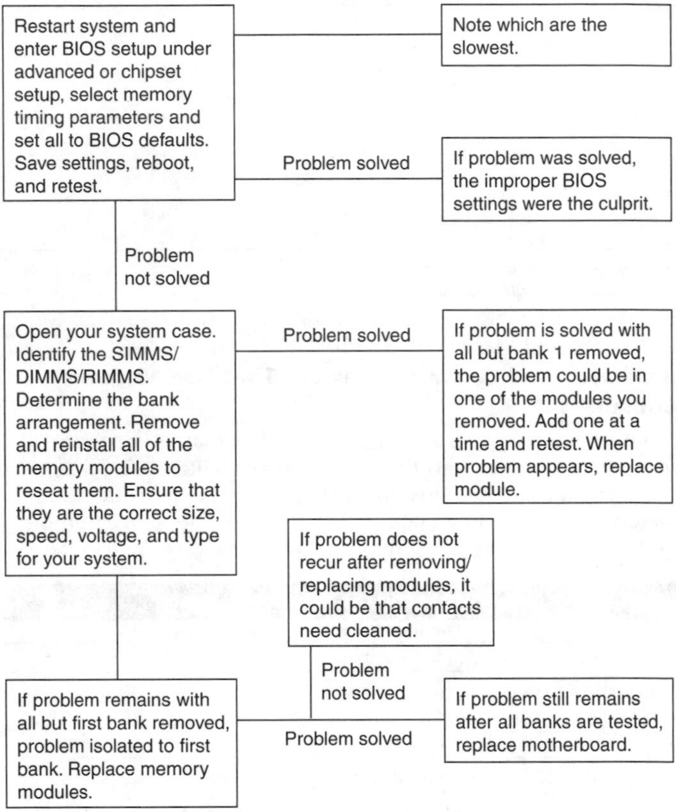

Restart system and enter BIOS setup under advanced or chipset setup, select memory timing parameters and set all to BIOS defaults. Save settings, reboot, and retest.

Note which are the slowest.

Problem solved

If problem was solved, the improper BIOS settings were the culprit.

Problem not solved

Open your system case. Identify the SIMMS/DIMMS/RIMMS. Determine the bank arrangement. Remove and reinstall all of the memory modules to reseat them. Ensure that they are the correct size, speed, voltage, and type for your system.

Problem solved

If problem is solved with all but bank 1 removed, the problem could be in one of the modules you removed. Add one at a time and retest. When problem appears, replace module.

If problem does not recur after removing/replacing modules, it could be that contacts need cleaned.

Problem not solved

If problem remains with all but first bank removed, problem isolated to first bank. Replace memory modules.

Problem solved

If problem still remains after all banks are tested, replace motherboard.

Figure 2.11   Testing and troubleshooting memory.

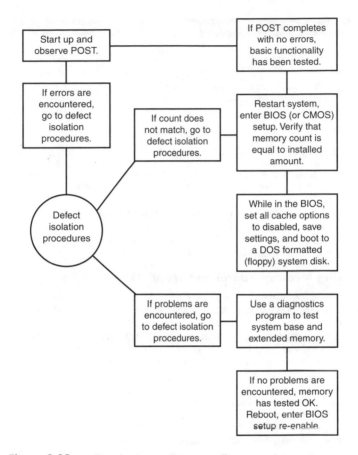

Figure 2.12   Follow these steps if you are still encountering memory errors after completing the steps in Figure 2.11.

If you are using an add-on card that uses a ROM BIOS chip onboard to overcome IDE hard drive limitations, overcome Y2K date rollover problems, or provide support for bootable SCSI hard drives, the BIOS chips on those cards must be placed in the unassigned memory range listed earlier. If you have two or more add-on cards that use memory address ranges, for best system performance, set the cards to use adjacent memory addresses.

Table 2.24 shows the typical memory uses for some common IDE and SCSI interface cards that use ROM BIOS chips.

	Onboard	
Adapter Type	**BIOS Size**	**BIOS Address Range**
Most XT-compatible controllers	8KB	0C8000–0C9FFF
Most AT controllers	None	Drivers in motherboard BIOS
Most standard IDE hard disk adapters	None	Drivers in motherboard BIOS
Most enhanced[1] IDE hard disk adapters	16KB	0C8000–0CBFFF
Some SCSI host adapters	16KB	0C8000–0CBFFF
Some SCSI host adapters	16KB	0DC000–0DFFFF

Table 2.24   Memory Addresses Used by Various Adapter Cards

1. *This type of adapter supplements the motherboard's IDE interface by supporting drives beyond 528MB (decimal) or 504MB (binary), or beyond 8.4GB (decimal) in size. Some of these adapters also can provide Y2K date-rollover support. Cards that combine both functions might use a larger (in KB) BIOS chip.*

Some older network cards also used memory addresses for RAM buffers or for ROM BIOS chips that permit diskless workstations to use a network copy of the operating system for booting. Network cards that use memory addresses are seldom used today.

Using Memory Addresses Beyond 1MB (0FFFFF)

Some older Super VGA cards, notably those from ATI, also could be set to use a 1MB extended memory address starting at 15MB for moving video data. This so-called *memory aperture* technique made the video cards using it faster but could not be used on systems with 16MB of RAM or above. If you use a video card that uses a fixed-memory aperture at 15MB on a system with less than 16MB of RAM, disable the memory aperture feature before you upgrade the RAM beyond 16MB. Some current PCI and AGP video cards also use memory apertures, but at addresses that generally do not interfere with today's larger amounts of system RAM.

Determining Memory Address Ranges in Use

On a system with Windows 9x, Windows 2000, Windows Me, or Windows XP, use the Device Manager's System Properties sheet to see overall memory address usage (see Figure 2.13).

Use add-on card documentation or a memory viewer, such as those included with AMIDiag, CheckIt, or Microsoft's MSD.EXE, to see memory usage on systems running Windows 3.1 or MS-DOS.

Note

To learn more about memory modules, see Chapter 6 of *Upgrading and Repairing PCs, 13th Edition*, published by Que.

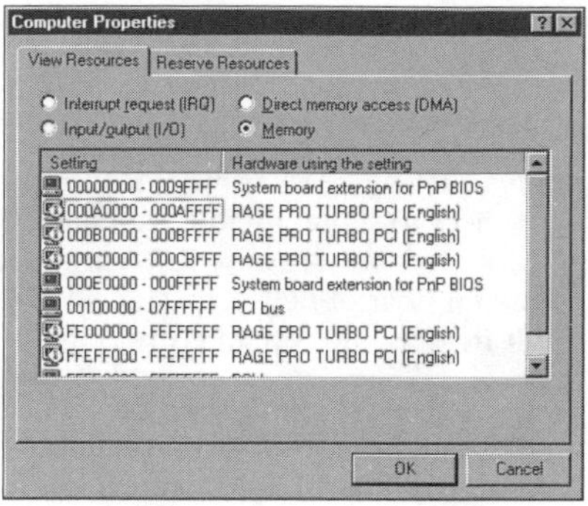

Figure 2.13   A system's upper memory usage as displayed by the
Windows 9*x* Device Manager. Addresses between 000CCFFFF and 000DFFFF
in upper memory are available for add-on cards. The ATI video card on board
also uses memory addresses above 1MB for a high-speed memory aperture.

Other Add-On Card Configuration Issues

When a card is installed into an expansion slot or a PCMCIA/PC
card device is installed into a PC card slot, the card must use at least
one of four hardware resources to be accessible to the system. All
add-on cards must use at least an I/O port address range or ranges,
most cards use an IRQ (interrupt request line), fewer cards use Direct
Memory Access (DMA), and memory addresses are used least of all.
Many cards use two or more of these hardware resources.

Note

For more information, see the section "Hardware and Firmware
Devices That Use Memory Addresses," earlier in this chapter.

If an add-on card is set to use the same hardware resource as an
existing card, it will not work unless that resource is designed to be
shared between cards. Although the capability to share IRQs has
existed (at least in theory) since the Micro Channel Architecture of
the late 1980s, even today the best rule of thumb for adding cards
is "each card has its own settings."

Plug-and-Play (PnP) configuration—introduced with Windows 95
and also present with Windows 98, Windows Me, Windows 2000,
and Windows XP—is designed to minimize much of the grief of
adding cards, but this technology has been in a state of flux since
it was introduced. To help you add cards, the following tables of

standard settings also list software and hardware tools that can help you find the settings already in use before you install your next card.

IRQs

Interrupt request channels (IRQs), or hardware interrupts, are used by various hardware devices to signal the motherboard that a request must be fulfilled. Most add-on cards use IRQs, and because systems today have the same number of IRQs available with the first IBM PC/AT systems built in 1984, IRQs frequently cause trouble in add-on card installations.

Table 2.25 shows IRQ assignments for 16-bit ISA and 32-bit VL-Bus/PCI expansion slots, listed by priority. Technically speaking, PCI interrupts can be shared, but, in practice, many older Pentium systems must use a unique IRQ value for each PCI card, as with ISA and VL-Bus cards.

Table 2.25   16/32-Bit ISA/VL-Bus/PCI Default Interrupt Assignments

IRQ	Standard Function	Bus Slot	Card Type	Recommended Use
0	System timer	No	—	—
1	Keyboard controller	No	—	—
2[1]	Second IRQ controller cascade	No	—	—
8	Real-time clock	No	—	—
9	Available (appears as IRQ 2)	Yes	8-/16-bit	Network interface card
10	Available	Yes	16-bit	USB
11	Available	Yes	16-bit	SCSI host adapter
12	Motherboard mouse port available	Yes	16-bit	Motherboard mouse port
13	Math coprocessor	No	—	—
14	Primary IDE	Yes	16-bit	Primary IDE (hard disks)
15	Secondary IDE/ available	Yes	16-bit	Secondary IDE (CD-ROM/tape)
3[4]	Serial Port 2 (COM 2:)	Yes	8-/16-bit	COM 2:/internal modem
4[3]	Serial Port 1 (COM 1:)	Yes	8-/16-bit	COM 1:
5[2]	Sound/Parallel Port 2 (LPT2:)	Yes	8-/16-bit	Sound card

	Standard			Recommended
IRQ	**Function**	**Bus Slot**	**Card Type**	**Use**
6	Floppy disk controller	Yes	8-/16-bit	Floppy controller
7	Parallel Port 1 (LPT1:)	Yes	8-/16-bit	LPT1:

Table 2.25   16/32-Bit ISA/VL-Bus/PCI Default Interrupt Assignments Continued

1. The original IBM PC/XT and compatible systems with 8-bit ISA slots did not assign any standard device to IRQ 2. When the 16-bit ISA slot was introduced, along with a second range of IRQs (8–15), this permitted the "cascading" of these interrupts via IRQ 2. Older cards that have IRQ 2 as a setting actually use IRQ 9 instead on 286-based and higher systems.

2. On original XT-class systems with 8-bit ISA slots, IRQ 5 was assigned to the hard disk controller card. Even though IRQ 5's "official" assignment is to handle LPT2 on systems with 16-bit ISA slots, only EPP and ECP (IEEE-1284) parallel port modes actually use an IRQ. This permits the use of IRQ 5 for sound cards in most systems without interfering with the use of LPT2.

3. Systems with COM 3 default to "sharing" COM 1's IRQ 4. This will cause system lockups in Windows if a serial mouse is used on COM 1 with a modem on COM 3. If you use the modem, the IRQ conflict crashes the system. To avoid problems, set the device using COM 3 to a different IRQ, or disable COM 2 and use COM 2 for the modem.

4. Systems with COM 4 default to "sharing" COM 2's IRQ 3. This will cause system lockups in Windows if a serial mouse is used on COM 2 with a modem on COM 4. If you use the modem, the IRQ conflict crashes the system. To avoid problems, set the device using COM 4 to a different IRQ, or disable COM 2 and use COM 2 for the modem.

Enabling IRQ Steering

Starting with Windows 95 OSR 2.*x* (Windows 95B), Microsoft Windows supports a feature called IRQ Steering, which enables two or more PCI cards to share a single IRQ. Systems that use IRQ steering will have an entry for the device using an IRQ and an entry indicating that IRQ Steering is taking place, as shown in Figure 2.14 later in this chapter.

For PCI IRQ Steering to take place, the following must be true:

• No ISA devices are using the IRQ.

• The BIOS and operating system support PCI IRQ Steering.

• PCI IRQ Steering is enabled.

To adjust the behavior of IRQ Steering using the Windows 98 Device Manager, perform these steps:

1. Click Start, Settings, Control Panel.

2. Open the System properties sheet.

3. Click the Device Manager tab.

4. Scroll down to the System Devices category and double-click to open it.

5. Select PCI Bus and click Properties.

6. Click the IRQ Steering tab to see or change the current settings.

For more information about troubleshooting IRQ Steering, see Chapter 4 of *Upgrading and Repairing PCs, 13th Edition.*

DMA

Direct Memory Access permits high-speed data transfer between I/O devices and memory without CPU management. This method of data transfer boosts performance for devices that use it, but because there is no CPU management, the possibility of data corruption is higher than for non-DMA transfers. Although DMA channels theoretically can be "shared" between devices that are not in use at the same time, this is not a recommended practice.

PCI cards don't use these DMA channels (with the exception of sound cards that are emulating the ISA-based Sound Blaster or compatibles—the major users of DMA channels today). See Table 2.26.

DMA	Standard Function	Bus Slot	Card Type	Transfer	Recommended Use
Table 2.26	**16/32-Bit ISA/PCI Default DMA-Channel Assignments**				
0	Available	Yes	16-bit	8-bit	Integrated sound
1	Available	Yes	8-/16-bit	8-bit	8-bit sound
2	Floppy disk controller	Yes	8-/16-bit	8-bit	Floppy controller
3	Available	Yes	8-/16-bit	8-bit	LPT1: in ECP mode
4	First DMA controller cascade	No	—	16-bit	—
5	Available	Yes	16-bit	16-bit	16-bit sound
6	Available	Yes	16-bit	16-bit	ISA SCSI adapter
7	Available	Yes	16-bit	16-bit	Available

Note that PCI adapters don't use these ISA DMA channels; these are only for ISA cards.

On PC/XT systems with only 8-bit ISA slots, only DMA channels 1–3 are available. DMA channel 2 was used for the floppy controller, as it is today, but channels 1 and 3 were not assigned to standard devices.

DMA transfers also can be performed by IDE/ATA hard drive interfaces, but because these are PCI devices, DMA channels are not needed.

Determining Actual IRQ and DMA Usage

Although these tables provide the "official" guidelines for IRQ and DMA usage, these settings might not be true for all systems at all times.

Add-on network, sound, serial, parallel, and SCSI cards often can be moved to different IRQ and DMA channels to work around conflicts. Nonstandard settings can be done manually with some cards, and this is a virtual certainty with PnP cards used with Windows 9*x*/Me/2000/XP. Well-designed PnP cards already installed in a system are designed to automatically move to nonconflicting settings when less-flexible PnP cards are inserted. Late-model Pentium-class systems using Windows 95 OSR 2.*x*, Windows 98, Windows 2000, Windows Me, or Windows XP also can use an IRQ holder for the PCI steering feature that allows multiple PCI devices to use a single IRQ, if the BIOS is designed to support it.

To view the current IRQ and DMA settings for systems using Windows 9*x* and later versions, use the Device Manager (a tab on the System Properties sheet). View the properties for the Computer icon at the top of the device list, and you can choose from IRQ, DMA, I/O port, and memory address information (see Figure 2.14).

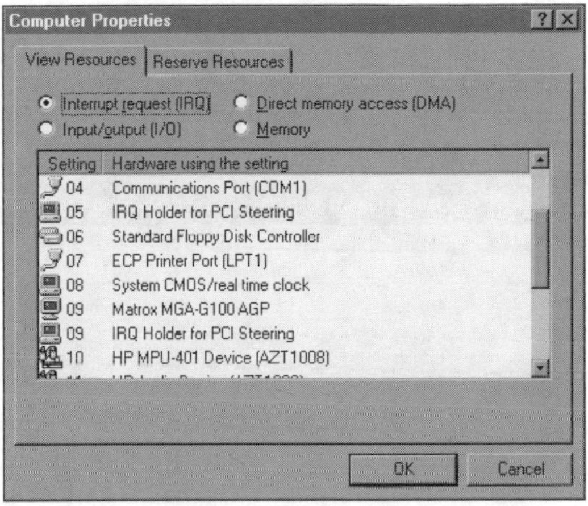

Figure 2.14   The Windows 9*x* Device Manager and Computer Properties sheet shows IRQs in use; available IRQs are not listed. The IRQ steering feature enables IRQ 5 to be shared between two different PCI-based cards without conflicts.

For other operating systems, we recommend an interface card with signal lights for IRQ and DMA usage. The Discovery Card, developed by John Rourke, pioneered this diagnostic category, and many vendors offer cards with this feature. Some vendors combine IRQ/DMA detection with POST code detection or active system testing.

To use an IRQ/DMA card, turn off the system, insert the card into an open slot, and turn on the system. As devices that use an IRQ or a DMA are activated, the corresponding signal light on the card is displayed. Most cards have a reset switch, which enables the card lights to be cleared, allowing you to test for possible conflicts. When combined with information from a system configuration template, this helps provide accurate IRQ and DMA usage information.

I/O Port Addresses

Your computer's I/O ports enable communication between devices and software in your system. They are equivalent to two-way radio channels. If you want to talk to your serial port, you need to know which I/O port (radio channel) it is listening on. Similarly, if you want to receive data from the serial port, you need to listen on the same channel on which it is transmitting.

One confusing issue is that I/O ports are designated by hexadecimal addresses similar to memory addresses. They are not memory; they are ports.

Motherboard and chipset devices normally are set to use I/O port addresses from 0h to FFh, and all other devices use from 100h to FFFFh. Table 2.27 shows motherboard and chipset-based I/O port usage.

Table 2.27	Motherboard and Chipset-Based Device Port Addresses	
Address (Hex)	**Size**	**Description**
0000–000F	16 bytes	Chipset—8237 DMA 1
0020–0021	2 bytes	Chipset—8259 interrupt controller 1
002E–002F	2 bytes	Super I/O controller configuration registers
0040–0043	4 bytes	Chipset—Counter/Timer 1
0048–004B	4 bytes	Chipset—Counter/Timer 2
0060	1 byte	Keyboard/mouse controller byte—reset IRQ
0061	1 byte	Chipset—NMI, speaker control
0064	1 byte	Keyboard/mouse controller, CMD/STAT byte
0070, bit 7	1 bit	Chipset—enable NMI
0070, bits 6:0	7 bits	MC146818—real-time clock, address
0071	1 byte	MC146818—real-time clock, data
0078	1 byte	Reserved—board configuration
0079	1 byte	Reserved—board configuration
0080–008F	16 bytes	Chipset—DMA page registers
00A0–00A1	2 bytes	Chipset—8259 interrupt controller 2
00B2	1 byte	APM control port
00B3	1 byte	APM status port

Table 2.27 Motherboard and Chipset-Based Device Port Addresses Continued		
Address (Hex)	**Size**	**Description**
00C0–00DE	31 bytes	Chipset—8237 DMA 2
00F0	1 byte	Math coprocessor reset numeric error

To find out exactly which port addresses are being used on your motherboard, consult the board documentation or look up the settings in the Windows Device Manager.

Bus-based devices (I/O devices found on the motherboard or on add-on cards) normally use the addresses from 100h on up. Table 2.28 lists the commonly used bus-based device addresses and some common adapter cards and their settings.

Table 2.28 Bus-Based Device Port Addresses		
Address (Hex)	**Size**	**Description**
0130–0133	4 bytes	Adaptec SCSI adapter (alternate)
0134–0137	4 bytes	Adaptec SCSI adapter (alternate)
0168–016F	8 bytes	Fourth IDE interface
0170–0177	8 bytes	Secondary IDE interface
01E8–01EF	8 bytes	Third IDE interface
01F0–01F7	8 bytes	Primary IDE/AT (16-bit) hard disk controller
0200–0207	8 bytes	Gameport or joystick adapter
0210–0217	8 bytes	IBM XT expansion chassis
0220–0233	20 bytes	Creative Labs Sound Blaster 16 audio (default)
0230–0233	4 bytes	Adaptec SCSI adapter (alternate)
0234–0237	4 bytes	Adaptec SCSI adapter (alternate)
0238–023B	4 bytes	MS bus mouse (alternate)
023C–023F	4 bytes	MS bus mouse (default)
0240–024F	16 bytes	SMC Ethernet adapter (default)
0240–0253	20 bytes	Creative Labs Sound Blaster 16 audio (alternate)
0258–025F	8 bytes	Intel above board
0260–026F	16 bytes	SMC Ethernet adapter (alternate)
0260–0273	20 bytes	Creative Labs Sound Blaster 16 audio (alternate)
0270–0273	4 bytes	Plug-and-Play I/O read ports
0278–027F	8 bytes	Parallel Port 2 (LPT2)
0280–028F	16 bytes	SMC Ethernet adapter (alternate)
0280–0293	20 bytes	Creative Labs Sound Blaster 16 audio (alternate)
02A0–02AF	16 bytes	SMC Ethernet adapter (alternate)
02C0–02CF	16 bytes	SMC Ethernet adapter (alternate)

Table 2.28 Bus-Based Device Port Addresses Continued		
Address (Hex)	**Size**	**Description**
02E0–02EF	16 bytes	SMC Ethernet adapter (alternate)
02E8–02EF	8 bytes	Serial Port 4 (COM 4)
02EC–02EF	4 bytes	Video, 8514, or ATI standard port
02F8–02FF	8 bytes	Serial port 2 (COM 2)
0300–0301	2 bytes	MPU-401 MIDI port (secondary)
0300–030F	16 bytes	SMC Ethernet adapter (alternate)
0320–0323	4 bytes	XT (8-bit) hard disk controller
0320–032F	16 bytes	SMC Ethernet adapter (alternate)
0330–0331	2 bytes	MPU-401 MIDI port (default)
0330–0333	4 bytes	Adaptec SCSI adapter (default)
0334–0337	4 bytes	Adaptec SCSI adapter (alternate)
0340–034F	16 bytes	SMC Ethernet adapter (alternate)
0360–036F	16 bytes	SMC Ethernet adapter (alternate)
0366	1 byte	Fourth IDE command port
0367, bits 6:0	7 bits	Fourth IDE status port
0370–0375	6 bytes	Secondary floppy controller
0376	1 byte	Secondary IDE command port
0377, bit 7	1 bit	Secondary floppy controller disk change
0377, bits 6:0	7 bits	Secondary IDE status port
0378–037F	8 bytes	Parallel port 1 (LPT1)
0380–038F	16 bytes	SMC Ethernet adapter (alternate)
0388–038B	4 bytes	Audio—FM synthesizer
03B0–03BB	12 bytes	Video, Mono/EGA/VGA standard ports
03BC–03BF	4 bytes	Parallel port 1 (LPT1) in some systems
03BC–03BF	4 bytes	Parallel port 3 (LPT3)
03C0–03CF	16 bytes	Video, EGA/VGA standard ports
03D0–03DF	16 bytes	Video, CGA/EGA/VGA standard ports
03E6	1 byte	Third IDE command port
03E7, bits 6:0	7 bits	Third IDE status port
03E8–03EF	8 bytes	Serial port 3 (COM 3)
03F0–03F5	6 bytes	Primary floppy controller
03F6	1 byte	Primary IDE command port
03F7, bit 7	1 bit	Primary floppy controller disk change
03F7, bits 6:0	7 bits	Primary IDE status port
03F8–03FF	8 bytes	Serial port 1 (COM 1)
04D0–04D1	2 bytes	Edge/level triggered PCI interrupt controller
0530–0537	8 bytes	Windows sound system (default)

Table 2.28	Bus-Based Device Port Addresses Continued	
Address (Hex)	**Size**	**Description**
0604–060B	8 bytes	Windows sound system (alternate)
0678–067F	8 bytes	LPT2 in ECP mode
0778–077F	8 bytes	LPT1 in ECP mode
0A20–0A23	4 bytes	IBM Token Ring adapter (default)
0A24–0A27	4 bytes	IBM Token Ring adapter (alternate)
0CF8–0CFB	4 bytes	PCI configuration address registers
0CF9	1 byte	Turbo and reset control register
0CFC–0CFF	4 bytes	PCI configuration data registers
FF00–FF07	8 bytes	IDE bus master registers
FF80–FF9F	32 bytes	Universal Serial Bus (USB)
FFA0–FFA7	8 bytes	Primary bus master IDE registers
FFA8–FFAF	8 bytes	Secondary bus master IDE registers

Determining Actual I/O Address Ranges in Use

To find out exactly what your devices are using, consult the documentation for the device or look up the device in the Windows 9*x* Device Manager. Note that some device documentation might list only the starting I/O address, not the full range of addresses used.

Virtually all devices on your system buses use I/O port addresses. Most of these are fairly standardized, meaning that you won't often have conflicts or problems with these settings.

Troubleshooting Add-On Card Resource Conflicts

The resources in a system are limited. Unfortunately, the demands on those resources seem to be unlimited. As you add more adapter cards to your system, you will find that the potential for resource conflicts increases.

Symptoms of a Potential Resource Conflict

- A device transfers data inaccurately.
- Your system frequently locks up.
- Your sound card doesn't sound quite right.
- Your mouse doesn't work.
- Garbage appears on your video screen for no apparent reason.
- Your printer prints gibberish.
- You cannot format a floppy disk.
- The PC starts in Safe mode (Windows 9*x*/2000/Me/XP).

Spotting Resource Conflicts with Windows 9x/2000/Me/XP

Windows 9x/Me/2000 also show conflicts by highlighting a device in yellow or red in the Device Manager representation. By using the Windows Device Manager, you usually can spot the conflicts quickly (see Figure 2.15).

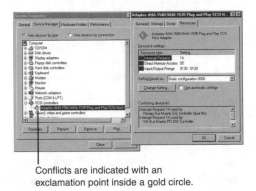

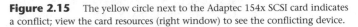

Conflicts are indicated with an
exclamation point inside a gold circle.

Figure 2.15   The yellow circle next to the Adaptec 154x SCSI card indicates a conflict; view the card resources (right window) to see the conflicting device.

Keep in mind that many computer viruses also can cause symptoms similar to hardware resource conflicts. Scan your system for viruses before you start working on it.

Recording System Settings

Use a System Configuration Template to record system settings. This sheet is resource-oriented, not device-oriented, to make finding conflicts easier. You can make a printout of the System Summary from the Windows 9x/Me/2000/XP Device Manager to get a lot of this information. For other operating systems, use the methods listed earlier.

The first system resource map is provided as a model for your use; it lists fixed resources on a modern PC. Add the other resources used on your PC. Note that many high-performance PCI or AGP video cards do use an IRQ, although some motherboard chipsets have a provision for disabling the IRQ usage.

Also note that you might see changes in the system configuration after you install a new Plug-and-Play (PnP) card. PnP cards might not only use additional resources, but they also might require that existing devices be moved to other resources to enable the new card to be installed. PnP cards also might receive IRQ assignments from the expansion slot used, and some motherboards share an IRQ between slots, or between a slot and an onboard device such as audio or network features. This is fine as long as IRQ Steering is enabled in the OS and supported by the BIOS.

System Resource Map

PC Make and Model: _____

Serial Number: _____

Date: _____

Interrupts (IRQs):	*I/O Port Addresses:*
0—Timer Circuits	040–04B
1—Keyboard/Mouse Controller	060 and 064
2—2nd 8259 IRQ Controller	0A0–0A1
8—Real-Time Clock/CMOS RAM	070–071
9— _____	_____
10— _____	_____
11— _____	_____
12— _____	_____
13—Math Coprocessor	0F0
14— _____	_____
15— _____	_____
3— _____	_____
4— _____	_____
5— _____	_____
6— _____	_____
7— _____	_____

Devices Not Using Interrupts:	*I/O Port Addresses:*
Mono/EGA/VGA Standard Ports	3B0–3BB
EGA/VGA Standard Ports	3C0–3CF
CGA/EGA/VGA Standard Ports	3D0–3DF
_____	_____
_____	_____
_____	_____
_____	_____
_____	_____

DMA Channels:

0— _____

1— _____

2— _____

3— _____

4—DMA Channel 0–3 Cascade

5— _____

6— _____

7— _____

Here's an example of how to fill out the worksheet:

System Resource Map

PC Make and Model: Intel SE440BX-2_____

Serial Number: 100000_____

Date: 06/09/99_____

Interrupts (IRQs):	*I/O Port Addresses:*
0—Timer Circuits	040–04B
1—Keyboard/Mouse Controller	060 and 064
2—2nd 8259 IRQ Controller	0A0–0A1
8—Real-Time Clock/CMOS RAM	070–071
9—SMC EtherEZ Ethernet card_____	340–35F_____
10—_____	_____
11—Adaptec 1542CF SCSI Adapter (scanner)	334–337[1]_____
12—Motherboard Mouse Port_____	060 and 064_____
13—Math Coprocessor	0F0
14—Primary IDE (hard disk 1 and 2)_____	1F0–1F7, 3F6_____
15—Secondary IDE (CD-ROM/tape)_____	170–177, 376_____
3—Serial Port 2 (Modem)_____	3F8–3FF_____
4—Serial Port 1 (COM1)_____	2F8–2FF_____
5—Sound Blaster 16 Audio_____	220–233_____
6—Floppy Controller_____	3F0–3F5_____
7—Parallel Port 1 (Printer)_____	378–37F_____

Devices Not Using Interrupts:	*I/O Port Addresses:*
Mono/EGA/VGA Standard Ports	3B0–3BB
EGA/VGA Standard Ports	3C0–3CF
CGA/EGA/VGA Standard Ports	3D0–3DF
ATI Mach 64 Video Card Additional Ports___	102, 1CE–1CF, 2EC–2EF
Sound Blaster 16 MIDI Port_____	330–331_____
Sound Blaster 16 Game Port (Joystick)_____	200–207_____
Sound Blaster 16 FM Synthesizer (Music)___	388–38B_____
_____	_____

DMA Channels:

0—_____

1—Sound Blaster 16 (8-bit DMA)_____

2—Floppy Controller_____

3—Parallel Port 1 (in ECP mode)_____

4—DMA Channel 0–3 Cascade

5—Sound Blaster 16 (16-bit DMA)_____

6—Adaptec 1542CF SCSI Adapter[1]_____

7—_____

1. Represents a resource setting that had to be changed to resolve a conflict.

After you've completed your system resource map by recording the current settings for hardware, you're ready to solve conflicts.

Note
Resource use can change whenever PnP or non-PnP hardware is installed or removed, so you should update this chart whenever you add or remove internal hardware.

Resolving Conflicts by Card and Operating System Type

Table 2.29 Guide to Resolving Conflicts		
Operating System	**Card Type**	**Notes**
Windows 9x/2000/Me/XP	PnP	Use Device Manager to change card settings, if possible. Remove and reinstall the card to redetect the card, and use new settings if that card can't be set manually. If the new card can't be detected when installed, remove other PnP cards and install the new card first.
	Non-PnP	Use Device Manager to see conflicting devices. Manually configure cards to non-conflicting settings by changing jumpers or DIP switches, or rerunning configuration programs.
Other operating systems	Any	*When did the conflict first become apparent?* If the conflict occurred after you installed a new adapter card, that new card probably is causing the conflict. If the conflict occurred after you started using new software, chances are good that the software uses a device that is taxing your system's resources in a new way.
		Are there two similar devices in your system that do not work? For example, if your modem, integrated serial ports, or mouse devices that use a COM port do not work, chances are good that these devices are conflicting with each other.
		Have other people had the same problem? And if so, how did they resolve it? Public forums such as those on CompuServe, Internet newsgroups, and America Online are great places to find other users who might be able to help you solve the conflict. Also check vendor forums for help.
		After you research these questions, make one (one!) change to your system configuration, reboot the computer and see whether the problem is now resolved. Repeat with a different setting until the problem is solved.

Table 2.29 Guide to Resolving Conflicts Continued		
Operating System	**Card Type**	**Notes**
		Test all components to make sure that "fixing" one component didn't cause a conflict with another.

Expansion Slots

If you want to add network, SCSI, modem, or sound capabilities to an existing system or upgrade your video card, you need to understand expansion slots. Expansion slots act as an extension of the system bus and permit you to connect cards with different features to your system.

ISA, EISA, and VL-Bus

Industry Standard Architecture (ISA) expansion slots are the oldest expansion slot design found in current PCs. The 8-bit versions go all the way back to the original IBM PC of 1981. Although 8-bit–only ISA slots have faded away, 16-bit ISA slots (introduced with the IBM PC/AT in 1984) are fully pin-compatible with 8-bit ISA cards.

The Enhanced ISA (EISA) bus was developed from the ISA architecture to provide 32-bit data transfers. The EISA expansion slot (introduced in 1988) is a deeper version of ISA, providing a second offset row of connectors that allows EISA slots to support ISA cards. Figure 2.16 compares an EISA slot to a 16-bit ISA slot. EISA slots primarily are found in 386, 486, and early Pentium servers.

Introduced in 1992, the VL-Bus (VESA Local-Bus) was an improved 32-bit version of ISA designed originally to provide faster video card performance on 486-based systems. This slot design, like EISA, is now obsolete. Although most VL-Bus slots were added to an ISA slot, the VL-Bus connector also could be added to an EISA slot. Thus, any VL-Bus slot is also an ISA or an ISA/EISA slot.

PCI

Intel developed Peripheral Component Interconnect (PCI) in 1992 to eventually replace ISA and its variations. Most PCI slots provide 32-bit transfers, with a 64-bit version of PCI being used in many late-model file servers.

Although most newer systems offer only PCI slots, many systems that you will encounter also will have one or more ISA slots, as in Figure 2.3.

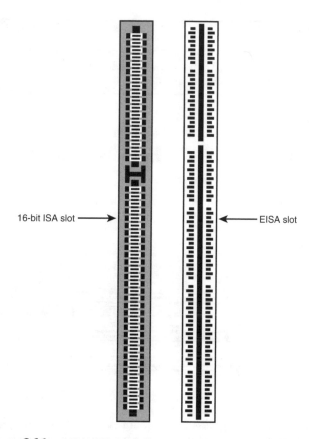

16-bit ISA slot ⟶   ⟵ EISA slot

Figure 2.16   A 16-bit ISA slot (left) compared to an EISA slot (right). The smaller teeth in the EISA slot enable the connector to use an offset design that can handle both EISA and ISA cards.

AGP

The latest expansion slot design is AGP (Accelerated Graphics Port), introduced in 1996 to provide faster video performance in a dedicated slot. AGP doesn't replace PCI for general purposes, but AGP video cards offer much faster performance than similar PCI cards, and can also "borrow" from main memory for 3D texturing. Most typical Pentium II/III, Celeron, Athlon, Duron, or Super Socket 7 systems include a single AGP slot as well as a mixture of PCI and ISA slots (see Figure 2.3).

> **Note**
>
> Although AGP video is standard on all desktop systems today, it is often implemented on very low-cost systems by means of onboard video rather than an AGP slot.

Types of AGP Slots

Three major types of AGP slots exist:

- AGP 1x/2x—Found on early AGP motherboards
- AGP 4x—The current standard
- AGP Pro—A modified AGP 4x slot that can provide more electrical power (wattage) for workstation-class AGP cards

These slots are pictured in Figure 2.17.

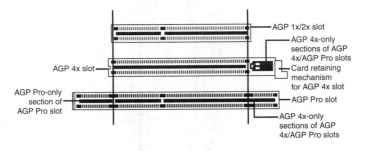

Figure 2.17   AGP standard (1x/2x), AGP 4x, and AGP Pro slots compared to each other. AGP 4x and AGP Pro can accept AGP 1x, 2x, and 4x cards.

Expansion Slot Comparison

Figure 2.18 and Table 2.30 provide a visual quick reference for expansion slots found in modern PCs.

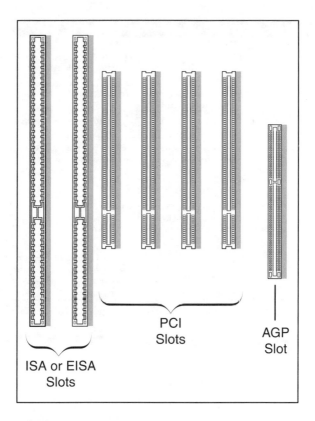

Figure 2.18   The AGP slot is located at the first (inside) slot position on motherboards with an AGP slot. Note the lack of space between the last PCI slot and the first ISA slot. This is called a *combo* or *shared* slot; only one of the slots actually can be used.

Table 2.30 Expansion Slot Quick-Reference Table			
Slot Type	**Bus Speed**	**Bus Width**	**Best Use**
ISA	8.33MHz	8-bit or 16-bit	Modems, serial, parallel ports; will be phased out in early 21st century
EISA	8.33MHz	32-bit with EISA cards; compatible with ISA cards	Obsolete for most uses; works well with server-optimized NIC cards
MCA	10MHz	16-bit or 32-bit	Introduced with IBM MicroChannel PS/2s in 1987; obsolete
VL-Bus	25–33MHz typical; can be run up to 40MHz on some systems	32-bit; slot also can be used as ISA	Obsolete; was popular for video cards and IDE hard disk interfaces
PCI	25–33MHz (depends on speed of motherboard)	Most are 32-bit; some 64-bit implementations used on file servers	Video, SCSI, sound, modems; replaced ISA as general-purpose bus
AGP	66MHz	64-bit	Dedicated high-speed video; motherboards can support 1x, 2x, or 4x speeds of AGP cards, depending on board design

Chapter 3

BIOS Configurations and Upgrades

What the BIOS Is and What It Does

The ROM (read only memory) BIOS (basic input/output system) chip on the computer's motherboard is designed to provide the essential interfacing between hardware (such as drives, the clock, the CPU, the chipset, ports, and video) and software (the operating system). Although video, some SCSI, and a few IDE add-on cards might also have BIOS chips that help manage those devices, whenever we refer to the computer's *BIOS chip*, we mean the one on the motherboard. The BIOS chip is often referred to as the *ROM BIOS* because, in its traditional form, it was a read-only memory chip with contents that could not be changed. Later versions could be reprogrammed with an EPROM programmer, and, beginning in the mid-1990s, BIOSes using flash memory (*flash BIOS*) began to appear. Flash BIOSes can be reprogrammed through software, and virtually all BIOSes on Pentium-class machines and beyond are flash-upgradeable.

Regardless of its form, the BIOS chip on the motherboard is also known as the *system BIOS*.

When a BIOS Update Is Necessary

The following list shows the primary benefits of a ROM BIOS upgrade:

- Adds LS-120 (120MB) floppy drive support (also known as a SuperDisk drive)

- Adds support for other ATAPI removable drives, such as Iomega Zip drives

- Adds support for hard drives greater than 8.4GB

- Adds support for Ultra-DMA/33, UDMA/66, UDMA/100, or faster IDE hard drives

- Adds support for bootable ATAPI CD-ROM drives (El Torito)

- Adds or improves Plug-and-Play support and compatibility

- Corrects calendar-related bugs

- Corrects known bugs or compatibility problems with certain hardware and software

- Adds support for newer or faster processors

In general, if your computer is incapable of using all the features of new software or hardware, you might need a BIOS upgrade.

Specific Tests to Determine Whether Your BIOS Needs an Update

To determine whether your BIOS needs to be updated because of hard drive capacity limitations, see Chapter 4, "SCSI and ATA Hard Drives and Optical Drives."

To determine whether your BIOS needs to be updated because of operating system or CPU upgrade issues, consult the technical-support Web sites for the operating system or CPU upgrade.

Fixing BIOS Limitations—BIOS Fixes and Alternatives

Use Table 3.1 to determine which options you can follow if a BIOS update isn't possible, depending on the BIOS problem noted.

Table 3.1	**Alternatives to BIOS Upgrades**		
Problem	**Alternative Fix**	**Benefits of Alternative Fix**	**Limitations of Alternative Fix**
IDE hard disk capacity limitations	See Chapter 4 for details of these fixes.		
Complete solution	Replace motherboard.	Provides both brand-new BIOS and new motherboard features at a price often just slightly higher than a third-party BIOS upgrade.	System must use standard MB form factor. Mix of ISA and PCI/AGP slots might mean some existing cards won't fit because latest motherboards have more PCI than ISA slots. Time-consuming hardware install; time-consuming redetection and configuration of hardware drivers in operating system.

How BIOS Updates Are Performed

Two different ways of updating a motherboard BIOS are available.

- **Replacing the physical BIOS chip**—With older systems, a physical *chip swap* (also called a *BIOS chip upgrade*) is necessary. The original BIOS chip is removed, and a new BIOS chip is inserted in its place. The new BIOS must be customized to match the old system's motherboard and chipset, use its existing CPU, and provide the enhanced features specified by the upgrade BIOS manufacturer. The typical cost range is around $30–$60 for a single BIOS chip.

- **Performing a flash upgrade**—With newer systems that have a flash-upgradeable BIOS, the update software is downloaded and installed onto a disk, which is used to boot the computer. Then the new BIOS code is copied to the BIOS chip in a process that takes about 3–5 minutes. If the BIOS update comes from a source *other* than the original system or motherboard maker, it will also cost as much as $60 for the update.

In either case, the system might need to be reconfigured, especially if the new BIOS was physically installed or if either a chip-based or flash-based BIOS is a different brand of BIOS than the original.

Where BIOS Updates Come From

The best (and cheapest) place to get a BIOS update is from your motherboard or system vendor. Most major system manufacturers offer free BIOS updates for their systems with flash BIOS chips on their Web sites. For generic systems with motherboards from various producers, see the section "Determining Which BIOS You Have," later in this chapter.

A second source for BIOS updates is from one of the following companies:

For systems that originally used the Phoenix BIOS, contact Micro Firmware (www.firmware.com or 800-767-5465). Micro Firmware typically supplies updated Phoenix flash BIOS code on disk for systems they support. See the Web site for the current list of supported systems and motherboards.

For systems that originally used the Award, AMI, MR BIOS, or Phoenix BIOS (including systems not supported by Micro Firmware), contact Unicore Software (www.unicore.com or 800-800-BIOS). Unicore might supply the update on disk or as a replacement MR BIOS chip. Contact these vendors for details and prices, which vary by system.

Precautions to Take Before Updating a BIOS

Use the following checklist to be safe, not sorry, when updating a BIOS:

1. First, back up your data. An "almost working" BIOS that doesn't quite work with your hard drive can blow away your data.

2. Back up your current BIOS code, if you can. Some BIOS update loader programs offer this option, but others don't. As an alternative, some BIOS chips keep a mini-BIOS onboard that can be reactivated if a botched update destroys the main BIOS. Some motherboards have a jumper that can be used to switch to the backup; check your system documentation. For others, check the Micro Firmware Web site for its Flash BIOS Recovery Disks page to find out whether your motherboard is listed. If the BIOS update isn't completed properly, you could have a dead system that will need a trip to the manufacturer for repair. See the section "How to Recover from a Failed BIOS Update Procedure," later in this chapter for a typical recovery procedure.

3. Record your hard drive configuration information. If you are switching to a different brand of BIOS, you might need to re-enter this information. The information that you should record includes

   - Cylinders

   - Heads

   - Sectors per track

   - Translation (Normal, LBA [greater than 528MB], Large, and so on)

4. Record other nonstandard BIOS settings, such as hard disk transfer rate settings, built-in serial and parallel port settings, and so on. A worksheet that you can use as a guide is found later in this chapter.

5. Read carefully and completely the information provided with the flash BIOS download or chip-type BIOS update kit. Check online or call the BIOS manufacturer if you have any questions before you ruin your BIOS.

6. Check to see whether your system has a *write-protect* setting jumper on the motherboard that must be adjusted to allow a BIOS update to take place. Some motherboards disable BIOS updates by default to protect your system's BIOS from unauthorized changes. Set your motherboard to allow the change before you install the flash BIOS update, and reset the protection after the update is complete.

How to Recover from a Failed BIOS Update Procedure

If your BIOS update procedure fails, your system will be useless until you replace the BIOS code. You have two options:

- Install a replacement BIOS chip (if the BIOS is located in a socketed chip).

- Use the BIOS recovery feature (available on many systems with surface-mounted or soldered-in-place BIOS chips).

If your BIOS is socketed, you will need to replace it with a compatible BIOS chip. Replacement BIOS chips are available from the BIOS upgrade sources listed earlier. However, if your system is still supported by BIOS updates from the manufacturer, you can order a BIOS replacement from BIOSWorld (www.biosworld.com), a company that will download the system or motherboard maker's latest BIOS into a replacement flash memory chip for about $30.

Most motherboards with soldered-in flash ROMs have a special BIOS recovery procedure that can be performed. This hinges on a special unerasable part of the flash ROM that is reserved for this purpose.

In the unlikely event that a flash upgrade is interrupted catastrophically, the BIOS might be left in an unusable state. Recovering from this condition requires the following steps. A minimum of a power supply, a speaker, and a floppy drive configured as drive A should be attached to the motherboard for this procedure to work.

1. Change the flash recovery jumper to the recovery mode position. Virtually all Intel motherboards and many third-party motherboards have a jumper or switch for BIOS recovery, which is normally labeled Recover/Normal.

2. Install the bootable BIOS upgrade disk that you previously created to perform the flash upgrade into drive A, and reboot the system.

Because of the small amount of code available in the
unerasable flash boot block area, no video prompts are available to direct the procedure. In other words, you will see
nothing onscreen. In fact, it is not even necessary for a video
card to be connected for this procedure to work. The procedure can be monitored by listening to the speaker and looking at the floppy drive LED. When the system beeps and the
floppy drive LED is lit, the system is copying the BIOS recovery code into the flash device.

3. As soon as the drive LED goes off, the recovery should be
   complete. Power off the system.

4. Change the flash recovery jumper back to the default position for normal operation.

When you power the system back on, the new BIOS should be
installed and functional. However, you might want to leave the
BIOS upgrade floppy in drive A and check to see that the proper
BIOS version was installed.

Note

Note that this BIOS recovery procedure is often the fastest way
to update a large number of machines, especially if you are performing other upgrades at the same time. This is how it is normally done in a system assembly or production environment.

Plug-and-Play BIOS

The role of the traditional BIOS was to manage the essential
devices in the system: the hard drive, floppy drive, video, parallel
and serial ports, and keyboard and system timer. Other devices
were left to fight for the remaining IRQs and other hardware
resources listed in Chapter 2, "System Components and
Configuration." When Windows 95 was introduced, the role of the
BIOS changed dramatically. To support Windows 95, the Plug-and-
Play BIOS was introduced, changing how cards were installed and
managed. Table 3.2 compares a Plug-and-Play (PnP) BIOS to a conventional BIOS.

Table 3.2   Plug-and-Play BIOS Versus Conventional BIOS

Task	Conventional BIOS	Plug-and-Play BIOS
Hardware configuration	Motherboard-based devices and video only	All PnP devices as well as motherboard devices
Configuration type	Static (fixed settings)	Dynamic (settings can be altered as various devices are installed)
Configuration method	Manual configuration	Manual, BIOS-assisted, or operating system assisted
Operating system relationship to BIOS	Accepts all BIOS settings without alteration	Receives PnP device information from BIOS and can alter settings as required

---

Note

A complete list of PnP device IDs is found in the Technical Reference section of the CD included with *Upgrading and Repairing PCs, 13th Edition.*

PnP BIOS Configuration Options

Although PnP BIOSes vary widely in their features, the following settings are typical. Use the list in Table 3.3, along with the tables that follow, to help you make configuration changes when necessary.

Resource Configuration

The Resource Configuration menu is used for configuring the memory and interrupt usage of non–Plug-and-Play (legacy) ISA bus-based devices. Table 3.3 shows the functions and options found in a typical modern BIOS.

Table 3.3   Typical Resource Configuration Menu[1]

Feature	Options	Description
Memory Reservation	C800 CBFF Available (default) I Reserved CC00 CFFF Available (default) I Reserved D000 D3FF Available (default) I Reserved D400 D7FF Available (default) I Reserved D800 DBFF Available (default) I Reserved DC00 DFFF Available (default) I Reserved	Reserves specific upper memory blocks for use by legacy ISA devices.
IRQ Reservation	IRQ 3 Available (default) I Reserved IRQ 4 Available (default) I Reserved IRQ 5 Available (default) I Reserved IRQ 7 Available (default) I Reserved IRQ 10 Available (default) I Reserved IRQ 11 Available (default) I Reserved	Reserves specific IRQs for use by legacy ISA devices. An asterisk (*) displayed next to an IRQ indicates an IRQ conflict.

1. Based on the Phoenix BIOS used by the Intel SE440BX2 motherboard. Used by permission of Intel Corporation.

Note that these settings are only for legacy (non–Plug-and-Play) ISA devices. For all Plug-and-Play ISA devices as well as PCI devices (which are Plug-and-Play by default), these resources are instead configured by the operating system or by software that comes with the cards.

Setting these resources here does not actually control the legacy ISA device; that usually must be done by moving jumpers on the card. By setting the resource as reserved here, you are telling the Plug-and-Play operating system that the reserved resources are off-limits, so it won't accidentally set a Plug-and-Play device to use the same resource as a legacy ISA device. Reserving resources in this manner is sometimes required because the Plug-and-Play software can't detect all legacy ISA devices and therefore won't know which settings the device might be using.

In a system with no legacy devices, reserving any resources via this menu is not necessary. To enable more options for the increasing number of PCI/PnP slots and cards found on recent systems, you can disable reservation for legacy devices that you don't use. For example, if you don't use LPT 1 (IRQ 7) and COM 2 (IRQ 3) ports, disable them in the BIOS and set these IRQs as available for PCI/PnP devices.

Some boards have additional configuration options for the Plug-and-Play (PnP) BIOS features as well as the PCI bus. These features are largely chipset-dependent, but some common examples are shown in Table 3.4.

Table 3.4 Typical PnP and PCI Options[1]	
DMA Assigned to	When resources are controlled manually, assign each system DMA channel as one of the following types, depending on the type of device using the interrupt: • Legacy ISA devices compliant with the original PC AT bus specification, requiring a specific DMA channel. • PCI/ISA PnP devices compliant with the Plug-and-Play standard, whether designed for PCI or ISA bus architecture.
PCI IRQ Activated by	Leave the IRQ trigger set at Level unless the PCI device assigned to the interrupt specifies edge-triggered interrupts.
PCI IDE IRQ Map to	This field enables you to select PCI IDE IRQ mapping or PC AT (ISA) interrupts. If your system does not have one or two PCI IDE connectors on the system board, select values according to the type of IDE interface(s) installed in your system (PCI or ISA). Standard ISA interrupts for IDE channels are IRQ 14 for primary and IRQ 15 for secondary.

Table 3.4   Typical PnP and PCI Options[1] Continued

Primary/Secondary IDE INT#	Each PCI peripheral connection is capable of activating up to four interrupts: INT# A, INT# B, INT# C, and INT# D. By default, a PCI connection is assigned INT# A. Assigning INT# B has no meaning unless the peripheral device requires two interrupt services rather than one. Because the PCI IDE interface in the chipset has two channels, it requires two interrupt services. The primary and secondary IDE INT# fields default to values appropriate for two PCI IDE channels, with the primary PCI IDE channel having a lower interrupt than the secondary.
	Note that all single-function PCI cards normally use INT# A, and each of these must be assigned to a different and unique ISA interrupt request (IRQ).
Used Mem Base Addr	Select a base address for the memory area used by any peripheral that requires high memory.
Used Mem Length	Select a length for the memory area specified in the previous field. This field does not appear if no base address is specified.
Assign IRQ for USB	Select Enabled if your system has a USB controller and you have one or more USB devices connected. If you are not using your system's USB controller, select Disabled to free the IRQ resource.

1. Based on the Phoenix BIOS used by the Intel SE440BX2 motherboard. Used by permission of Intel Corporation.

When to Use the PnP BIOS Configuration Options

In an ideal situation involving PnP-aware operating systems such as Windows 9x/Me or 2000/XP, a computer with a PnP BIOS, and a PnP device, the BIOS detects the PnP device and Windows configures it without user intervention. Table 3.5 lists the circumstances under which you might need to use PnP BIOS configuration options.

Table 3.5   Solving Configuration Problems with the PnP BIOS Configuration Options

Problem	Solution	Notes
Legacy (non-PnP) card needs particular IRQ or DMA setting already in use by PnP device.	Set DMA and IRQ used by legacy card to ISA option in BIOS.	This prevents PnP devices from using the resource; verify that legacy card setting matches BIOS selections.
Windows 9x/Me/2000/XP is not detecting and configuring PnP devices not needed at boot time (such as modems, printers, and so on).	Set Plug and Play Aware Operating System option to Yes in BIOS.	

Table 3.5   Solving Configuration Problems with the PnP BIOS Configuration Options Continued

Problem	Solution	Notes
PCI video card is assigned an IRQ that you need for another device.	Set Assign IRQ to VGA option to No in BIOS.	This frees up the IRQ without ill effects in some cases; might not work if the card is used for MPEG movie playback. Do not use for AGP video cards.
New PnP device can't be detected by the system.	Set PCI Slot x IRQ Priority to desired (unused) IRQ; install card into designated PCI slot.	If setting the IRQ for the PCI slot doesn't work, remove all non-essential PnP cards, install new PnP card first, and then reinstall others.
New PnP device interferes with existing PnP device.	Check system manual to determine whether the slot that is used shares an IRQ with another slot or with an onboard device.	Using a different slot for the new PnP device can avoid conflicts.

Other BIOS Troubleshooting Tips

Use Table 3.6 to help solve some other typical system problems through BIOS configuration settings.

Table 3.6   Troubleshooting Common BIOS-Related System Problems

Problem	Solution	Notes
Can't access system because password(s) for startup or setup access aren't known.	Passwords are stored in CMOS nonvolatile RAM (NVRAM) and are configured through BIOS.	Remove battery on motherboard and wait for all CMOS settings to be lost, or use MB jumper called clear CMOS; before clearing CMOS, view bootup configuration information and note hard drive and other configuration information because all setup information must be reentered after CMOS is cleared.
System wastes time detecting hard drives at every bootup.	Disable automatic drive detection in BIOS; lock in settings for drives by using Detect Drives option in BIOS.	Use automatic drive detection if you are frequently changing drives.
System drops network or modem connection when system is idle.	Power management not set correctly for IRQs in use by modem or network card.	Determine which IRQs are used by devices, and adjust power management for those devices; disable power management in BIOS.

Table 3.6 Troubleshooting Common BIOS-Related System Problems Continued		
Problem	**Solution**	**Notes**
Parallel or serial port conflicts.	Change configuration in BIOS.	See Chapter 6, "Serial and Parallel Ports and Devices," and Chapter 7, "USB and IEEE-1394 Ports and Devices," for details.

For more about troubleshooting and adjusting BIOS configuration settings, see Chapter 5 of *Upgrading and Repairing PCs, 13th Edition*, published by Que.

Soft BIOS CPU Speed and Multiplier Settings

Conventional motherboards might require the user to configure CPU speed, FSB (motherboard or system bus) speed, and clock multipliers through a series of jumpers or switches or through BIOS configuration screens. One danger to BIOS configuration is that the user might create a configuration that won't allow the system to boot and might require the CMOS configuration to be deleted to enable the user to try another option.

A number of different motherboards now offer BIOS-controlled configuration of CPU speeds, clock multipliers, FSB (motherboard/system bus) speeds, and CPU core voltage.

Determining Which BIOS You Have

It's important to know which BIOS brand and version a computer has, for two reasons.

First, if a boot failure occurs, BIOS error codes, which vary by brand and model, can be used to help you find the cause of the problem and lead you to a solution.

Second, knowing which BIOS brand and version you have can enable you to get help from the BIOS or system vendor for certain chipset configuration issues.

To determine which BIOS you have, use the following methods:

- Watch your system startup screen for information about the BIOS brand and version, such as Award BIOS v4.51PG.

- Use a hardware test-and-reporting utility, such as AMIDiag, CheckIt, or others.

Note that the best source for machine-specific information about
error codes and other BIOS issues is your system manufacturer.
Major vendors such as IBM, Dell, Compaq, Gateway, Hewlett-
Packard, and others maintain excellent Web sites that list specific
information for your system. However, if you are working with a
white-box clone system made from generic components, BIOS-level
information might be the best information you can get.

Determining the Motherboard Manufacturer for BIOS Upgrades

Although knowing the BIOS brand and version is sufficient for
troubleshooting a system that won't start, solving problems with
issues such as large hard disk support and power management
requires knowing exactly which motherboard you have and who
produced it. Because motherboard manufacturers tailor BIOS code
to the needs of each motherboard model, the motherboard or system vendor—not the BIOS vendor—is the source to turn to for
BIOS upgrades and other BIOS configuration issues.

Identifying Motherboards with AMI BIOS

Motherboards using AMI BIOS versions built from 1991 to the present (AMI's High-Flex BIOS or WinBIOS) display a long string of
numbers at the bottom of the first screen that is displayed when
the system is powered on or restarted:

    51-0411-001771-00111111-071595-82439HX-F

Interpret a number such as this one with the following numerical
key (see Table 3.7):

    AB-CCCC-DDDDDD-EFGHIJKL-mmddyy-MMMMMMM-N

Table 3.7	AB-CCCC-DDDDDD-EFGHIJKL-mmddyy-MMMMMMM-N
Position	**Description**
A	Processor type:
	0 = 8086 or 8088
	2 = 286
	3 = 386
	4 = 486
	5 = Pentium
	6 = Pentium Pro/II/III/Celeron/Athlon/Duron
B	Size of BIOS:
	0 = 64K BIOS
	1 = 128K BIOS
	2 = 256K BIOS

Table 3.7 AB-CCCC-DDDDDD-EFGHIJKL-mmddyy-MMMMMMM-N Continued

Position	Description
CCCC	Major and minor BIOS version number
DDDDDD	Manufacturer license code reference number:
	0036xx = AMI 386 motherboard, xx = Series #
	0046xx = AMI 486 motherboard, xx = Series #
	0056xx = AMI Pentium motherboard, xx = Series #
	0066xx = AMI Pentium Pro motherboard, xx = Series #
	(For other numbers, see the following note)
E	1 = Halt on POST error
F	1 = Initialize CMOS every boot
G	1 = Block pins 22 and 23 of the keyboard controller
H	1 = Mouse support in BIOS/keyboard controller
I	1 = Wait for F1 key on POST errors
J	1 = Display floppy error during POST
K	1 = Display video error during POST
L	1 = Display keyboard error during POST
mmddyy	BIOS Date, mm/dd/yy
MMMMMMM	Chipset identifier or BIOS name
N	Keyboard controller version number

Note

Use the following resources to determine the manufacturer of non-AMI motherboards using the AMI BIOS:

AMI has a listing of U.S. and non-U.S. motherboard manufacturers at http://www.ami.com/support/bios.html.

AMI also offers a downloadable utility program called AMIMBID for use with Windows 9x/2000/NT/Me/XP, and MS-DOS. Download it from http://www.ami.com/support/mbid.html.

A more detailed listing, including complete identification of particular motherboard models, is available at Wim's BIOS site (http://www.wimsbios.com). This site also has links to motherboard manufacturers for BIOS upgrades.

Identifying Motherboards with Award BIOS

Motherboards with the Award Software BIOS also use a numerical code, although the structure is different from that for the AMI Hi-Flex BIOS.

The following is a typical Award BIOS ID:

```
2A59IABDC-00
```

The sixth and seventh characters (bolded for emphasis) indicate the motherboard manufacturer, whereas the eighth character can be used for the model number or the motherboard family (various motherboards using the same chipset).

Note

For lookup tables of these codes, see the following Web sites:

Award Software's official table for manufacturers only is available at http://www.phoenix.com/pcuser/phoenixbios/
motherboard.html.

An expanded list, also containing chipset information (stored in the first five characters of the Award BIOS ID), is available at Wim's BIOS site (http://www.wimsbios.com).

Identifying Motherboards with Phoenix or Microid Research BIOS

Unfortunately, neither Phoenix nor Microid Research (MR BIOS) uses any type of a standardized motherboard ID number system.

For systems using a Phoenix BIOS, see whether your motherboard or system is listed on the Micro Firmware BIOS upgrades page. Links from this page for Intel and Micronics motherboards list the codes that show up onscreen during boot. Match these codes to your system, and you might be able to use a Micro Firmware upgrade. Most MR BIOS (Microid Research BIOS) installations are done as upgrades rather than in original equipment. See the list of supported chipsets (identified by chipset brand and model, not motherboard vendor) and motherboards using Intel's Triton-series chipsets to see whether your system can use an MR BIOS, or contact Microid Research directly for system-specific information.

Accessing the BIOS Setup Programs

The BIOS is configured in one of several ways. Early computers, such as the IBM PC and PC/XT, used DIP switches on the motherboard to set a limited range of BIOS options, including memory size and the number of floppy disk drives. The IBM PC/AT introduced a disk-based configuration utility to cope with the many additional options on 286-based CPUs. Since the late 1980s, most computers have had their BIOS Setup programs incorporated into the BIOS chip itself. The Setup program is accessed on these systems by pressing a key or key combination early in the system startup procedure. Most recent computers display the correct keystroke(s) to use during the system startup. If not, use Table 3.8 to learn the keystrokes used to start common BIOS types.

Table 3.8 Common Keystrokes Used to Access the BIOS Setup Program		
BIOS	**Keystrokes**	**Notes**
Phoenix BIOS	Ctrl+Alt+Esc	
	Ctrl+Alt+F1	
	Ctrl+Alt+S	
	Ctrl+Alt+Enter	
	Ctrl+Alt+F11	
	Ctrl+Alt+Ins	
Award BIOS	Ctrl+Alt+Esc	
	Esc	
	Del	
AMI BIOS	Del	
IBM BIOS	Ctrl+Alt+Ins* F1	*Early notebook models; press when cursor is in upper-right corner of screen.
Compaq BIOS	F10*	Keystroke actually loads Compaq Setup program from hard disk partition; press when cursor is in upper-right corner of screen.

Note

See Chapter 5 of *Upgrading and Repairing PCs, 13th Edition*, published by Que, to see how a typical BIOS Setup program operates.

How the BIOS Reports Errors

The BIOS uses three methods for reporting errors: beep codes, error/status codes, and onscreen messages. Error/status codes must be read with a special interface board, whereas the others require no special equipment.

BIOS Beep Codes and Their Purposes

Virtually all systems make a polite "beep" noise when started, but most systems have a special series of beep codes that serve the following purposes:

- Beeps alert you to serious system problems, many of which can prevent your system from even starting (a so-called *fatal error*) or from working to its full potential (a so-called *nonfatal error*).

- Because most fatal and many nonfatal errors take place before the video subsystem is initialized (or might indicate that the video isn't working), beeps can be used to determine the cause of the problem.

- A system that can't start and is reporting a problem with beep codes will give the code once and then halt. To hear the code again, restart the computer.

Use the following tables of beep codes to determine why your system will not start. To solve the problem reported by the beep codes, repair or replace the device listed in the description. If your repair or replacement has solved the problem, the beep code will no longer sound when you restart the system.

For errors involving removable devices (socketed chips, memory, or video), an easy fix is to remove and replace the item because a device that's not securely in its socket will cause the test to fail.

Note

For an exhaustive list of BIOS codes, beep codes, and error messages, see the CD accompanying *Upgrading and Repairing PCs, 13th Edition.*

AMI BIOS Beep Codes and Solutions

Note

AMI BIOS beep codes are used by permission of American Megatrends, Inc.

Beeps	Error Message	Description	Explanation
1	DRAM Refresh Failure	The memory refresh circuitry on the motherboard is faulty.	Remove and reinstall memory, and retry. Replace memory with known working memory.
2	Parity Error	A parity error occurred in system memory.	Remove and reinstall memory, and retry. Replace memory with known working memory. Disable parity checking in BIOS if you are using nonparity memory.
3	Base 64K (First Bank) Memory Failure	Memory failure in the first bank of memory.	Remove and reinstall memory, and retry. Replace memory with known working memory.
4	System Timer Failure	Memory failure in the first bank of memory, or Timer 1 on the motherboard is not functioning.	Remove and reinstall memory, and retry. Replace memory with known working memory. Replace motherboard if memory swap doesn't help.
5	Processor Error	The processor on the motherboard generated an error.	Remove and reinstall processor. Replace processor with known working processor. Replace motherboard if processor swap doesn't help.
6	Keyboard Controller Gate A20 Failure	The keyboard controller might be bad. The BIOS cannot switch to protected mode.	Remove and reinstall keyboard controller chip (if socketed). Replace and reinstall keyboard; look for blown keyboard fuse on motherboard and replace.
7	Virtual Mode Processor Exception Interrupt Error	The processor generated an exception interrupt.	Remove and reinstall processor. Replace processor with known working processor. Replace motherboard if processor swap doesn't help.
8	Display Memory Read/Write Error	Either the system video adapter is missing or its memory is faulty.	Remove and reinstall memory on video card (if memory removable). Remove and reinstall video card. Replace video card with known working unit.
9	ROM Checksum Error	ROM checksum value does not match the value encoded in BIOS.	Faulty BIOS chip; replace BIOS chip, if socketed, or replace motherboard.
10	CMOS Shutdown Register Read/Write Error	The shutdown register for CMOS RAM failed.	Replace motherboard.

Beeps	Error Message	Description	Explanation
11	Cache Error/L2 Cache Bad	The L2 cache is faulty.	Locate L2 cache.
			If built into processor, remove and reinstall processor. Replace processor with known working unit.
			If built into motherboard, replace motherboard.
			If socketed, remove and reinstall cache RAM chips or module. Replace with known working cache RAM or replace motherboard.
1 long, 3 short	Conventional/ extended memory failure	The motherboard memory is faulty.	Remove and reinstall memory, and retry. Replace memory with known working memory.
1 long, 8 short	Display/retrace test failure	The video card is faulty.	Reseat the video card in its slot, or move it to a different slot.

Award BIOS Beep Codes

Currently only one beep code exists in the Award BIOS. A single long beep followed by two short beeps indicates that a video error has occurred and the BIOS cannot initialize the video screen to display any additional information.

Phoenix BIOS Beep Codes

The following beep codes are for the current version of Phoenix BIOS, version 4.0, release 6. Other versions will have somewhat different beeps and Port 80h codes. To view the Port 80h codes, you will need a POST diagnostics card with a two-digit LED readout, available from many sources for diagnostic tools. I recommend a PCI-based POST card because ISA slots are becoming obsolete.

Note

Phoenix BIOS beep codes are used by permission of Phoenix Technologies, Ltd.

Beeps	Port 80h Code	Explanation
1-2-2-3	16h	BIOS ROM checksum
1-3-1-1	20h	Test DRAM refresh
1-3-1-3	22h	Test keyboard controller

Beeps	Port 80h Code	Explanation
1-3-3-1	28h	Autosize DRAM
1-3-3-2	29h	Initialize POST memory manager
1-3-3-3	2Ah	Clear 512KB base RAM
1-3-4-1	2Ch	RAM failure on address line xxxx
1-3-4-3	2Eh	RAM failure on data bits xxxx of low byte of memory bus
1-4-1-1	30h	RAM failure on data bits xxxx of high byte of memory bus
2-1-2-2	45h	POST device initialization
2-1-2-3	46h	Check ROM copyright notice
2-2-3-1	58h	Test for unexpected interrupts
2-2-4-1	5Ch	Test RAM between 512KB and 640KB
1-2	98h	Search for option ROMs; one long, two short beeps on checksum failure
1	B4h	One short beep before boot

IBM BIOS Beep and Alphanumeric Error Codes

After completing the power-on self-test (POST), an audio code indicates either a normal condition or that one of several errors has occurred.

> ### Note
>
> IBM BIOS and alphanumeric error codes used by permission of IBM.

Audio Code	Sound Graph	Description
1 short beep	•	Normal POST—system okay
2 short beeps	••	POST error—error code on display
No beep		Power supply, system board
Continuous beep	——————	Power supply, system board
Repeating short beeps	••••	Power supply,
	••	system board
1 long, 1 short beep	—•	System board
1 long, 2 short beeps	—••	Video adapter (MDA/CGA)
1 long, 3 short beeps	—•••	Video adapter (EGA/VGA)
3 long beeps	——————	3270 keyboard card

Microid Research Beep Codes

The MR BIOS generates patterns of high and low beeps to signal an error condition. For Microid Research beep codes, see the Technical Reference on the CD packaged with *Upgrading and Repairing PCs, 13th Edition,* or see http://www.mrbios.com/postcode.html.

Other BIOS and Motherboard Manufacturers' Beep and POST Codes

Beep and POST codes for other manufacturers from Acer to Zenith are available from BIOS Central, at http://www.bioscentral.com.

Reading BIOS Error Codes

Because beep codes can indicate only some of the problems in a system at startup, most BIOSes also output a series of status codes during the boot procedure. These codes are sent to an I/O port address that can be read by specialized diagnostic cards, which you can purchase from many different vendors. These *POST cards* (so named from the power-on self test) feature a two-digit LED panel that displays the status codes output by the BIOS. The simpler POST cards are hard-wired to pick up signals from the most commonly used I/O port address 80hex, but more expensive models can be adjusted with jumper blocks to use other addresses used by certain BIOSes (such as Compaq).

These cards are normally sold with manuals that list the error/status codes. Although the cards are durable, the codes can become outdated. To get an updated list of codes, contact the system or BIOS vendor's Web site.

Most POST cards have been based on the ISA bus, but the latest models are now being made to fit into PCI slots because ISA is becoming obsolete. For diagnosing portable systems, and to avoid the need to open a system to insert a POST card, Ultra-X offers a MicroPOST display unit that attaches to the parallel port. Contact Ultra-X at http://www.uxd.com for more information. For standard ISA and PCI POST cards, see JDR Computer Products at http://www.jdr.com.

Onscreen Error Messages

An onscreen error message is often the easiest of the error methods to understand because you don't need to count beeps or open the system to install a POST card. However, because some systems use numeric error codes, and because even "plain English" codes need interpretation, these messages can still be a challenge to interpret.

Because the video circuits are tested after components such as the motherboard, CPU, and BIOS, an onscreen error message is usually indicative of a less-serious error than one that is reported with beep codes.

Interpreting Error Codes and Messages

Because beep codes, error/status codes, and onscreen messages vary a great deal by BIOS vendor (and sometimes BIOS model), you must know what BIOS a system has before you can choose the correct table. With major-brand systems (and some others), you'll typically find a list of error codes and messages in the system documentation. You can also contact the BIOS or system vendors' Web sites for this information, or check the CD included with *Upgrading and Repairing PCs, 13th Edition*, published by Que.

BIOS Configuration Worksheet

BIOS configuration options vary a great deal, and incorrect settings can cause a system to fail, lose data, or not work correctly with PnP-compatible operating systems, such as Windows 9x/2000/Me/XP. The following worksheet can be used to record the most critical BIOS configuration information. Use it when you are unable to print out the actual configuration screens.

System ID_____**Brand & Model #** _____

Date Recorded_____**Operating System**_____

Hard Disk Partitions_____

Notes_____

_____

Standard CMOS/BIOS Configuration

(Configuration Option)	(Setting—circle or write down setting used)
Drive A	1.44MB
	2.88MB
	Other_____
	None
Drive B	1.44MB
	2.88MB
	Other_____
	None
1st IDE Drive	Drive type:
	Hard disk
	CD-ROM

	Other (specify)
	_____
	Hard disk geometry
	Cyl:_____
	Sectors/track: ____
	Heads: _____
	LBA Y/N:
2nd IDE Drive	*Drive type:*
	Hard disk
	CD-ROM
	Other (specify)
	_____
	Hard disk geometry
	Cyl:_____
	Sectors/track: ____
	Heads: _____
	LBA Y/N:
3rd IDE Drive	*Drive type:*
	Hard disk
	CD-ROM
	Other (specify)
	_____
	Hard disk geometry
	Cyl:_____
	Sectors/track: ____
	Heads: _____
	LBA Y/N:
4th IDE Drive	*Drive type:*
	Hard disk
	CD-ROM
	Other (specify)
	_____
	Hard disk geometry
	Cyl:_____
	Sectors/track: ____
	Heads: _____
	LBA Y/N:
Other BIOS Configuration Screens	
Boot Sequence	*1st drive: _____*
	2nd drive:_____

	3rd drive:_____
	4th drive:_____
Antivirus or Write-Protect Boot Sector	Enable/Disable
PS/2 Mouse	Enable/Disable
Password	Power on
	Password: _____
	Setup
	Password: _____
External Memory Cache (Level 2)	Enable/Disable
Internal Memory Cache (Level 1)	Enable/Disable
Shadow RAM/ROM Shadowing	*Specify range(s) in use:*
	_____
	_____
	_____
	_____
USB Ports	Enable/Disable
USB Legacy Support (Keyboard and Mouse)	Enable/Disable
Memory Timing Configuration	Auto/Manual
	If manual, specify changes from system default here:
	_____
	_____
	_____
	_____
	_____
Power Management	Enable/Disable
	If enabled, specify changes from system default here:
	_____
	_____
	_____
	_____
	_____
Plug and Play (PnP)	Enable/Disable
	If enabled, specify changes from system default here:
	_____
	_____

	_____
	_____
	_____
LPT Port	*Mode selected:*
	Standard EPP ECP Bi-Di
	Disabled
	EPP version # _____
	IRQ: 7 5 _____
	DMA for ECP mode: _____
	I/O Port address:
	378H
	278H
	3BCH
	Disabled
Serial (COM) Port 1	*I/O port address:*
	3FH (COM1)
	2FH (COM2)
	3EH (COM3)
	2EH (COM4)
	Disabled
	Notes: _____
Serial (COM) Port 2	*I/O port address:*
	3FH (COM1)
	2FH (COM2)
	3EH (COM3)
	2EH (COM4)
	Disabled
	Notes: _____
IDE Hard Disk Interface #1	*Interface:*
	Enable/Disable
	32-bit mode: Enable/Disable
	PIO mode: 0 1 2 3 4
	UDMA mode: 33MHz 66MHz 100MHz
	Block mode: Enable/Disable
	# of blocks: _____
IDE Hard Disk Interface #2	*Interface:*
	Enable/Disable
	32-bit mode: Enable/Disable
	PIO mode: 0 1 2 3 4

UDMA mode: 33MHz 66MHz 100MHz

Block mode: Enable/Disable

# of blocks: _____

Chapter 4

SCSI and ATA Hard Drives and Optical Drives

Understanding Hard Disk Terminology

When installing ATA hard disks in particular, at least three parameters must be indicated in the BIOS Setup program to define a hard disk:

- The number of read/write heads (H)
- The number of sectors per track (S)
- The number of cylinders (C)

The CHS values (also known as *hard disk geometry)* are used to calculate the capacity of the drive.

> **Note**
>
> Understanding how hard drives store data is an enormous topic. If you'd like to learn more, see Chapters 9 and 10 of *Upgrading and Repairing PCs, 13th Edition,* also published by Que.

Heads, Sectors per Track, and Cylinders

If the CHS information is not accurately listed in the BIOS configuration for ATA drives, the full capacity of the drive will not be available unless special hard disk drivers or supplementary BIOS cards are used. Whenever possible, the computer's own ROM BIOS should fully support the drive's capacity.

For drives larger than 504MB (binary) or 528 million bytes, additional translation options also are required with MS-DOS and Windows to achieve full capacity.

SCSI drives are supported by a special BIOS on hard disk–compatible SCSI host adapters, not by the system BIOS.

Hard-Drive Heads

A hard drive is comprised of one or more platters, normally made of aluminum but occasionally made of glass. These platters are covered with a thin, rigid film of magnetized material. The magnetic structures of the platters are read or changed by read/write heads that move across the surface of the platters but are separated from it by a thin cushion of air. Virtually all platters are read from both sides.

Sectors per Track

The magnetic structures stored on the hard-disk platters are organized into sectors of 512 data bytes each, plus additional areas in each sector for identifying the sector location on the hard disk. These sectors form concentric circles numbering from the outside of each platter to the hub area of the platter.

Cylinders

The third factor used to calculate the size of the hard disk is the number of cylinders on the hard disk. The identically positioned tracks on each side of every platter together make up a cylinder.

The BIOS calculates the size of the hard disk from the number of cylinders, the number of heads, and the number of sectors per track. Most system BIOSes calculate the size of the hard drive in mibibytes (Mi) or gibibytes (Gi) (the same way as hard-disk preparation programs such as FDISK or Disk Management do), but a few make the calculation in megabytes (MB) or gigabytes (GB) (see Chapter 1, "General Technical Reference," for the differences in these numbering methods). BIOSes that use megabyte or gigabyte calculations report the size of the drive the same way that drive manufacturers do. Either way, the same number of bytes will be available *if* the drive is fully and accurately handled by the ROM BIOS and operating system. Most recent and current drives print the cylinder, head, and sectors per track information (collectively called the drive's *geometry*) on a label on the top of the drive for easy reference during installation. Mibibytes and Gibibytes previously were called binary megabytes and binary gigabytes.

Note that all three elements of the drive geometry are actually logical, not physical, on ATA drives. This factor explains why the geometry can be translated (see the following) and why some ATA drives in older machines are working, despite being installed with "incorrect" geometries.

Use the worksheet at the end of Chapter 3, "BIOS Configurations and Upgrades," to record your hard drive geometry and other information for each system you manage.

IDE/ATA Hard Drive Identification

Integrated Drive Electronics (IDE), more properly called ATA drives (AT Attachment), are the overwhelming favorite for client PC installations. Although SCSI hard drives (see the following) offer benefits for network and high-performance workstation use, the combination of constantly improving performance, rock-bottom pricing per megabyte (less than 1 cent and falling), and enormous capacities (up to 100GB and climbing) will continue to make IDE/ATA drives the choice of most users. Figure 4.1 shows the typical ATA drive connectors.

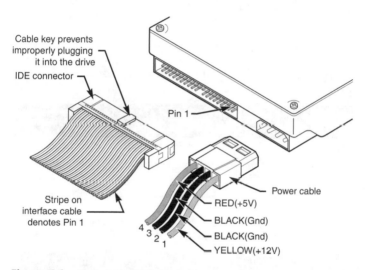

Figure 4.1 Typical ATA (IDE) hard-drive connectors.

Master and Slave Drives

Virtually every ATA drive interface is designed to handle two drives with a single 40-pin interface cable.

Because the cable has no twist, unlike a typical 34-pin floppy inter-face cable, jumper blocks on each hard drive must be set to distin-guish between the first (or *master*) drive on the cable and the second (or *slave*) drive on the cable.

Most ATA drives can be configured with four possible settings:

* Master (single-drive), also called Single
* Master (dual-drive)

- Slave (dual-drive)
- Cable Select

When the traditional 40-pin, 40-wire non–Cable Select ATA cable is used, the Cable Select setting can be ignored. If the cable does support Cable Select, then setting all drives that way makes installation easier: After that, the jumpers will never need to be changed—Cable Select will automatically configure one drive as master and the other as slave. However, drives that support UDMA/66, UDMA/ 100, or faster UDMA modes use a new 40-pin, 80-wire cable that always supports Cable Select. In other words, all 80-conductor cables support Cable Select, while only some 40-conductor cables do. Those that don't support Cable Select require that the drives be jumpered as master/slave. Table 4.1 lists the jumper settings used with 40-wire cables, while Table 4.2 lists the jumper and drive position settings required for the 80-wire UDMA cable.

Table 4.1 Jumper Settings for Typical ATA IDE-Compatible Drives Using a 40-Wire Non–Cable Select ATA Cable			
Jumper Name	**Single-Drive**	**Dual-Drive Master**	**Dual-Drive Slave**
Master (M/S)	On or off[1]	On	Off
Slave Present (SP)	Off	On	Off
Cable Select	Not Used	Not Used	Not Used

1. Varies with drive; check user documentation.

Use Table 4.1 as a general guideline only. Follow your drive manu-facturer's recommendations if they vary.

Table 4.2 Connector Colors and Jumpering for ATA IDE-Compatible Drives Using an 80-Wire UDMA ATA Cable		
Connector Color	**Used For**	**Drive Jumpering**
Blue	ATA host adapter	N/A
Black	Primary drive	CS[1]
Gray	Slave drive	CS[1]

1. Cable Select.

The jumpers on the hard drive might be located on the back of the drive (between the power and data connectors) or on the bottom of the drive. Typical hard disk jumpers are shown in Figure 4.2.

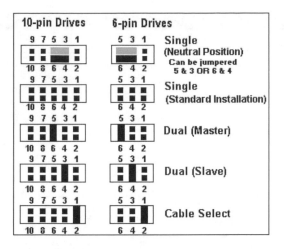

Figure 4.2   ATA (IDE) drive jumpers. Many drives now have 8, 9, or 10 jumper pins to allow for special configurations required on some systems to break the 528MB drive barrier (see the following sections).

ATA Standards

IDE drives originally were developed in the late 1980s as a proprietary drive interface used by Compaq and a few other brands. Later, formal standards for the most common type of IDE drive, the AT Attachment (ATA) drive, were developed. Table 4.3 provides a quick reference to ATA standards, which are frequently used to describe the features provided by the system BIOS, ATA host adapters, and ATA drives.

Table 4.3	ATA Standards				
Standard	Timeframe	PIO Modes	DMA Modes	Ultra-DMA Modes	Speed Features[1]
ATA-1	1986–1994	0–2	0	—	8.33 Drive support up to 136.9GB; BIOS issues not addressed
ATA-2	1995–1996	0–4	0–2	—	16.67 Faster PIO modes; CHS/LBA BIOS translation defined up to 8.4GB, PC Card
ATA-3	1997	0–4	0–2	—	16.67 SMART[2]; improved signal integrity, LBA support mandatory; eliminated single word DMA modes

Table 4.3	ATA Standards Continued				
Standard	**Timeframe**	**PIO Modes**	**DMA Modes**	**Ultra-DMA Modes**	**Speed Features**[1]
ATA-4	1998	0–4	0–2	0–2	33.33 Ultra-DMA modes; BIOS supports up to 136.9GB
ATA-5	1999–2000	0–4	0–2	0–4	66.67 Faster UDMA modes, 80-pin cable with autodetection
ATA-6	2001–present	0–4	0–2	0–5	100.00 100MBps UDMA mode; extended drive and BIOS support of up to 144PB[3]

1. Speed is megabytes per second (MBps).

2. SMART = Self-monitoring, analysis, and reporting technology.

3. PB = Petabyte; 1 PB is equal to 1 quadrillion bytes.

MB = Millions of bytes

GB = Billions of bytes

CHS = Cylinder head sector

LBA = Logical block address

UDMA = Ultra DMA (Direct Memory Access)

ATA/IDE Drive Capacity Limits

ATA interface versions up through ATA-5 suffered from a drive capacity limitation of 136.9GB (billion bytes). Depending on the BIOS used, this limitation can be further reduced to 8.4GB, or even as low as 528MB (million bytes). This is due to limitations in both the BIOS and the ATA interface, which, when combined, create even further limitations. To understand these limits, you have to look at the BIOS and ATA interface.

Table 4.4	ATA/IDE Drive Capacity Limitations	
Specification	**Max. Sectors**	
Standard CHS BIOS	1,032,192	
CHS BIOS with translation	16,515,072	
ATA-1 through 5 interface	267,386,880	
ATA-6 interface	281,474,976,710,655	
Enhanced (EDD BIOS)	18,446,744,073,709,551,600	

1. Maximum capacity in bytes.

ATA = AT Attachment

CHS = Cylinder head sector

EDD = Enhanced disk drive

The pertinent limitations are those of the ATA interface itself, as well as the BIOS (drivers) used to talk to the interface. A summary of the limitations is shown in Table 4.4.

The first specification, standard CHS BIOS, lists the maximum drive capacity possible on old systems that lack any means of translating the drive's geometry to achieve larger capacities. The 528MB limit also applies to newer systems in which disk translation (see the next section) has been disabled.

Breaking the 528MB Drive Barrier

Three factors contribute to the CHS limit of 528MB (504MiB) for ATA hard drives:

- The BIOS, as well as MS-DOS and DOS-based operating systems such as Windows, can access only 1024 cylinders.

- The ATA interface can address only 16 heads.

- The BIOS can address only 63 sectors per track.

$1,024 \times 16 \times 63 = 1,032,192$ sectors per drive (see Table 4.4).

This limit was merely theoretical until 1994, when Phoenix released the Enhanced Disk Drive specification (EDD 1.0), which defined an enhanced BIOS to circumvent these limits.

An enhanced BIOS circumvents the limits by using a different geometry when talking to the drive than when talking to the software. What happens in between is called *translation*. For example, if your drive has 2000 cylinders and 16 heads, a translating BIOS will define the drive as having 1000 cylinders and 32 heads. Newer versions of ATA standards have added more translation methods. The most common translation methods are listed in Table 4.5.

Capacity[1]	Max Capacity
528,482,304	528.5MB
8,455,716,864	8.4GB
136,902,082,560	136.9GB
144,115,188,075,855,360	144.12PB
9,444,732,965,739,290,430,000	9.4ZB

MB = Million bytes

GB = Billion bytes

PB = Petabytes; 1PB equals a quadrillion bytes

ZB = Zettabytes, 1ZB equals a billion trillion bytes

Table 4.5 Drive Sector Addressing Methods		
BIOS Mode	**Operating System to BIOS**	**BIOS to Drive**
Standard (normal) No translation	Physical CHS parameters	Physical CHS parameters
Extended CHS (large) Translation	Logical CHS parameters	Physical CHS parameters
LBA Translation	Logical CHS parameters	LBA parameters
Pure LBA (EDD BIOS)	LBA parameters	LBA parameters

A BIOS that supports only Standard CHS recognizes only a maximum of 1024 cylinders, 16 heads, and 63 sectors per track for any IDE/ATA drive. Thus, if you install a 6.4GB IDE/ATA drive in a system with this type of BIOS, it will recognize only 528MB with MS-DOS and Windows. Non-DOS operating systems such as Novell NetWare, UNIX, and Linux don't require translation if they will be the only operating system on the disk partition.

On systems that provide translation, this BIOS mode is called *Normal* because the geometry isn't changed. Configuring a drive to use Normal mode is correct for operating systems such as UNIX, Linux, and Novell NetWare, but not for systems that use MS-DOS file structures, including MS-DOS itself, Windows 9*x*/NT/2000/Me/XP, and OS/2.

The next two modes, Extended CHS and LBA (Logical Block Addressing), do translate the geometry. Extended CHS is also called *Large* mode and is recommended only for drives larger than 528.5MB that cannot be operated in LBA mode. Most enhanced BIOSes don't offer Large mode, but all offer LBA mode, which numbers sectors sequentially. Thus, LBA mode is the best option to select if you might need to move a drive from system to system because most BIOSes will be capable of recognizing the drive once its CHS parameters have been entered and LBA mode has been enabled. However, a few (such as older Acer BIOSes) might call LBA mode something different, such as DOS mode or >504Mi mode.

Using LBA Mode

LBA mode can be enabled in two ways, depending on the BIOS. On most current BIOSes, using the automatic-detection option in the BIOS or during system boot will detect the basic hard-drive geometry and select LBA mode automatically. On some BIOSes, though, the automatic detection sets up the basic cylinder-head-sectors per track drive geometry, but it doesn't enable LBA mode unless you set it yourself. Depending on the BIOS release used by a given system, the LBA mode setting can be performed on the same BIOS

configuration screen used for standard drive configuration, or it
might be located on an Advanced CMOS configuration or peripheral setup screen.

A BIOS that performs LBA translation should enable you to use an
ATA hard drive as large as 8.4GB with MS-DOS. If you find that you
can use a 2.1GB hard disk but not larger ones, the version of LBA
mode supported by your BIOS is a very early version, and your
BIOS should be updated. Support for drives larger than 8.4GB is
discussed later in this chapter.

When LBA Mode Is Necessary—and When Not to Use It

Use Table 4.6 to determine when to use LBA mode.

Table 4.6	Using LBA Mode		
Drive Size	**Operating System**	**Use LBA Mode**	**Reason**
<=528MB	Any	No	Not necessary
>528MB	Linux, UNIX, Novell NetWare	No	No 1024-cylinder limit with these operating systems[1]

1. *Recent versions of Linux include LBA-compatible drivers that allow Linux to operate on drives
configured with LBA.*

Problems with LBA Support in the BIOS

Ideally, LBA mode would be automatically enabled in a clearly
understood way on every system with an enhanced BIOS. It also
would be easy to know when you did *not* need to use it.
Unfortunately, this is often not the case.

Many 1994–1996 versions of the AMI text-based and graphical
(WinBIOS) BIOSes listed the basic hard-drive geometry on one
screen and listed the LBA mode option on a different screen alto-
gether. To make matters worse, the automatic drive setup options
on many of these BIOSes didn't set the LBA mode for you; you had
to find it and then set it. But perhaps the worst problem of all was
for users who had carefully set the LBA mode and then ran into
problems with other BIOS configurations. Most AMI BIOS versions
offer a feature called *automatic configuration* with either BIOS/
Optimal defaults (high performance) or Power-On/Fail-Safe defaults
(low performance). In AMI BIOSes in which the LBA mode was *not*
listed on the same screen with the hard disk geometry, *any* automatic
configuration would reset LBA mode to its default setting—off.

Although newer versions of the AMI BIOS and other BIOSes place
the LBA option on the hard disk configuration screen, it's still easy
to disable it if you're not careful. The Award BIOS, for example,
offers LBA, Large, and Normal configurations when it autodetects
hard drives; the user can select any of the three options. With any
BIOS, you can disable LBA mode if you use a user-defined drive
configuration rather than autodetection.

Because the location of the LBA setting can vary from system to system, always verify that LBA mode is still enabled if you make any changes to a BIOS configuration on systems that use LBA mode.

Dangers of Altering Translation Settings

Depending on the operating system and drive configuration, one of several unpleasant events takes place when LBA translation is turned off after a drive is configured using LBA. Table 4.7 summarizes these problems, some of which can be fatal to data.

Table 4.7   Problems Associated with Disabling LBA Mode

Drive Configuration	Operating System	Symptom	End Result
Primary (C:) and extended (D: and above) partitions on a single physical drive	MS-DOS	Can't access drive letters in extended partition because part of capacity is located beyond cylinder 1024.	Usually no harm to data because drive is inaccessible until LBA mode is re-enabled.
C: or C:, D:, and so on	Windows 9x, Windows 2000, Windows NT, Windows Me, Windows XP	Can't boot drive because of incorrect geometry.	Usually no harm to data because drive is inaccessible until LBA mode is reset.
C: only	MS-DOS	System boots and operates normally until data is written to a cylinder beyond 1024.	Drive wraps around to cylinder 0 (location of partition table and other vital disk structures) because LBA translation to access cylinders past 1024 is absent. Drive overwrites beginning of disk, causing loss of all data.

We used the last scenario in a computer troubleshooting class a few times, and it was quite a surprise to see a hard disk "eat" itself! However, it is never a good idea to "play" with LBA translation after it has been set in a system.

Detecting Lack of LBA Mode Support in Your System

To determine whether your system lacks LBA support or doesn't have LBA support enabled, do the following:

1. Install the hard drive set for Master, Slave, or Cable Select, as appropriate.

2. Turn on the computer and detect the drive in the BIOS Setup program. Note the size of the drive reported.

3. Run your operating system's drive partitioning program (FDISK with MS-DOS or Windows 9*x*/Me) or Disk Management (Windows 2000/XP).

4. Select the new drive and view its capacity.

5. If the drive size is listed as only 504Mi and the drive is larger, LBA support is lacking or is not enabled.

6. Restart the computer, enable LBA mode in the BIOS, and try steps 3–5 again. If your disk-partitioning program reports the same or similar size to what the BIOS reports, your drive is being translated correctly by the BIOS if your hard disk is <=8.4.GB/7.8Gi. If FDISK still reports a size significantly less than your hard disk's actual capacity, see Table 4.8 for solutions.

7. If your hard disk is >8.4GB/7.8Gi *and* you are using Windows 9*x*/2000/Me/NT/XP, the size that FDISK should report might be *greater* than what the BIOS displays. If FDISK reports only 8192Mi (8.4GB) and the hard disk is larger, see Table 4.8 for solutions.

Note

Remember that hard-drive manufacturers rate their hard disks in megabytes or gigabytes, and most BIOSes follow the FDISK standard for rating drives in mibibytes or gibibytes (binary megabytes or binary gigabytes). See Table 1.2 in Chapter 1 for equivalents.

---

8. If you can't start the computer after installing the new hard drive, the BIOS is incapable of handling the drive's geometry. See Table 4.8 for solutions.

Using FDISK to Determine Compatibility Problems Between the Hard Disk and the BIOS

A mismatch between the capacity that FDISK reports for a hard disk and what the BIOS reports for the hard disk indicates a problem with LBA translation or with support for hard disks above 8.4GB.

FDISK also can be used to determine when the dangerous "DOS wraparound" condition exists, in which a drive prepared with LBA translation has the LBA translation turned off.

We've included a mock-up of how the FDISK Display Partition Information screen appears. See the discussion of LBA mode earlier in this chapter for solutions. In the following example, FDISK indicates no problems, because the values for X (size of hard disk partition) and Y (total size of drive) are equal. Note that the term "Mbytes" used by FDISK is equivalent to mebibytes, as described in Table 1.2 in Chapter 1.

```
Display Partition Information      Current fixed
disk drive: 1
Label   Mbytes    System      Usage      C: 1
A       PRI DOS
Partition   Status    Type      Volume
W95US1U         1626  FAT16         100%
                    X


    Total disk space is 1626 Mbytes (1 Mbyte =
1048576 bytes)
                              Y


Press Esc to continue
```

X = Size of hard disk partition (drive has already been FDISKed)

Y = Total disk space (as seen by FDISK)

Use Table 4.8 to determine what the FDISK total disk space figure is telling you about your system.

Table 4.8	FDISK Disk Space Detected as a Guide to Disk Problems		
X Value[1]	Y Value[2]	Drive Size	Underlying Cause
>504MiB	=504MiB	>504MiB (528MB)	Drive was prepared with LBA mode enabled, but LBA mode has been disabled in BIOS.
			See "Dangers of Altering Translation Settings," earlier in this chapter.
Not listed	=504MiB	>504MiB	LBA mode not enabled in BIOS or not present.
Not listed	8064MiB	>8064MiB (8.4GB)	BIOS supports LBA mode, but not EDD modes.

1. The X value appears only when a drive has already been FDISKed.

2. The Y value appears on any drive being viewed through FDISK, whether the FDISK process has been completed or not.

For more information about using FDISK, see the section "Using FDISK," later in this chapter.

If you use Windows 2000 or Windows XP, Disk Management will report 504MiB if you install a larger drive and don't enable LBA mode, or 8064MiB if you enable LBA mode but your BIOS doesn't support BIOS Enhanced Disk Drive (EDD) functions.

The BIOS Enhanced Disk Drive (EDD) Specification

LBA mode translation of CHS drive parameters works only up to 8.4GB, a drive capacity that is now routinely exceeded by even the lowest-cost IDE/ATA drives. BIOSes compatible with larger drives must support the BIOS Enhanced Disk Drive (EDD) specification released in 1998. EDD also has been called Extended Int13h support. EDD uses pure LBA values to access all drive sectors, rather than translating CHS to LBA values as with the original LBA translating BIOS.

Most system BIOSes dated 1998 to the present will have EDD support, which is enabled automatically as needed whenever LBA mode is enabled for drives larger than 8.4GB.

Getting LBA and BIOS Enhanced Disk Drive (EDD) Support for Your System

If your computer is incapable of detecting the full capacity of your hard disk or locks up after you install the hard drive, your BIOS is not compatible with your hard drive. Use Table 4.9 to determine the causes and solutions that will help you get full capacity from your new hard disk with maximum safety.

Table 4.9   Why ATA Drive Is Not Detected at Full Capacity

Symptom	Drive Size	Operating System	Cause	Solution
System locks up after installing new drive.	>2.1GB	Any	BIOS cannot handle 4096 cylinders or more, even with LBA enabled.	Upgrade BIOS (see Table 4.7) or install drive with third-party disk tools.
	>32GB	Any	BIOS cannot handle capacity even with LBA enabled.	Upgrade BIOS (see Table 4.7) or install drive with third-party disk tools.
Full capacity not available.	>528MB– 8.4GB	MS-DOS, Windows 9x/NT/2000/ XP, OS/2	No LBA mode or inadequate LBA support in BIOS.	Upgrade BIOS (see Table 4.7) or install drive with third-party disk tools.
	>8.4GB	Windows NT	Atapi.sys not correct version; BIOS lacks EDD support required for large drives.	Update Atapi.sys (included in SP3 or above of NT 4.0), and upgrade BIOS, if necessary (see Table 4.7); install drive with third-party disk tools.

Table 4.9	Why ATA Drive Is Not Detected at Full Capacity Continued			
Symptom	Drive Size	Operating System	Cause	Solution
	>8.4GB	Novell NetWare 4.11	Drivers needed to support drive at full capacity.	Contact Novell for drivers. NetWare 5.x will support >8.4GB drives. Upgrade BIOS, if necessary.
	>8.4GB	IBM OS/2 Warp	Patch needed to support drive at full capacity.	Contact IBM for patch file; upgrade BIOS, if necessary.
	>8.4GB	Windows 9x, Windows 2000, Windows Me, Windows XP	Windows 9x has EDD for drive, but BIOS lacks support.	Upgrade BIOS (see Table 4.7) or install drive with third-party disk tools.
	>8.4GB	MS-DOS	MS-DOS can't use ATA drives above 8.4GB unless a third-party disk tool is used to prepare drive in place of FDISK and FORMAT.	Buy 8.4GB drive or smaller; upgrade to Windows 9x or newer versions; install drive with third-party disk tools.

For details about third-party disk tools that can be used to overcome capacity limits, see "Third-Party Hard-Disk Installation Programs," later in this chapter.

Determining Whether Your System Supports EDD

Drives that are 8.4GB or larger require EDD support in the BIOS to be accessible at full capacity. This size represents a second barrier to drive capacity for MS-DOS, and one that cannot be overcome without changing to a different type of drive (SCSI), making the move to Windows 9x/2000/Me/XP, or using a third-party disk-partitioning tool.

Even if you have updated versions of operating systems that support ATA capacities beyond 8.4GB, your BIOS also must offer this support. Table 4.10 describes the differences between how LBA and EDD support work.

Table 4.10	LBA Mode Versus EDD	
Mode	Setting	BIOS Drive Capacity Listing
LBA	Must be set in BIOS by user or automatically by drive-type detection.	Indicates full capacity of drive if drive is under 8.4GB in size. Some BIOSes might display translated geometry values.

Table 4.10	LBA Mode Versus EDD Continued	
Mode	**Setting**	**BIOS Drive Capacity Listing**
EDD	Automatically enabled when LBA mode is enabled on systems that support EDD functions.	BIOS configuration might or might not indicate full capacity of drive.

This support is not "visible" in the BIOS; there is no Enhanced Int13h option to enable, as there is with LBA mode.

Also, in some cases, the geometry reported by drives of varying sizes doesn't change, either. On a system that supports EDD but doesn't display the full drive capacity in the BIOS configuration, an 8.4GB hard disk will report a geometry to the BIOS of 16 heads, 16,383 cylinders, and 63 sectors per track; a 80GB hard disk reports the same geometry! Support of hard disks beyond 8.4GB on some systems breaks the usual rule about the BIOS configuration matching the drive's capacity.

As with the previously mentioned LBA mode issues, use FDISK or Disk Management to determine whether your system supports an ATA hard drive of greater than 8.4GB at full capacity.

Drive Capacity Issues in Microsoft Windows 95 and 98

Table 4.11 lists the capacity limitations and issues for Windows 95 and 98.

Table 4.11	Drive Capacity Issues for Windows 95 and 98	
Windows Version	**Drive Capacity Limitation**	**Fix**
Windows 95 (all releases)	32GB	Third-party disk tools can be used to bypass the 32GB limit; however, the drive will be software-supported rather than BIOS supported.
		We recommend upgrading to Windows 98, NT, 2000, XP, or Me before installing a larger hard drive instead.
		See Microsoft online document Q246818 for details.
Windows 98 (all releases)	32GB and up	Graphical version of ScanDisk lists errors for all sectors beyond 32GB on some systems using Phoenix BIOS with BitShift ATA drive translation.
		See Microsoft online document Q243450 for download (Microsoft Knowledgebase). Use command-line ScanDisk as a workaround.

Table 4.11   Drive Capacity Issues for Windows 95 and 98 Continued

Windows Version	Drive Capacity Limitation	Fix
Windows 98 (all releases)	64GB and up	Drive works at full capacity, but FDISK reports capacity as 64GB lower than actual; see Microsoft online document Q263044 for patch download instructions.
Windows 98 (all releases)	64GB and up	FORMAT run from command line reports capacity as 64GB lower than actual, but FORMAT works correctly; use the FORMAT option within Windows Explorer as a workaround. See Microsoft online document Q263045.

Sources for BIOS Upgrades and Alternatives for Large ATA Hard Disk Support

If your BIOS doesn't support the full capacity of your hard disk, use Table 4.12 to choose your best solution.

Table 4.12   Sources for BIOS and Alternative Support for Large Hard Drives

Solution	Benefits	Cost	Concerns
Upgrade BIOS.	Best all-around solution to hard disk and other support issues.	Free if BIOS is Flash type and is supported by motherboard or system maker.	Be sure to correctly identify your system or motherboard before installing the upgrade; test afterward (see Chapter 3 for details).
		If BIOS is no longer supported by MB or manufacturer, purchase upgrade.	See Chapter 3 for sources and system details.
Purchase BIOS upgrade card.	Might be less expensive than purchasing BIOS replacement or new motherboard; fast, easy install.	$35–$75; can be combined with UDMA 66/100 support and might include additional ATA host Adapters.	Make sure the card supports 136.9GB (ATA-5) size limit for disk; many early versions had 2.1GB or 8.4GB limits. Requires open ISA or PCI slot.
Use BIOS replacement feature in hard disk installation software supplied with drive.	None.	Free with drive.	Worst choice for large hard disk support because software drivers and nonstandard disk structures can be altered and destroyed very easily. This is absolutely *not* recommended.

> **Caution**
>
> Note that we believe that only a BIOS or BIOS adapter solution should be used. We absolutely *do not* recommend using any of the software that comes with the drives for patching the system to recognize a drive beyond the BIOS capability. You can get a BIOS card such as the ATA Pro Flash from MicroFirmware (http://www.firmware.com) for only $35. For that price, it is simply not worth the dangers involved in messing with the BIOS and OS extension software that often come with the drives.

After you decide on a strategy for handling the full capacity of your hard disk, don't change it! Don't use a BIOS replacement option in a program such as Disk Manager or EZ-Drive and then decide to install a BIOS upgrade (flash, chip, or card). The BIOS support won't be capable of working with your drive because it's already being translated by the software. Make your choice before you finish your drive installation.

Standard and Alternative Jumper Settings

If you decide to use the BIOS replacement software shipped with the hard drive instead of downloading or purchasing a BIOS upgrade, you might need to use alternative jumper settings on your hard disk. These typically involve the use of two jumpers rather than one for configuring a master, a slave, or single drive; the normal master and slave jumper block plus a second jumper block reduces the reported capacity of the drive. Check your drive's documentation for details.

A drive configured with the Alternate configuration requires the use of EZ-Drive, MAXBlast, or other drive manufacturer–supplied disk utility programs to access the full capacity of the drive. In some cases, the system might need to be shut down at the end of a session rather than warm-booted. Check with the drive manufacturer for details on using this configuration with Windows NT/2000 or with Linux, UNIX, or Novell NetWare. We recommend a system BIOS or BIOS card upgrade instead of using this feature, if possible.

Improving Hard-Disk Speed

A major benefit of ATA-2 was improving data-transfer rates, as shown in Table 4.13.

PIO Mode	Cycle Time (ns)	Transfer Rate (MB/Sec)	Specification
0	600	3.33	ATA
1	383	5.22	ATA
2	240	8.33	ATA
3	180	11.11	ATA-2, EIDE, fast-ATA
4	120	16.67	ATA-2, EIDE, fast-ATA

Table 4.13 PIO Modes and Transfer Rates

PIO modes 0–2 could be achieved with the original 16-bit mother-board or expansion slot-based IDE/ATA host adapters, but PIO modes 3 and above require a local-bus connection—either VL-Bus, PCI card, or (most often) a PCI motherboard connection.

The first ATA-2/EIDE hard drives introduced in 1994 were capable of PIO 3 transfer rates, but newer drives run at PIO 4 transfer rates or above. Most recent BIOSes detect the correct PIO mode as well as the basic drive geometry and set it for you. On BIOSes that offer a PIO mode setting that you must make manually, consult the drive vendor for the correct mode. Setting the PIO mode too high will cause data corruption.

Ultra DMA

The newest hard drives and motherboards support an even faster method of data transfer called Ultra DMA, or UDMA. See Table 4.14 for common Ultra DMA modes.

UDMA Mode	Transfer Rate (MBps)	Specification
2	33.33	ATA-4, Ultra-ATA/33
4	66.67	ATA-5, Ultra-ATA/66
5	100.00	Ultra-ATA/100
6	133.00	Ultra-ATA/133

Table 4.14 Common Ultra DMA Modes

With both PIO and UDMA modes, the transfer rates listed are maxi-mum (burst) transfer rates; sustained rates are much slower. Nevertheless, you will want to run your hard disk at the highest PIO or UDMA mode that it's capable of.

UDMA/66 and UDMA/100 Issues

Virtually all hard drives now on the market are designed to support UDMA/66 (also called Ultra ATA-66) or UDMA/100 transfer rates *if* certain requirements are met; Maxtor released the latest standard,

UDMA/133 (Ultra ATA-133), in July 2001. Table 4.15 lists the
requirements for UDMA/66, UDMA/100, and UDMA/133 compliance.

**Table 4.15   Ultra DMA/66, UDMA/100, and UDMA/133
Requirements**

Item	Features	Notes
Drive	Drive must have firmware for desired mode.	Some drives automatically sense compliance; others require you to run a configuration program to enable the mode. Consult the drive vendor.
Motherboard chipset	Must support same mode used by the drive, or the drive will operate more slowly than designed.	Check system or MB vendor for compliance; for highest performance, you should also install a bus-mastering device driver (see Table 4.13).
		If the motherboard can't run the drive at full speed, you can add a UDMA/66 or UDMA/100 PCI-based ATA interface card from sources such
		as MicroFirmware (http://www.firmware.com) or Promise Technologies (http://www.promise.com).
Cable	Cable must be 80-wire cable (40 data wires separated by 40 ground wires).	Connect blue end of UDMA/66 and UDMA/100 data cable to motherboard to ensure proper operation.

Any system that cannot run the drive at UDMA/66 or UDMA/100
can use the drive at the system's maximum speed (UDMA/33,
PIO 4, and so on).

See Figure 4.3 for a comparison of a standard ATA 40-wire cable
with an 80-wire cable required for UDMA/66 and faster operation.

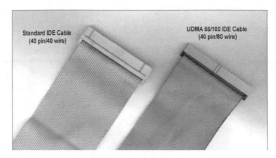

Figure 4.3   A standard 40-wire ATA cable (left) compared to an 80-wire UDMA/66-100 ATA cable (right). Both cables use the same 40-pin connector. The standard cable's 40 wires give the cable a pronounced ridged appearance when compared to the smaller and finer wires in the 80-wire cable.

Bus-Mastering Chipsets for ATA

Most late-model Pentium-class and more recent motherboards can support bus-mastering drivers for their ATA interfaces. The benefits of bus-mastering include faster ATA data transfer for CD-ROM, CD-R/CD-RW, and hard drives, and lower CPU utilization rates (the percentage of total time that the CPU spends handling a particular task). Table 4.16 lists the major chipsets providing bus-mastering features and tells where to get the driver. Be sure that you install the correct driver for your chipset.

Even if you enable UDMA/33 or faster UDMA modes in your system BIOS, you must install the bus-mastering driver for your hardware and operating system to get the maximum benefit out of your UDMA-compatible drives.

Table 4.16   Bus-Mastering Chipsets by Vendor and Operating System

Vendor	Chipsets	Driver Source by Operating System
Intel	430FX 430HX 430VX	(Same driver for all Intel chipsets at left) Windows 95 original and OSR1 (95a): Download BM-ATA 3.02 or greater driver from the Intel Web site.
	440FX 430TX 440LX 440BX 440EX 440GX 440ZX 440ZX-66 450NX	Windows 95B, 95C (OSR 2.x), Windows 98, Windows Me: included on Windows CD-ROM.

Table 4.16   Bus-Mastering Chipsets by Vendor and Operating System Continued

Vendor	Chipsets	Driver Source by Operating System
Intel	800-series	Download Ultra ATA Storage Driver chipsets (all) from Intel Web site (http://developer.intel.com). Works with Windows 98, 98SE, Windows Me, Windows 2000, and Windows NT 4.0. All versions except for Windows NT 4.0 require that you first install the Intel Chipset Software Installation Utility, also available from the Intel Web site.
VIA Apollo	Pro 266 Pro 133A Pro 133 ProSavage PM133 PLE133 KT266 KT133A ProSavage KM133 KT133 KX133 MVP4 MVP3	For Windows 95 (any version) and NT 4.0 and higher: Download the drivers from the VIA Web site. For Windows 98, 2000, Me, and XP: Drivers for some chipsets are included on Windows CD. Newer versions can be downloaded from the VIA Web site separately or are incorporated into the VIA 4-in-1 driver (AGP, ATA, IRQ routing and (INF).
SiS	Various chipsets	See Support FAQs on the SiS Web site (http://www.sis.com) for details of which chipsets and drivers require specific driver support and for driver downloads.
ETEQ	Various motherboard models	See http://www.soyo.com.tw to look up models and drivers; download there or from a related FTP site.
PCChips	Various motherboard models	See http://www.pcchips.com to look up ATA drivers by model and operating system (Windows 95, 98, Windows NT 4.0, and Windows 2000).
ALi (Acer Labs)	ALiMAGiK 1 ALADDiN-Pro 5 ALADDiN-Pro 4 CyberBLADE ALADDiN i1 ALADDiN TNT2 ALADDiN-Pro 2 ALADDiN 7 ALADDiN 5 ALADDiN 4	M1533 and M1543C South Bridge ATA driver available from the ALI Web site (http://www.acerlabs.com); other South Bridge chips use default ATA drivers provided with Windows 95 OSR 2.1 and newer releases.

Table 4.16 Bus-Mastering Chipsets by Vendor and Operating System Continued		
Vendor	**Chipsets**	**Driver Source by Operating System**
	ALADDiN 3	M1523B South Bridge driver for Windows 95 is available from the Acer Labs Web site (http://www.acerlabs.com); use the default Windows driver for later Windows versions.

All Intel chipsets that contain a PIIXn device (PIIX, PIIX3, PIIX4, PIIX4E, and so on) are bus-mastering chipsets.

Although PCChips chipset names are similar to certain Intel Pentium chipsets (Triton series TX, HX, and VX), the drivers listed are strictly for PCChips chipsets, not Intel's.

Acer Labs and VIA recommend checking with motherboard manufacturers' Web sites first for drivers because drivers might be customized for a particular vendor's products.

Benefits of Manual Drive Typing

Even though virtually every BIOS used since the mid-1990s supports automatic drive detection (also called *drive typing*) at startup, a couple of benefits to performing this task within the BIOS configuration screen do exist:

- If you need to move the drive to another system, you'll know the drive geometry and translation scheme (such as LBA) that was used to access the drive. If the drive is moved to another computer, the identical drive geometry (cylinder, head, sectors per track) and translation scheme must be used in the other computer; otherwise, the data on the drive will not be accessible and can be lost. Because many systems with autoconfiguration don't display these settings during the startup process, performing the drive-typing operation yourself might be the only way to get this information.

- If you want to remove a drive that is already in use and the BIOS displays the drive geometry, write it down! Because the ATA interface enables a drive to work with *any* defined geometry that doesn't exceed the drive's capacity, the current BIOS configuration for any given drive might *not* be what the manufacturer recommends (and what would be detected by the BIOS, using the ATA identify drive command). We ran a 203MB Conner drive successfully for years with an incorrect BIOS setting that provided 202MB because technical information about drives in the early days of ATA wasn't always easy to get. Drives working with the "wrong" geometry should *not* be "corrected" because this would require a complete backup of the drive and resetting the geometry in the BIOS, repartitioning and reformatting the drive, and restoring the data. Just label the drive with the actual head, cylinder, and sectors per track that it uses now.

Troubleshooting ATA Installation

In addition to the BIOS capacity and PIO/UDMA mode configuration issues, you might run into other problems during an ATA drive installation. Use Table 4.17 to determine problems, causes, and solutions.

Table 4.17 Other ATA Drive Installation Problems and Solutions		
Problem	**Causes**	**Solution**
Drive is not recognized by BIOS, but system will boot from floppy (drive is spinning).	Drive cabling installed incorrectly.	Make sure that pin 1 on the ATA Interface, and ATA drive are connected to pin 1 (colored edge) of ATA cable; some cables are keyed with a plugged hole at pin 20 or with a "bump" over the middle of the cable that corresponds to a cutout in the plastic skirt that surrounds the cable. On nonskirted motherboard ATA connectors, make sure that pins are connected to both rows of the cable, without any offsets.
System display remains blank after power on. No boot or other activity.	Drive cabling reversed; pin 1 is connected to pin 39 at either drive or interface connector.	Many systems cannot initialize the video card until the ATA hard drive is successfully initialized. Use of keyed cables will help to eliminate this problem (see previous tip).
Drive not recognized by BIOS, but system will boot from floppy (drive is not spinning).	Drive power cable not connected or defective.	If a Y-splitter or power extender is in use, check it for damage, or remove it and plug the drive directly to the power supply; make sure that the power connector is tightly inserted into the drive; use a Digital Multimeter (DMM) to check power leads; the drive might be defective if the power checks out okay.
One or both ATA drives on a single cable are not recognized by system (drives are spinning).	Drives might be jumpered incorrectly: both as master or both as slave, or as Cable Select with a standard 40-wire ATA cable.	Jumper the boot drive as the master, second drive.
One or both ATA drives on a single cable are not recognized by the system (drives are spinning	Drives might not be 100% compliant with ATA standards (very likely when trying to mix various brands	Reverse master and slave jumpering; move the second drive to the other ATA connector, and jumper both drives accordingly.

Table 4.17 Other ATA Drive Installation Problems and Solutions Continued		
Problem	**Causes**	**Solution**
and are jumpered correctly).	of ATA drives, especially older ones).	

Serial ATA

Serial ATA, which defines a brand-new high-speed drive interface, is the eventual successor to ATA-6 and earlier ATA standards; look for Serial ATA systems, drives, and add-on cards to appear in 2002. Serial ATA uses a thin seven-wire signal cable instead of the 40-wire or 80-wire cable used by current ATA/IDE and UDMA ATA/IDE standards, and it transmits signals at one of three signaling rates, as shown in Table 4.18. SATA-150, which is the speed used by the first SATA devices, is 50% faster than UDMA-100's maximum speed and much faster than UDMA-100's sustained transfer rate.

Table 4.18 SATA Standards Specifications				
Serial ATA Type	**Bus Width (Bits)**	**Bus Speed (MHz)**	**Data Cycles per Clock**	**Bandwidth (MBps)**
SATA-150	1	1500	1	150
SATA-300	1	3000	1	300
SATA-600	1	6000	1	600

Serial ATA transmits data serially (1 bit at a time), just as other recent I/O interfaces such as USB and IEEE-1394 do (see Chapter 6, "Serial and Parallel Ports and Devices," for details). Other differences between Serial ATA and current ATA/IDE standards include these:

- **No master/slave/cable select jumpers**—Each drive is connected directly to the Serial ATA host adapter.

- **A maximum cable length of 1 meter (over 39 inches)**—More than twice as long as the 18-inch cables used with UDMA/66 and faster UDMA drives.

- **Industry-standard 4-pin or optional 15-pin (12-wire) power connectors**—The optional 15-pin power connector will provide 3.3V of power and additional amperage for each drive.

See Figure 4.4 for the details of SATA signal and power connectors.

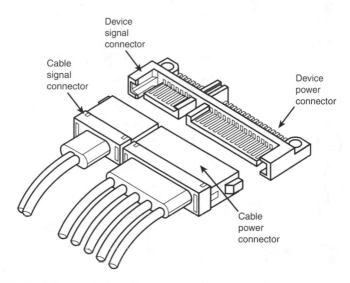

Figure 4.4   SATA (Serial ATA) signal and power connectors.

SCSI

The small computer system interface (SCSI) is a very flexible and high-performance drive and device interface. In addition to supporting hard drives, it also can support nonbootable optical and tape storage, scanners, and many other device types.

SCSI Types and Data Transfer Rates

Although many types of SCSI exist, different SCSI types can be mixed on the same host adapter. For best results, you should buy a host adapter capable of running your fastest devices at their top speeds *and* one that enables various types of devices to run without slowing each other down. Use Table 4.19 to learn common SCSI types and their characteristics.

Table 4.19 SCSI Types

Marketing Term	SCSI Standard	SCSI Technology Term	Transfer Speed (MBps)	Transfer Width	Cable Type
Asynchronous	SCSI-1	Async	4	8-bit	A
Synchronous	SCSI-1	Fast-5	5	8-bit	A
Fast	SCSI-2	Fast-10	10	8-bit	A
Wide	SCSI-2	Fast-10/Wide	20	16-bit	P
Ultra	SPI	Fast-20	20	8-bit	A
Ultra/Wide	SPI	Fast-20/Wide	40	16-bit	P
Ultra2	SPI-2	Fast-40	40	8-bit	A
Ultra2/Wide	SPI-2	Fast-40/Wide	80	16-bit	P
Ultra 160 (Ultra 3)	SPI-3	Fast-80DT	160	16-bit	P
Ultra 320 (Ultra 4)	SPI-4	Fast-160DT	320	16-bit	P

SPI = SCSI Parallel Interface; replaces the former SCSI-3 terminology.

The A cable is the standard 50-pin SCSI cable, whereas the P cable is a 68-pin cable designed for 16-bit. The maximum cable length is 6 meters (about 20 feet) for standard speed SCSI, and only 3 meters (about 10 feet) for Fast/Fast-20/Fast-40 (Ultra) SCSI; that drops to 1.5 meters if more than three devices are attached. SPI-2, SPI-3, and SPI-4 allow cable lengths of up to 12 meters (40 feet) if only one device is attached to the host adapter (point-to-point interconnect).

See Chapter 12, "Connector Quick Reference," for illustrations of SCSI cable connectors.

Single-Ended Versus Differential SCSI

SCSI is not only a flexible interface; it's also a multiplatform interface. Traditionally, PCs have used single-ended SCSI, whereas other platforms use differential SCSI. Because these two types of SCSI are not interchangeable, you should never mix them on a host adapter designed for single-ended SCSI. Use the markings in Figure 4.5 to distinguish between these.

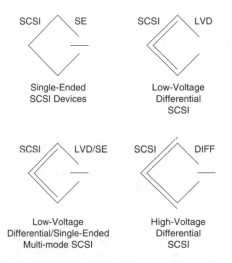

Figure 4.5   Single-ended and differential SCSI universal symbols.

Low-Voltage Differential Devices

Ultra2Wide SCSI devices, which run at 80MBps maximum transfer rates, use a modified version of differential SCSI called low-voltage differential (LVD). Workstation-oriented cards, such as Adaptec's AHA-2940U2W, enable the use of LVD Ultra2Wide devices and standard single-ended SCSI devices on the same card. Cards with this feature use two buses—one for LVD and one for standard SCSI devices.

> **Note**
>
> If you do need to use single-ended and differential SCSI devices
> on the same cable, adapters are available that will safely handle
> the connection. Paralan Corporation (4655 Ruffner St., San
> Diego, CA 92111, phone 858-560-7266; fax 858-560-8929,
> http://www.paralan.com) offers several off-the-shelf models
> and can create custom SCSI solutions.

SCSI Drive and Device Configuration

SCSI drives and devices require two configuration settings:

- SCSI ID setting (0–7 or 0–15, depending on the SCSI host adapter)

- Terminating resistors

The number of SCSI IDs available on a host adapter depends on its
design: 0–7 on SCSI adapters with an 8-bit bus (also called *narrow
SCSI*); 0–15 on SCSI adapters with a 16-bit bus (also called *wide
SCSI*); and two groups of 0–15 on a 16-bit bus with a dual-processor
host bus adapter.

SCSI Device ID

Up to seven SCSI devices (plus the adapter, for a total of eight) can
be used on a single narrow SCSI bus (8-bit), or up to 15 devices
(plus the adapter, for a total of 16) can be used on a wide (16-bit)
SCSI bus. Now dual-processor, 16-bit host adapters are available
that can operate up to 30 devices plus the host adapter. In every
case, each device must have a unique SCSI ID address. The host
adapter takes one address, so the rest are free for up to seven SCSI
peripherals (or more, as defined by the host adapter). Most SCSI
host adapters are factory-set to an ID of 7 or 15, which is the highest priority ID. All other devices must have unique IDs that do not
conflict with one another. Some host adapters boot only from a
hard disk set to a specific ID. Older Adaptec host adapters required
the boot hard disk to be ID 0; newer ones can boot from any ID. A
SCSI device containing multiple drives (such as a CD-ROM tower or
changer) will have a single ID, but each physical drive or logical
drive will also be known by a logical unit number (LUN). For example, a five-CD changer is SCSI ID 3. Each "virtual drive" or disc
position within SCSI ID 3 has a LUN of 0–4. So, the last "drive" has
drive letter J and is also identified by Windows as SCSI ID#3,
LUN 4.

Setting the SCSI ID

The methods for setting the SCSI ID vary with the device. For internal drives, the settings are made with jumper blocks. Use Table 4.20 to set the jumpers. Note that the column to the left is the lowest-numbered ID jumper, which may be identified as A0 or SCSI ID0, depending on the drive vendor.

Table 4.20	SCSI ID Jumper Settings				
SCSI ID #	ID A0 ID0	Jumper A1 ID1	Settings A2 ID2	A3 ID3	(WD and Quantum Markings) (Seagate Markings)
00	0	0	0	0	
01	1	0	0	0	
02	0	1	0	0	
03	1	1	0	0	
04	0	0	1	0	
05	1	0	1	0	
06	0	1	1	0	
07	1	1	1	0	
08	0	0	0	1	
09	1	0	0	1	
10	0	1	0	1	
11	1	1	0	1	
12	0	0	1	1	
13	1	0	1	1	
14	0	1	1	1	
15	1	1	1	1	

1 = Jumper on, 0 = Jumper off

SCAM—Automatic ID Setting

Some SCSI hard drives and host adapters support SCAM (SCSI Configure AutoMagically), which automatically assigns the drive a unique SCSI ID number. To use SCAM, both the host adapter and the drive must support SCAM, and SCAM must be enabled (usually by a jumper on the drive).

SCSI ID Setting for External Devices

SCSI drives and devices can be used both internally and externally, often with the same interface card. For external devices, one of the following methods will apply for each device in the SCSI daisy-chain. Use Table 4.14 as a general reference. Typically, the ID setting control is at the back of the device, near the SCSI interface cable. Depending on the device, the device ID can be set by a rotary dial, a push-button control, or a sliding switch. Not all SCSI

ID numbers are available with every device; many low-cost devices allow a choice of only two or three numbers. Regardless of the setting method, each internal and external device on a single SCSI daisy-chain of devices must have a unique ID. If you use Adaptec SCSI interface cards, use the SCSI Interrogator program before you add a new SCSI device to determine which device IDs you have remaining. If you are adding a new SCSI device with limited ID choices (such as the Iomega Zip 100 SCSI drive), you might need to move an existing device to another ID to make room for the new device.

For high-performance SCSI cards that offer multiple buses, you should be able to reuse device numbers 0–7 for each separate bus on the card. If you have problems with duplicate ID numbers on various buses, the device drivers for either the device or the interface card might not be up-to-date. Contact the device and card maker for assistance.

SCSI Termination

SCSI termination is simple. Termination is required at both ends of the bus; there are no exceptions. If the host adapter is at one end of the bus, it must have termination enabled. On the other hand, if the host adapter is in the middle of the bus—and if both internal and external bus links are present—the host adapter must have its termination disabled, and the devices at each end of the bus must have terminators installed. Unfortunately, the majority of problems that we see with SCSI installations are the result of improper termination.

Terminators can be external or internal (set with a jumper block or with switches or sliders). Some devices also terminate themselves automatically.

The pass-through models are required when a device is at the end of the bus and only one SCSI connector is available.

SCSI Configuration Troubleshooting

When you are installing a chain of devices on a single SCSI bus, the installation can get complicated very quickly. Here are some tips for getting your setup to function quickly and efficiently:

- **Start by adding one device at a time**—Rather than plugging numerous peripherals into a single SCSI card and then trying to configure them at the same time, start by installing the host adapter and a single hard disk. Then you

can continue installing devices one at a time, checking to
make sure that everything works before moving on.

- **Keep good documentation**—When you add a SCSI
  peripheral, write down the SCSI ID address and any other
  switch and jumper settings, such as SCSI parity, terminator
  power, and delayed or remote start. For the host adapter,
  record the BIOS addresses, IRQ, DMA channel, and I/O port
  addresses used by the adapter, and any other jumper or configuration settings (such as termination) that might be
  important to know later.

- **Use proper termination**—Each end of the bus must be
  terminated, preferably with active or Forced Perfect (FPT) terminators. If you are using any Fast SCSI-2 device, you must
  use active terminators rather than the cheaper passive types.
  Even with standard (slow) SCSI devices, active termination is
  highly recommended. If you have only internal or external
  devices on the bus, the host adapter and the last device on
  the chain should be terminated. If you have external and
  internal devices on the chain, you generally will terminate
  the first and last of these devices but not the SCSI host
  adapter (which is in the middle of the bus).

- **Use high-quality shielded SCSI cables**—Make sure that
  your cable connectors match your devices. Use high-quality
  shielded cables, and observe the SCSI bus-length limitations.
  Use cables designed for SCSI use, and, if possible, stick to the
  same brand of cable throughout a single SCSI bus. Various
  brands of cables have different impedance values, which
  sometimes causes problems, especially in long or high-speed
  SCSI implementations.

- **Have the correct driver for your SCSI host adapter
  and for each device**—SCSI, unlike ATA, is controlled not
  by your computer's motherboard BIOS, but by software drivers. A SCSI device cannot be used unless the appropriate software drivers are installed for it. As with any other
  software-driven peripheral, these drivers often are updated
  periodically. Check for improved drivers, and install them as
  needed.

Following these tips will help minimize problems and leave you
with a trouble-free SCSI installation.

Use Table 4.21 to help you record SCSI information. Table 4.22
shows a form that we use to record data about our systems. You
can attach this information to the system template referred to in
Chapter 2, "System Components and Configuration."

Table 4.21   SCSI Device Data Sheet

Interface Card	IRQ	DMA	I/O Port Address	Slot Type
Notes and details				
Device information				
Include SCSI interface card and all devices below				

Device ID Y/N	Device Name	Internal or External	Cable/ Connector Type	Terminated?
0				
1				
2				
3				
4				
5				
6				
7				
8				
9				
10				
11				
12				
13				
14				
15				

Table 4.22   Completed SCSI Device Data Sheet

Interface Card	IRQ	DMA	I/O Port Address	Slot Type
Adaptec AHA-1535	10	5	0130h–0133h	ISA
Notes and details	Bus-mastering card with internal and external cable connectors; allows pass-through so that both connectors can be used at once			

Table 4.22 Completed SCSI Device Data Sheet Continued				
Interface Card	IRQ	DMA	I/O Port Address	Slot Type
Device Information				
Include SCSI interface card and all devices				
Device ID Y/N	Device Name	Internal or External	Cable/ Connector Type	Terminated?
0				
1	(No device)			
2	Epson Expression 636 flatbed scanner with transparency adapter	External	50-pin Centronics	No
3	Polaroid SprintScan 35Plus slide and filmstrip scanner	External	50-pin Centronics and DB-25 25-pin	Yes
4	Philips CDD2600 CD-Recorder (CD-R)	Internal	50-pin ribbon cable	Yes
5	(No device)			
6	Iomega Zip 100 Zip drive	External	DB-25 25-pin	No
7	Adaptec AHA-1535 SCSI host adapter card	Internal	50-pin ribbon (internal)	
			50-pin high-density (external)	No
8–15	(No devices)			

Note that both ends of the daisy-chain are terminated and that the actual end of the internal daisy-chain is *not* the AHA-1535 SCSI host adapter, but the Philips CDD2600 drive. Also note that some SCSI devices support different types of cables.

Use the worksheet shown in Figure 4.6 to help you plan your SCSI cabling and physical layout. Start with the host adapter card. Figure 4.7 shows a completed worksheet.

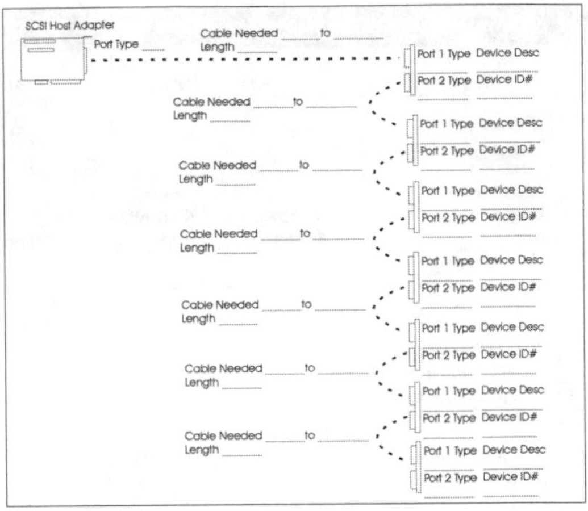

Figure 4.6   SCSI cabling worksheet (blank). See Figure 4.7 for a completed example. Use data recorded on the SCSI device data sheet shown in Table 4.22.

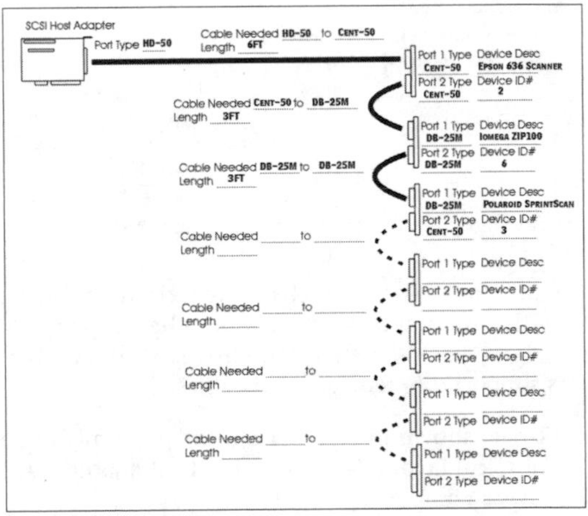

Figure 4.7   SCSI cabling worksheet (completed). This uses data from the completed SCSI device data sheet from Table 4.22.

Hard Disk Preparation

The formatting process for a hard disk drive subsystem has three major steps:

1. Low-level formatting

2. Partitioning

3. High-level formatting

Table 4.23 outlines the steps for preparing a drive for use after installation.

Table 4.23	Comparing the Steps in the Formatting Process	
Process Step	**When Necessary**	**How Performed**
Low-level formatting (LLF)	ATA and SCSI hard drives are low-level formatted at the factory; reformat only to correct errors.	
	With SCSI only, to configure the drive for use with a specified host adapter and its driver software. This is required for Windows 3.x/MS-DOS systems, but not for 32-bit Windows systems.	Use factory-supplied LLF or diagnostic utilities; use Ontrack Disk Manager or MicroScope v.9 for IDE/EIDE/ATA drives. For SCSI, use the host adapter's BIOS or software routines (such as Adaptec's EZ-SCSI), if necessary.
Partitioning	Always required for both SCSI and ATA hard drives. Indicates which portion of the drive will be used for each operating system and how the drive letters will be defined.	Use operating system utility (FDISK or equivalent) if BIOS provides full support for drive capacity. EZ-Drive, Disk Manager, and similar products can be used for both FDISK and FORMAT options for Windows 9x/Me systems. Use Disk Management for Windows 2000/XP. With SCSI drives under Windows 3.x/MS-DOS, host-adapter–specific partitioning and formatting routines are normally used.

Table 4.23 Comparing the Steps in the Formatting Process Continued

Process Step	When Necessary	How Performed
High-level formatting	Always required for all drive letters defined by FDISK or partitioning utility.	Use operating system utility (FORMAT or equivalent). EZ-Drive, Disk Manager, and similar products can be used for both FDISK and FORMAT options with Windows 9x/Me. Disk Management for Windows 2000/XP also formats drive. With SCSI drives under Windows 3.x/MS-DOS, host-adapter–specific partitioning and formatting routines normally are used.

Using FDISK

FDISK is the partitioning utility used with MS-DOS, Windows 9x, and Windows Me, and it has equivalents in all other operating systems. Disk Management performs the same task (plus high-level formatting) for Windows 2000 and Windows XP. In most cases with SCSI and all cases with ATA drives, it's the first software program that you run after you physically install a hard disk and properly detect or configure it in the BIOS.

FDISK is used to set aside disk space (or an entire physical drive) for use by an operating system, as well as to specify how many and what size the logical drives will be within that space. By default, the MS-DOS and Windows 9x/Me versions of FDISK prepare a single physical drive as a single drive letter (up to the limits listed), but FDISK also can be used to create multiple drives. By not preparing all of a hard disk's capacity with FDISK, you can use the remaining room on the hard disk for another operating system.

Drive-Letter Size Limits

We've already considered the physical drive size limits caused by BIOS limitations and how to overcome them. Those limits define the maximum size that a *physical* hard drive can be. However, depending on the version of Windows in use (and with any version of MS-DOS), it might be necessary to subdivide a hard drive through the use of FDISK to allow its full capacity to be used through the creation of multiple logical drive letters.

The original release of Windows 95 and all versions of MS-DOS from DOS 3.3x up support FAT16, which allows no more than 65,536 files per drive and a single drive letter no more than 2.1GB in size. Thus, a 6GB hard disk prepared with MS-DOS or the original Windows 95 must have at a minimum three drive letters and could have more (see Figure 4.8). The primary disk partition (C: on a single drive system) can be bootable and contains only a single drive letter. An extended partition, which cannot be bootable, contains the remainder of the drive letters (called *logical DOS drives* in most versions of FDISK).

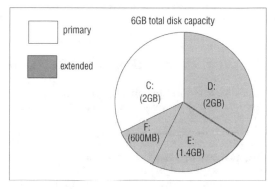

Figure 4.8   Adding a hard drive above 2.1GB in size to a computer running MS-DOS or original Windows 95 computer forces the user to create multiple drive letters in an extended disk partition to use the entire drive capacity.

Large Hard Disk Support

If you use the Windows 95B or above (Win95 OSR 2.x), Windows 98, or Windows Me versions of FDISK with a hard drive greater than 512MB, FDISK offers to enable large hard disk support.

Choosing to enable large hard disk support provides several benefits:

- You can use a large hard disk (greater than 2.1GB) as a single drive letter; in fact, your drive can be as large as 2TB and still be identified by a single drive letter. This is because of the FAT32 file system, which allows for many more files per drive than FAT16.

- Because of the more efficient storage methods of FAT32, your files will use less hard disk space. FAT32 is not supported by Windows NT 4.0 or earlier, but it is supported by Windows 2000 and Windows XP.

- Note that a FAT32 drive cannot be directly accessed by older versions (pre–OSR 2.x) of Windows 95, Windows 3.1x/MS-DOS, or any other operating system. If you occasionally need to run older applications that cannot run under Windows 95B or Windows 98 and you want to store those applications on a hard drive, be sure that you create a hard drive letter that uses FAT16. This way, you can boot your older operating system and still access your program files. You can, of course, access data on a FAT32 drive over a network with any computer using a compatible network protocol. Also, the windowed MS-DOS sessions that you can run with 32-bit Windows programs will enable MS-DOS programs to be run from and access a FAT32 drive.

Benefits of Hard-Disk Partitioning

Even though it might seem like a lot of trouble to partition a single physical hard disk into multiple drive letters, especially with FAT32, several good reasons exist for both FAT16 and FAT32 users to partition their hard disks:

- **Multiple partitions can be used to separate the operating system, application programs, and data for easier backup and greater security**—This method for dividing a hard disk into C: (Windows and drivers), D: (applications), and E: (data) is recommended by PowerQuest (makers of the popular PartitionMagic disk utility), and we've followed their advice for awhile. Some time ago, we lost both C: and D: to a completely unexpected disk crash, but our data on E: stayed safe.

- **For FAT16 operating systems in particular (MS-DOS, Windows 95/95a, and others using FAT16), partitioning the drive results in significantly less disk space wasted**—Because files actually are stored in clusters (or allocation units) that are multiples of the 512-byte disk sector, a small file must occupy an entire cluster. As Table 4.24 indicates, the bigger the drive is, the greater the space is wasted.

Table 4.24	FAT16 Cluster Sizes		
Drive Size (Defined by FDISK) Binary MB/GB	**Drive Size (Defined by Drive Maker) Decimal MB/GB**	**Cluster Size in Binary KB**	**Cluster Size in Bytes**
0–127MB[1]	0–133MB[1]	2KB	2,048
128–255MB	134–267MB	4KB	4,096

Table 4.24	FAT16 Cluster Sizes Continued		
Drive Size (Defined by FDISK) Binary MB/GB	Drive Size (Defined by Drive Maker) Decimal MB/GB	Cluster Size in Binary KB	Cluster Size in Bytes
256–511MB	268–537MB	8KB	8,192
512MB–1,023MB	538MB–1,073MB	16KB	16,384
1,024MB (1GB)– 2,048MB (2GB)	1,074MB–2,113MB	32KB	32,768

1. *If you create a partition less than 15MB (binary) in size, the operating system actually uses the old FAT12 file system, which results in a cluster size of 8KB.*

FAT32 Versus FAT16 Cluster Sizes

FAT32 is far more efficient than FAT16 and is used by virtually every recent system with a preinstalled copy of Windows 95 OSR 2.*x* (95B/95C), Windows 98, or Windows Me. If you are installing an additional hard disk on a system that uses these operating systems, use Table 4.25 to determine the relative efficiencies of FAT16 versus FAT32 because you can choose either FAT type for the entire new drive or any partitions on it. This chart uses MiB/GiB sizes (used by FDISK and most system BIOSes) only.

Table 4.25	FAT16 Versus FAT32	
Cluster Size	FAT16 Partition Size	FAT32 Partition Size
4KB	128MiB—255MiB	260MiB—8GiB
8KB	256MiB—511MiB	8GiB—16GiB
16KB	512MiB—1,024MiB	16GiB—32GiB
32KB	1,025MiB—2,048MiB	32GiB—2TiB

Converting FAT16 Partition to FAT32

If your existing hard disk uses FAT16, you can convert any partition on it to FAT32 *if* one of the following is true:

- You have Windows 95B or above (OSR 2.*x*) *and* PowerQuest's PartitionMagic v3.*x* or newer. PartitionMagic has a FAT1–to–FAT32 converter, which also can reverse the process (FAT32 to FAT16).

- You have Windows 98 or Windows Me. Windows 98 comes with its own FAT16–to–FAT32 converter, and it also can use PartitionMagic version 4.*x* or newer.

NTFS Considerations and Default Cluster Sizes

New Technology File System (NTFS) is the high-performance file system that can be used on Windows NT, Windows 2000, and Windows XP systems. It has much more efficient storage by default than FAT16, but it can't be directly accessed by other versions of Windows or MS-DOS. The version of NTFS in Windows 2000 and Windows XP (NTFS 5) also supports encryption and the merging of several physical drives into a single logical folder.

Use the following guidelines when considering the use of NTFS:

- Windows 2000 and Windows XP can install a drive of any size recognized by the BIOS as a single NTFS volume up to the limits of the BIOS.

- Windows NT 4.0 must partition a drive of more than 4GB into at least two drive letters because its boot drive cannot exceed 4GB.

- Windows 2000 and Windows XP can be used in a dual-boot environment with Windows 98 or Me, but if NTFS is installed on the same hard drive partition as Windows 98 or Windows Me, it cannot be used.

- NTFS drives require special disk utility programs for defragmentation and disk maintenance because their internal structure is different from FAT16 and FAT32 drives.

The default cluster sizes for NTFS in Windows 3.51 and above (including Windows NT 4.0, Windows 2000, and Windows XP) are listed in Table 4.26.

Table 4.26 Default NTFS Cluster Sizes	
Drive Size	**NTFS Cluster Size**
512MiB or less	512 bytes
513MiB–1,024MiB(1GiB)	1,024 bytes (1KiB)
1,025MiB–2,048MiB(2GiB)	2,048 bytes (2KiB)
2,049MiB and larger	4,096 bytes (4KiB)

Note that NTFS drives can be larger than FAT16 drives and are even more efficient than FAT32 drives.

The default cluster sizes for FAT16 drives under Windows NT 4.0, Windows 2000, and Windows XP are the same as for Windows 9x and MS-DOS. In addition, three more large drive sizes are supported by Windows NT 4.0 only (see Table 4.27).

Table 4.27 Additional FAT16 Cluster Sizes Supported by Windows NT 4.0	
Drive Capacity	Size of FAT (Using FAT16)
2,048–4,096MiB (2–4GiB)	64KiB
4,096–8,192MiB (4–8GiB)	128KiB
8,192–16,384MiB (8–16GiB)	256KiB

How Disk Partitioning and the Operating System Create and Allocate Drive Letters

Two types of partitions can be created with disk-partitioning programs (FDISK or Disk Management) in 32-bit Windows and MS-DOS: *primary* and *extended*. The primary partition can be bootable and can occupy all, part, or none of a hard disk's capacity. If you have only one hard disk in a system and it's bootable, at least a portion of that drive's partition is primary.

An extended partition is similar to a "pocket" that holds one or more logical drives inside it. Table 4.28 shows how FDISK identifies these various disk structures as they might be found in a typical 13GB hard disk divided into three drives—C:, D:, and E:.

Table 4.28 FDISK Primary, Extended, and Logical Drives Compared (example 13GB Hard Disk)					
Partition Type	Size	Contained Within	Bootable?	% of Total Disk Space	% of Partition
Primary	4GB	—	Yes	32.5%	—
Drive C:	4GB	Primary	Yes	32.5%	100% of primary
Extended	9GB	—	No	67.5%	—
Logical drive D:	4GB	Extended	No	32.5%	44.4% of extended
Logical drive E:	5GB	Extended	No	35.0%	55.6% of extended

With FDISK, the partitions shown earlier must be created in the following order:

1. Create the primary partition to occupy less than 100% of disk space at the size that you choose, up to any limits imposed by your operating system.

2. Create an extended partition to use the *remainder* of disk space unused by the primary partition.

3. Create one or more logical drives to occupy the extended partition.

4. Before leaving FDISK, make the primary partition (C:) active to enable it to boot.

Assigning Drive Letters with FDISK

You can use FDISK in many ways, depending on the number of hard drives that you have in your system and the number of drive letters that you want to create.

With a single drive, creating a primary partition (C:) and an extended partition with two logical DOS drives within it will result in the following drives, as you saw earlier:

Partition Type	*Contains Drive Letter(s)*
Primary	C:
Extended	D: and E:

A second drive added to this system should have drive letters that follow the E: drive, to preserve paths to data and program files.

However, you must understand how drive letters are allocated by the system to know how to use FDISK correctly in this situation. Table 4.29 shows how FDISK assigns drive letters by drive and partition type.

Table 4.29   Drive Letter Allocations by Drive and Partition Type

Drive	Partition	Order	First Drive Letter
1st	Primary	1st	C
2nd	Primary	2nd	D
1st	Extended	3rd	E
2nd	Extended	4th	F or higher

How does this affect you when you add another hard drive? If you prepare the second hard drive with a primary partition and your first hard drive has an extended partition on it, the second hard drive will take the primary partition's D drive letter. This moves all the drive letters in the first hard drive's extended partition up at least one drive letter.

This example lists a drive with C:, D:, and E: as the drive letters (D: and E: were in the extended partition). Table 4.30 indicates what happens if a second drive is added with a primary partition on it.

Table 4.30 Drive Letter Changes Caused by Addition of Second Drive with Primary Partition				
Drive	Partition Type	Order	Original Drive Letter(s) (First Drive Only)	New Drive Letter(s) After Adding Second Drive
1st	Primary	1st	C	C
2nd	Primary	2nd	—	D
1st	Extended	3rd	D, E	E, F

This principle extends to third and fourth physical drives as well: The primary partitions on each drive get their drive letters first, followed by logical DOS drives in the extended partitions.

How can you avoid the problem of changing drive letters? If you're installing an additional hard drive (not a replacement), remember that it can't be a bootable drive. If it can't be bootable, there's no reason to make it a primary partition. FDISK will enable you to create an extended partition using 100% of the space on any drive.

Table 4.31 shows the same example used in Table 4.29, with the second drive installed as an extended partition.

Table 4.31 Drive Letter Allocations After the Addition of a Second Drive with an Extended Partition Only				
Drive	Partition Type	Order	Original Drive Letter(s) (First Drive Only)	New Drive Letter(s) After Adding Second Drive
1st	Primary	1st	C	C
1st	Extended	2nd	D, E	D, E
2nd	Extended	3rd	—	F

This operating system behavior also explains why some of the first computers with ATA-based (ATAPI) Iomega Zip drives identified the Zip drive as D:, with a single 2.5GB or larger hard disk identified as C: and E:—the Zip drive was treated as the second hard drive with a primary partition because of the drivers used. Later Zip drive software drivers treated the drive as a removable-media drive and avoided conflicts with drive letters in the extended partition.

Differences Between FDISK and Disk Management

Windows 2000 and Windows XP use a graphical Disk Management program in place of the command-line FDISK program used by earlier Windows versions. The major differences between Disk Management and FDISK include these:

- Disk Management is launched from the Computer Management program; FDISK is launched from the command line.

- Disk Management provides a wizard-driven interface; FDISK uses a cryptic menu-driven interface.

- Disk Management allows new drive letters in either primary or extended partitions to be mapped around existing drive letters on hard disk, removable media, and optical drives; drive letters created with FDISK may replace existing drive letters.

- Disk Management also formats drives; FDISK requires the user to run a separate FORMAT program.

High-Level (DOS) Format

The final step in the installation of a hard disk drive is the high-level format. Similar to the partitioning process, the high-level format is specific to the file system that you've chosen to use on the drive. On 32-bit Windows and MS-DOS systems, the primary function of the high-level format is to create a FAT and directory system on the disk so that the operating system can manage files. With Windows 9x/Me, you must run FDISK before formatting a drive. Each drive letter created by FDISK must be formatted before it can be used for data storage. This process might be automated with setup programs for some operating systems, such as Windows 9x retail versions. In the following notes, we provide the steps for a manual drive preparation in which you'll install a full operating system copy later.

Usually, you perform the high-level format with the FORMAT.COM program or the formatting utility in Windows 9*x*/Me Explorer. FORMAT.COM uses the following syntax:

```
FORMAT C: /S /V
```

This high-level command formats drive C, writes the hidden operating system files in the first part of the partition (/S), and prompts for the entry of a volume label (/V) to be stored on the disk at the completion of the process.

The FAT high-level format program performs the following functions and procedures:

1. Scans the disk (read only) for tracks and sectors marked as bad during the LLF, and notes these tracks as being unreadable.

2. Returns the drive heads to the first cylinder of the partition; at that cylinder (Head 1, Sector 1), it writes a DOS volume boot sector.

3. Writes a FAT at Head 1, Sector 2. Immediately after this FAT, it writes a second copy of the FAT. These FATs essentially are blank except for bad-cluster marks noting areas of the disk that were found to be unreadable during the marked-defect scan.

4. Writes a blank root directory.

5. If the /S parameter is specified, copies the system files, IO.SYS and MSDOS.SYS (or IBMBIO.COM and IBMDOS.COM, depending on which DOS you run) and COMMAND.COM to the disk (in that order).

6. If the /V parameter is specified, prompts the user for a volume label, which is written as the fourth file entry in the root directory.

Now the operating system can use the disk for storing and retrieving files, and the disk is a bootable disk.

> **Note**
>
> Because the high-level format doesn't overwrite data areas
> beyond the root directory of the hard disk, using programs such
> as Norton Utilities to unformat the hard disk that contains data
> from previous operations is possible—provided that no pro-
> grams or data has been copied to the drive after high-level
> formatting. Unformatting can be performed because the data
> from the drive's previous use is still present.

If you create an extended partition, the logical DOS drive letters
located in the extended partition need a simpler FORMAT command
because system files aren't necessary—for example, FORMAT D:/V
for drive D, FORMAT E:/V for drive E, and so on. Windows
2000/XP's Disk Management partitions and formats drives in a
single operation.

Third-Party Hard-Disk Installation Programs

Windows, DOS, and OS/2 users can enjoy easier disk installation by
using the automatic disk-installation programs supplied by hard
disk vendors or available for retail purchase. Table 4.32 provides an
overview of these products.

Table 4.32   Overview of Automatic Disk-Installation Programs

Vendor Web Site	Software	Current Version	OEM	Retail	OS Supported
Ontrack http://www.ontrack.com (includes Disk Manager 9.5x)	Disk Manager 2000	4.x	Yes	Yes	9x, Me
Ontrack	Disk Manager	9.5x	Yes	No	Win 3.x, DOS, OS/2
StorageSoft http://www.storagesoft.com	EZ-Drive	9.1x	Yes	Yes	9x, Me, NT (FAT)
Seagate[1] www.seagate.com	DiscWizard 2000	2.4x	Yes	No	9x, Me NT4, 2000
Maxtor[2] www.maxtor.com	MaxBlast Plus	1.2x	Yes	No	9x, Me,
	MaxBlast	9.x	Yes	No	DOS
Western Digital[3] http://www.wdc.com	Data Lifeguard Tools	2.6x	Yes	No	DOS, 9x, Me NT4, OS/2

1. Seagate's DiscWizard 2000 was codeveloped with Ontrack and contains an OEM version of Disk Manager v9.x. Seagate also offers a Web-based version of DiscWizard called DiscWizard Online, a 16-bit Windows 3.x version of DiscWizard and an OEM version of Disk Manager.

2. Maxtor's MaxBlast Plus software is a customized version of StorageSoft's DriveGuide disk installation program. MaxBlast 9.x is a customized version of EZ-Drive. Maxtor also provides OEM versions of DiskManager 2000 and Disk Manager 9.5x for Quantum drives (Quantum's hard disk division is now owned by Maxtor).

3. Western Digital's Data Lifeguard Tools includes an OEM version of EZ-Drive.

Drive Migration Data-Transfer Methods

After you have installed your drive, partitioned it, and formatted it, you can use one of these methods to place information from your old drive onto your new drive, if desired:

- XCOPY

- Drive-copying utilities

XCOPY

The major virtue of using the XCOPY utility is its low cost; it's free because it's included in current Windows operating systems as well as in late versions of MS-DOS.

Because 32-bit Windows uses many hidden files and folders, you cannot run XCOPY by booting from a disk and running it directly from the command line because the DOS version of XCOPY can't copy hidden files and folders and can't preserve file and folder attributes. Instead, you need to use XCOPY within a command-prompt window after launching Windows. When XCOPY is run from a command-prompt window, an enhanced version (XCOPY32) is used that supports options for copying hidden files and folders and handling errors that can happen when open files such as the swapfile are copied. The following command runs Xcopy32 to copy the entire contents of C: drive to a newly installed D: drive with Windows 9*x*/Me. The D: drive must be configured as a primary partition if you plan to use it to replace the C: drive after copying files.

```
xcopy32 c:\. d:\/s/c/h/e/r/k
```

The command switches are explained here:

- **/S**—Copies folders beneath the starting folder.

- **/C**—Continues to copy after errors. (The Windows swap file can't be copied because it is in use.)

- **/H**—Copies hidden and system files.

- **/E**—Copies folders, even if empty.

- **/R**—Overwrites read-only files.

- **/K**—Preserves file attributes.

Repeat the command with appropriate drive-letter changes for any additional drive letters on your old drive.

After the original drive is removed from the system, the new drive needs to be jumpered as master (or single); the operating system will assign it C:. You also must run FDISK from a floppy and set the primary partition on the new C: drive as Active. Then exit FDISK, and the drive will boot.

This process can take a long time because of the overhead of running an MS-DOS session beneath Windows.

> **Caution**
>
> Beware that this technique can result in problems with the short filenames when files are copied. The short names won't be preserved, and if any registry entries refer to these short names (often some do), those files will no longer be found. Although XCOPY can work in a pinch, it is recommended that you use a professional disk-migration program instead of XCOPY.

Drive-Copying Utilities

Because of the long time that XCOPY32 data transfer can take and the potential problems that can take place during data transfer, we recommend using a specialized drive-copying program. Most drive-installation products listed in Table 4.32 include drive-copying utilities. Table 4.33 lists additional drive-copying options.

Table 4.33   Drive-Copying Utilities

Program	Vendor Web Site	Retail or OEM	Operating Systems Supported
DriveCopy 4.x	PowerQuest http://www.powerquest.com	Retail	9x, Me, 2000, NT, DOS, OS/2
EZ-Copy	StorageSoft http://www.storagesoft.com	Retail and OEM	9x, Me, 2000, NT (FAT only) with ATA drives only

Windows XP users can use the Files and Settings Transfer Wizard to copy data files and configuration information between systems. However, you will need to install Windows XP and your applications manually before using the wizard to customize your new system.

Hard-Disk Drive Troubleshooting and Repair

Hard-disk problems fall into two categories: hard and soft. *Hard* problems are triggered by mechanical problems that cause the drive to emit strange grinding or knocking noises (or no noise at all), whereas *soft* problems are read and write errors that occur in a drive that sounds normal. Before deciding that a hard disk is defective, test it on another known working system. If the problem goes away on another system, the drive is not the problem (see Table 4.34).

> **Note**
>
> Before using this table, verify that your drive's BIOS configuration is correct. If your system's LBA or other drive-translation settings are disabled and your drive needs them, it will appear to hang.

Table 4.34   Hard and Soft Problems and Solutions

Symptom	Cause	Solution
Drive makes banging noise on initial powerup; can't boot without restarting the computer a couple of times. Usually found on very old (under 100MB) RLL or MFM hard disks only. These drives use two (20-pin and 34-pin) data and signal cables.	*Stiction* (static friction) is causing the heads to stick to the media because of an aging mechanism and lubrication problems internally.	If the drive hangs, try tapping gently on one corner to free the heads or mount the drive upside down. Back up data and replace the drive as soon as possible.
Drive makes scratching or "boinging" noise internally; won't boot.	Severe head damage, probably caused by impact (fall or drop).	Replace the drive.
Drive spins normally but can't be recognized.	If cable and jumpering okay, probably failed logic board.	Replace the logic board or replace the drive.

Table 4.34 Hard and Soft Problems and Solutions Continued		
Symptom	**Cause**	**Solution**
Drive has repetitive errors detected by SCANDISK or other disk-testing utility.	If system rebooted or was turned off without proper shutdown, these are temporary files that weren't closed. This does not indicate a hardware problem.	Remind the user to shut down the computer normally.
	If the normal shutdown procedure was followed, might indicate marginal disk surface.	If the normal shutdown procedure was followed, get a manufacturer utility to detect and remap sectors, and retest the drive frequently. If the drive doesn't improve, replace it as soon as possible.

If replacing the logic assembly does not solve the problem, contact the manufacturer or a specialized repair shop that has clean-room facilities for hard-disk repair.

Drive and System Configuration Errors

Table 4.35 lists common configuration problems that can take place with drives that are electronically and mechanically sound but that require adjustments to the drive or system setup to work correctly.

Table 4.35 Drive and System Configuration Errors and Solutions		
Symptom	**Problem**	**Solution**
Drive won't boot on initial powerup, but it boots when system is reset. "Drive not ready" error is displayed	Drive is not spinning fast enough to be recognized by BIOS.	Enable or increase hard disk predelay time factor in BIOS setup.
UDMA/66 or faster ATA drive is recognized as UDMA/33 only	Wrong cable could be in use.	Use 80-wire UDMA cable, and rejumper drives as Cable Select.
	Drive firmware might not have faster UDMA modes enabled.	Run the drive manufacturer's utility for enabling the fastest UDMA mode available on the drive; download from the drive vendor.

Table 4.35   Drive and System Configuration Errors and Solutions Continued

Symptom	Problem	Solution
"Immediately back up your data and replace your hard disk drive. A failure may be imminent" error	The drive uses S.M.A.R.T. to predict failures, and the S.M.A.R.T. system has detected a serious problem with the drive.	Follow the onscreen instructions to back up your drive. Replace your drive immediately.
"Invalid Drive Specification" error	Drive has not been partitioned or high-level formatted, or wrong OS is being used to view drive.	Verify that the drive is empty with recent Windows versions before running FDISK and FORMAT.
"Invalid Media Type" error	Drive has not been FDISKed or drive's format is corrupt.	View the drive with FDISK's #4 option, and create new partitions as needed.

Optical Drive Interface Types

Most internal CD-ROM, CD-R, and CD-RW drives are ATAPI-based (ATAPI uses the standard ATA interface). Some high-performance drives in either internal or external form factors are SCSI based. Physical installation and cabling is the same as for any other ATA (ATAPI) or SCSI device, as seen earlier in this chapter.

Some external drives use parallel-port, USBm or IEEE-1394 port connectors. See Chapter 6 and Chapter 7, "USB and IEEE-1394 Ports and Devices," for troubleshooting and configuration tips for drives using these interface types.

MS-DOS Command-Line Access to CD-ROM Drives for Reloading Windows

CD-ROM drives normally are controlled in Windows 9*x* and Me by 32-bit drivers, but these drivers *will not work* if the operating system becomes corrupted or if Windows will work only in Safe mode. In those cases, having access to the CD-ROM drive becomes critical to enable you to reload the operating system.

In Windows 98 and Me, the emergency disk that you can create during initial installation or later contains drivers that work for most ATA/ATAPI- and SCSI-based CD-ROM drives. In addition, the disk will try each driver until it finds one that works.

In Windows 95, the emergency disk does *not* contain drivers for the
CD-ROM. Follow these general guidelines to create a working boot
disk with CD-ROM support. This same process will work for MS-
DOS/Windows 3.1 users.

The following instructions are for ATA (ATAPI) CD-ROM drives.
SCSI-based CD-ROM drives also will require SCSI device drivers for
the host adapter and devices attached.

1. Create the Windows 95 emergency disk (it's bootable) from
    the Control Panel's Add/Remove Programs icon Windows
    Setup tab. This process destroys all previous contents on the
    disk.

2. Copy the following files to your bootable disk in the A:
    drive:

    - **MYCDROM.SYS**—Use the actual driver name for your
      CD-ROM drive, and copy it from the file's actual loca-
      tion. If you don't have an MS-DOS driver, you can
      download one from the drive's manufacturer, or you
      can download an ATAPI driver called AOATAPI.SYS
      available from several Web sites.

    - **MSCDEX.EXE**—Copy from C:\WINDOWS\
      COMMAND or your CD-ROM drive's folder; it's the
      same file for any CD-ROM drive.

Next, you'll need to create a CONFIG.SYS file that will load the CD-
ROM device driver and an AUTOEXEC.BAT that will load the
MSCDEX.EXE CD-ROM extensions for MS-DOS program. Use a text
editor, such as the Windows Notepad.

Contents of CONFIG.SYS include:

- `DEVICE=MYCDROM.SYS /D:mscd001`

- `Lastdrive=M`

Contents of AUTOEXEC.BAT include:

- `MSCDEX.EXE /d:mscd001 /m:10 /L:M`

Note

Note that the /d: switch refers to the same device name, which
could be Charlie or Kumquat or anything that matches! A mismatch will cause the loading process to fail.

Check your computer's BIOS setup and verify that the floppy drive is the first bootable device. Then restart the computer with this floppy in drive A, and you should see the CD-ROM driver initialize. Next, MSCDEX should assign the CD-ROM the drive letter listed after the /L: option (M:).

If you don't have a suitable Windows 95 disk with CD-ROM support, a popular workaround is to use a Windows 98 or Windows Me startup disk because they both contain the CD-ROM drivers that you need to access your CD for reinstallation of files or the entire operating system.

Troubleshooting Optical Drives
Failure Reading a CD

If your CD-ROM drive fails to read a CD, try the following solutions:

- Check for scratches on the CD's data surface.

- Check the drive for dust and dirt; use a cleaning CD.

- Make sure that the drive shows up as a working device in System Properties.

- Try a CD that you know works.

- Restart the computer (the magic cure-all).

- Remove the drive from the Device Manager in Windows 9x, allow the system to redetect the drive, and reinstall drivers (if it's a PnP-based system).

Failure Reading CD-R and CD-RW Disks in a CD-ROM or DVD-ROM Drive

If your CD-ROM or DVD drive fails to read CD-R and CD-RW disks, try the following solutions:

- Check compatibility; some very old 1x CD-ROM drives can't read CD-R media. Replace the drive with a newer, faster, cheaper model.

- Many early model DVD drives can't read CD-R and CD-RW media; check compatibility.

- The CD-ROM drive must be Multi-Read—compatible to read CD-RW because of the lower reflectivity of the media; replace the drive.

- If some CD-Rs but not others can be read, check the media color combination to see whether some color combinations work better than others. Change the brand of media.

- Packet-written CD-Rs (from Adaptec DirectCD and backup programs) can't be read on MS-DOS/Windows 3.1 CD-ROM drives because of limitations of the operating system.

ATA/ATAPI CD-ROM Drive Runs Slowly

If your ATA/ATAPI CD-ROM drive performs poorly, check the following items:

- Check the cache size in the Performance tab of the System Properties Control Panel. Select the quad-speed setting (largest cache size).

- Check to see whether the CD-ROM drive is set as the slave to your hard disk; move the CD-ROM to the secondary controller, if possible.

- Your PIO or UDMA mode might not be set correctly for your drive in the BIOS; check the drive specs and use autodetect in BIOS for best results.

- Check to see that you are using bus-mastering drivers on compatible systems; install the appropriate drivers for the motherboard's chipset and operating system in use.

- Check to see whether you are using the CD-ROM interface on your sound card instead of an ATA connection on the motherboard. Move the drive connection to the ATA interface on the motherboard, and disable the sound card ATA, if possible, to free up IRQ and I/O port address ranges.

- Open the System Properties Control Panel, and select the Performance tab to see whether the system is using MS-DOS Compatibility mode for the CD-ROM drive. If all the ATA drives are running in this mode, see http://www.microsoft.com and query on "MS-DOS Compatibility Mode" for a troubleshooter. If only the CD-ROM drive is in this mode, see whether you're using CD-ROM drivers in CONFIG.SYS and AUTOEXEC.BAT. Remove the lines containing references to the CD-ROM drivers (don't actually delete the lines—REM them), reboot the system, and verify that your CD-ROM drive still works and that it's running in 32-bit mode. Some older drives require at least the CONFIG.SYS driver to operate.

Trouble Using Bootable CDs

Bootable CDs are terrific vehicles for installing a standard software image on a series of computers, or as a "bulletproof" method of running antivirus software, but they can be tricky to use.

If you are having problems using a bootable CD, try these possible solutions:

- Check the contents of the bootable floppy disk from which you copied the boot image during the creation of the bootable CD. To access the entire contents of a CD-R, a bootable disk must contain CD-ROM drivers, AUTOEXEC.BAT, and CONFIG.SYS. Test the bootable disk by starting the system with it and seeing whether you can access the CD-ROM drive afterward.

- Use ISO 9660 format. Don't use the Joliet format because it is for long-filename CDs and can't be used for bootable CDs.

- Check your system's BIOS for boot compliance and boot order; CD-ROM should be listed first.

- Check the drive for boot compliance.

- SCSI CD-ROMs need a SCSI card with BIOS and bootable capability, as well as special motherboard BIOS settings.

- You must use your mastering software's Bootable CD option to create the bootable CD-ROM from the files on the bootable floppy. The bootable disk's AUTOEXEC.BAT, CONFIG.SYS, and basic boot files are stored on a bootable CD as files called BOOTIMG.BIN and BOOTCAT.BIN by the mastering software's Bootable CD mastering option.

- If you cannot boot from the Windows 2000 CD-ROM for installation, create boot disks and use them to start the system and activate CD-ROM support.

Chapter 5

Floppy, Removable, Tape, and Flash Memory Storage

Floppy Drives

A 3 1/2-inch 1.44MB floppy drive, the most common type of floppy drive in use today, isn't very expensive to replace. However, when it stops working, you might *not* need to replace it right away, if you have the "inside story." Figure 5.1 shows an exploded view of a typical 3 1/2-inch 1.44MB floppy drive after the dust shield has been removed.

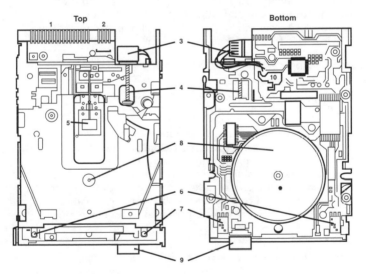

Figure 5.1   A typical 3 1/2-inch floppy disk drive.

1. 34-pin data cable connector

2. 4-pin power connector

3. Head-actuator motor

4. Worm gear to drive actuator motor

5. Read-write head (one of two)

6. Write-protect sensor

7. Media sensor (720KB or 1.44MB)

8. Spindle (left) and drive motor (right)

9. Disk ejector button

10. Logic board

Where Floppy Drives Fail—and Simple Fixes

Five common failure points exist on floppy drives:

- Dust shield
- Stepper motor
- Circuit board
- Read-write heads
- Cabling

If your drive fails for one of these reasons, you might be able to get it back into operation without replacing it, which is useful to know if a spare drive isn't readily available.

The Dust Shield

The metal plate on the top of the drive is called the dust shield. It protects the floppy disk's flexible magnetic media and the read-write heads from contamination and damage. However, a damaged or bent drive cover can bind the disk ejector, preventing it from moving. The drive cover can easily be removed and bent back into shape.

The Stepper Motor

The stepper motor moves the head actuator across the surface of the floppy disk media, reading or writing data (see Figure 5.2).

On a 3 1/2-inch drive, the stepper motor is often a worm-gear arrangement. The worm gear is very compact but can be jammed by shock. To free it up, carefully unscrew the stepper motor from the rear of the drive frame, and move the head actuator back and forth gently until the worm gear moves freely again. Reassemble the drive and test it outside the case by running the data and power cable to it before you secure it into its normal position.

Interface Circuit Boards

A drive's *interface circuit board* (also called a *logic board*) can be damaged by shock, static electricity, or a power surge. Usually, it can easily be removed from the bottom of the drive and replaced by a spare circuit board from an identical drive with a bad read/write head or stepper motor. Keep such failures around for spare parts.

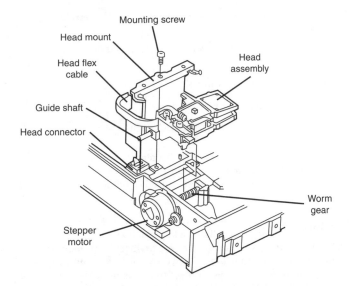

Figure 5.2   An expanded view of a stepper motor and head actuator.

Read/Write Heads

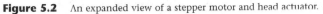

Because of the contact between the heads and disk, a buildup of the magnetic material from the disk eventually forms on the heads. The buildup should periodically be cleaned off the heads as part of a preventive-maintenance or normal service program.

The best method for cleaning the heads involves the use of a commercial wet-method disk head cleaner and a program that spins the cleaning disk and moves the heads around the cleaning media. MicroSystems Development (http://www.msd.com) offers the TestDrive floppy drive testing program, which contains such a cleaning utility. Depending on the drive use and the amount of contaminants (smoke, dust, soot) in the air, you should clean the read/write heads on a floppy drive only about once every six months to a year.

Do *not* use standard 3 1/2-inch floppy head cleaners with LS-120 or LS-240 SuperDisk floppy drives; although these drives can read and write to standard disks as well as the SuperDisk media, a conventional cleaner will damage their special read/write heads. The SuperDisk head-cleaning kit is Imation part number 0-51122-41066-6. If you are unable to order it from your favorite vendor, contact Imation (http://www.imation.com) Customer Service at 800-854-0033.

Floppy Drive Hardware Resources and Potential Conflicts

All primary floppy controllers use a standard set of system resources:

- IRQ 6 (Interrupt Request)

- DMA 2 (Direct Memory Address)

- I/O ports 3F0-3F5, 3F7 (Input/Output)

These system resources are standardized and generally are not changeable. This normally does not present a problem because no other devices will try to use these resources (which would result in a conflict).

The only major device that could cause a conflict with a floppy drive is a floppy-interface tape backup, such as those which use the QIC-80, Travan-1, and Travan-3 tape cartridges. Although these drives are obsolete, they are still used by some computers. Because floppy-interface tape drives connect to the same cable as the floppy drive, attempting to use the floppy drive while the tape drive is running will result in an IRQ and DMA conflict, with possible data loss on either or both drives. Newer tape drives that interface via other port types will not conflict with floppy drives.

Disk Drive Power and Data Connectors

Two sizes are used for disk drive power connectors. Figure 5.3 shows the original Molex power connector used on 5 1/4-inch floppy drives. Most 3 1/2-inch floppy drives and tape backups use a smaller connector, but either size normally has the same four-wire pinout shown in the figure.

Some 3 1/2-inch tape drives come with an extension cable with only two wires—a ground wire (black) and a +5v wire (red)—because their motors use the same +5v power as the logic board does.

Figure 5.4 shows a typical five-connector floppy data cable. Typically, the 5 1/4-inch edge connectors are seldom used today, unless a 3 1/2-inch drive has a pin-to-edge connector adapter attached.

Table 5.1 compares floppy and hard disk ribbon cables.

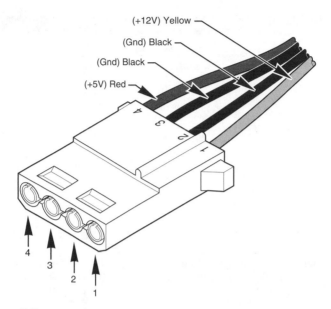

(+12V) Yellow

(Gnd) Black

(Gnd) Black

(+5V) Red

4
3
2
1

Figure 5.3 A disk drive female power supply cable connector.

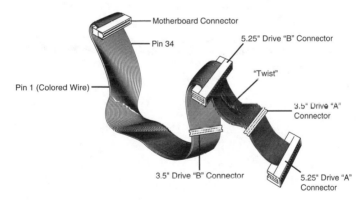

Motherboard Connector

Pin 34

5.25" Drive "B" Connector

"Twist"

Pin 1 (Colored Wire)

3.5" Drive "A" Connector

3.5" Drive "B" Connector

5.25" Drive "A" Connector

Figure 5.4 Standard five-connector floppy interface cable.

Table 5.1	**Comparing Ribbon Cables—Floppy Versus Hard Disk**			
Interface Type	Floppy	ST-506 ESDI	IDE	SCSI
Cable Width	34-pin	34-pin	40-pin or 80-strand	50-pin or 68-pin
Notes	Almost all have twist between A drive connectors and B drive connectors; twist toward pin 1 (colored edge of cable)	Can be straight or twisted; twist away from pin 1. This is obsolete and seldom seen today; it is used with 20-pin ribbon cable	80-strand cable has 40 pins; designed for use with UDMA/66 and faster motherboards and drives	

Table 5.2 lists the parameters for current and obsolete disk drives used on PCs. If you are preparing a drive with FORMAT that is smaller than the drive's capacity, you will need to set the FORMAT parameters manually.

A damaged media descriptor byte will prevent programs from properly accessing the disk; however, this problem can be fixed with Norton Utilities.

Table 5.2	**Floppy Disk Logical Formatted Parameters**							
	Current Formats					**Obsolete Formats**		
Disk size (inches)	3 1/2	3 1/2	3 1/2	5 1/4	5 1/4	5 1/4	5 1/4	5 1/4
Disk capacity (KB)	2,880	1,440	720	1,200	360	320	180	160
Media descriptor byte	F0h	F0h	F9h	F9h	FDh	FFh	FCh	Feh
Sides (heads)	2	2	2	2	2	2	1	1
Tracks per side	80	80	80	80	40	40	40	40
Sectors per track	36	18	9	15	9	8	9	8
Bytes per sector	512	512	512	512	512	512	512	512
Sectors per cluster	2	1	2	1	2	2	1	1
FAT length (sectors)	9	9	3	7	2	1	2	1

Table 5.2 Floppy Disk Logical Formatted Parameters Continued							
	Current Formats					**Obsolete Formats**	
Number of FATs	2	2	2	2	2	2	2	2
Root dir. length (sectors)	15	14	7	14	7	7	4	4
Maximum root entries	240	224	112	224	112	112	64	64
Total sectors per disk	5,760	2,880	1,440	2,400	720	640	360	320
Total available sectors	5,726	2,847	1,426	2,371	708	630	351	313
Total available clusters	2,863	2,847	713	2,371	354	315	351	313

Floppy Drive Troubleshooting

Table 5.3 Floppy Drive Troubleshooting Tips		
Problem	**Cause**	**Solution**
Dead drive— the drive does not spin, and the LED never comes on.	Bad power supply or power cable.	Measure the power at the cable with a voltmeter; ensure that 12V and 5V are available to the drive.
	Drive or controller not properly configured in BIOS setup.	Check BIOS setup for proper drive type and ensure that the controller is enabled if built into the motherboard; if an add-on card contains a floppy controller and the motherboard also has one, disable one of them.
	Bad data cable.	Replace the cable, and retest.
	Defective drive.	Replace the drive, and retest.
	Defective controller.	Replace the controller and retest. If the controller is built into the motherboard, disable it via the BIOS setup, install a card-based controller, and retest, or replace the entire motherboard and retest.
Drive LED remains on continuously.	Data cable on backward at either the drive or the controller connection.	Reinstall the cable properly and retest.

Table 5.3   Floppy Drive Troubleshooting Tips Continued

Problem	Cause	Solution
	The data cable could be offset on the connector by one or more pins.	Reinstall the cable properly and retest; replace cable if this doesn't work.
Phantom directories— you have exchanged disks in the drive, but the system still believes that the previous disk is inserted, and it even shows directories of the previous disk.	Defective cable.	Replace the cable and retest.
	Improper drive configuration.	Older drives must have their DC jumper (for Drive Changeline support) enabled.
	Defective drive or interface.	Replace the drive and retest.

Note

Windows users: Windows does *not* automatically refresh the display with File Manager, Explorer, and so on by default. Use the F5 key or click Refresh to reread the disk.

Common Floppy Drive Error Messages—Causes and Solutions

Table 5.4   Handling Floppy Drive Error Messages

Error Message	Cause	Solution
Invalid Media or Track Zero Bad, Disk Unusable	You are formatting the disk, and the disk media type does not match the format parameters.	Make sure you are using the right type of disk for your drive and are formatting the disk to its correct capacity.
	Disk is defective or damaged.	Replace the disk and retest.
	Read/ write heads are dirty.	Clean the drive, allow the heads to dry, and retest.

Table 5.4 Handling Floppy Drive Error Messages Continued

Error Message	Cause	Solution
CRC Error or Disk Error 23	The data read from the disk does not match the data that was originally written. (CRC stands for cyclic redundancy check.)	Replace the disk and retest. Clean the drive heads, allow them to dry, and retest. Use Norton Utilities or SpinRite to recover data from the disk.
General Failure Reading Drive A, Abort, Retry, Fail, or Disk Error 31	The disk is not formatted or has been formatted for a different operating system (Macintosh, for example).	Reformat the disk and retest.
	There are damaged areas on the disk medium.	Replace the disk and retest. Use Norton Utilities or SpinRite to recover data from the disk.
	The disk is not seated properly in the drive.	Remove and reinsert the disk in the drive. Try holding the disk in place with your hand. If you can read the data, copy it to a reliable disk.
Access Denied	You are trying to write to a write-protected disk or file.	Move the write-protect switch to allow writing on the disk, or remove the read-only file attribute from the file(s). File attributes can be changed by the ATTRIB command or through the file properties in Windows.
Insufficient Disk Space or Disk Full	The disk is filled, or the root directory is filled.	Check to see if sufficient free space is available on the disk for your intended operation. Use folders on the disk to store files, or change to a new disk.
Bytes in Bad Sectors (greater than 0)	This is displayed after FORMAT, CHKDSK, or ScanDisk if allocation units (clusters) have been marked bad.	The operating system will not use bad sectors, but this is a sign of a marginal disk; reformat or discard, and use a new disk with no bad sectors.
Disk Type or Drive Type Incompatible or Bad	You are attempting to DISKCOPY between two incompatible drive or disk types.	Disks can be copied only between drives using the same disk density and size. Use COPY or XCOPY instead, unless you are trying to create an exact copy.

Removable Storage Drives

For backup or alternative main storage, many users today are de-emphasizing floppy disks in favor of alternative storage media. Table 5.5 describes the varying types of storage media, and Table 5.6 provides an overview of storage types. Of the drives listed, only the LS120/SuperDisk, Sony HiFD, and Caleb it drives are also read/write–compatible with standard 3 1/2-inch floppy media.

Drives that use SCSI or IDE (ATAPI) interfaces are installed the same way as other SCSI or IDE devices. See Chapter 4, "SCSI and ATA Hard Drives and Optical Drives," for details.

Table 5.5   Quick Reference to Removable Magnetic and Flash Storage Devices (in Order by Capacity)

Media Type	Media Brands	Mfrs.	Capacity	Interface Type	Best Use
Flash memory	SmartMedia, ATA Data Flash, Compact Flash, Memory Stick, MultiMedia Card	Various	2MB–512MB, depending on brand and model	Proprietary, PC Card or floppy via adapters, PC Card Type II	Digital camera "film," storage for PDAs, portable devices
Flexible magnetic disk	Zip, LS-120 SuperDisk, LS-240, SuperDisk PocketZip (formerly Clik!), PhotoShow	Various	40MB–250M3, depending on brand and model	Parallel, IDE, SCSI, USB, PC Card (PCMCIA)	Data and program backups and storage for direct access
Hard disk	MicroDrive	IBM	340MB, 1GB	CF+ Type II, PC Card via adapter	Digital camera "film," program and data storage for notebook computers
High-performance, flexible magnetic disk	Jaz	Iomega	1GB and 2GB	SCSI	Program storage, data and program backups

Table 5.5   Quick Reference to Removable Magnetic and Flash Storage Devices (In Order by Capacity) Continued

Media Type	Media Brands	Mfrs.	Capacity	Interface Type	Best Use
High-performance hard disk cartridge	Orb	Castlewood	2.2GB, 5.7GB (IDE)	IDE, SCSI, USB, Parallel	Program storage, data and program backups
High-performance hard disk cartridge	Peerless	Iomega	10GB, 20GB	IEEE-1394, USB	Program storage, full drive backups
.315-inch magnetic tape cartridge	Travan and Travan NS	Various	Up to 10GB[1], depending on brand and model	IDE, SCSI, parallel, USB	Data and program backups, full drive backup
ADR magnetic tape cartridge	ADR 30GB and 50GB	OnStream	15GB[1] and 25GB[1]	IDE, SCSI, parallel, USB, IEEE-1394	Data and program backups, full drive backup; works in progress storage and playback
DAT, Exabyte 8MM, AIT, DDS magnetic tape	Various	Various	Up to 50GB1	SCSI	Data and program backups, full drive backup

1. Uncompressed capacity: Tape drives are usually rated at 2:1 compression; multiply uncompressed capacity by actual compression ratio obtained to determine your nominal working capacity.

Table 5.6	Removable Drive Specifications (in Order by Capacity)		
Drive Type Mfr.	**Disk/Cartridge Capacity/Type**	**Average Seek Time**	**Data Transfer Rate (Sustained)**
Iomega PocketZip (formerly Clik!) Parallel	40MB PocketZip	Not listed	620KBps
Iomega Zip Parallel[1]	100MB Zip	29ms	1.4MBps
Iomega Zip IDE/ATAPI	100MB Zip	29ms	1.4Mbps
Iomega Zip SCSI[1]	100MB Zip	29ms	1.4MBps
Iomega Zip USB	100MB Zip	29ms	1.2MBps
Imation LS-120 IDE Internal[2]	120MB SuperDisk	60ms	1.1MBps
Imation LS-120 Parallel[2]	120MB SuperDisk	60ms	750KBps
Imation LS-120 USB[2]	120MB SuperDisk	60ms	700KBps
Imation LS-120 PCMCIA[2]	120MB SuperDisk	70ms	440KBps
Que! SuperDisk 240MB FD32 USB[3]	240MB SuperDisk	65ms	600KBps
Iomega Zip 250 SCSI[4]	250MB Zip	29ms	2.4MBps
Iomega Zip 250 Parallel[4]	250MB Zip	29ms	800KBps
Iomega Zip 250 ATAPI/IDE[4]	250MB Zip	29ms	2.4MBps
Iomega Zip 250 USB[4]	250MB Zip	<50ms	900KBps
Iomega Zip 250 USB with FireWire adapter[4]	250MB Zip	29ms	>2.0MBps
Iomega Jaz (SCSI)[4]	2GB Jaz	12ms	7.35MBps
Castlewood ORB IDE	2.2GB ORB	12ms	12.2MBps
Castlewood ORB SCSI	2.2GB ORB	12ms	12.2MBps
Castlewood ORB Parallel	2.2GB ORB	12ms	2MBps
Castlewood ORB IDE	5.7GB ORB		

Table 5.6 Removable Drive Specifications (in Order by Capacity) Continued			
Drive Type Mfr.	**Disk/Cartridge Capacity/Type**	**Average Seek Time**	**Data Transfer Rate (Sustained)**
Iomega Peerless USB	10GB/20GB Peerless	12ms	1MBps
Iomega Peerless IEEE-1394/FireWire Peerless	10GB/20GB	12ms	15MBps

1. Although Iomega rates ZIP 100 parallel and SCSI versions as having the same transfer rate, SCSI versions are as much as eight times faster in actual use.

2. This has been discontinued by Imation, but the product might still be available from some suppliers. Performance of OEM versions might vary. All LS-120 SuperDisk models can read/write standard 1.44MB/720KB 3.50-inch floppy media.

3. LS-240 drives also can read/write LS-120 SuperDisk and standard 3.5-inch 720KB and 1.44MB floppy disks. LS-240 drives also can format standard 1.44MB 3.5-inch floppy disks at 32MB. Performance of other versions of the LS-240 drive might vary.

4. Zip 250 drives also can read/write Zip 100 media, although performance is slower than with Zip 250 media.

5. Jaz 2GB drive also can read/write Jaz 1GB cartridges.

Sources for "Orphan" Drive Media, Repairs, Drivers, and Support

Several removable-media drives have become "orphans" over the last few years. Although the best long-term recommendation that you can make is to copy all readable data off an orphan drive and transfer it to industry-standard storage devices, you might need to buy replacement drives, media, repairs, or parts to enable your clients to complete the move to new storage devices. Use Table 5.7 to help you locate these sources.

Table 5.7 Sources for "Orphan" Drive Parts, Service, and Media			
Drive	**Status**	**Parts or Repairs**	**Media Drivers**
Avatar Shark 250	Manufacturer out of business.	Weymouth Technologies (508)735-3513 www.weymouthtech.com	www.windrivers.com/ company.htm ("Dead Boards" section)
Iomega Alpha 8 inch, Beta 5.25 inch, 21MB floptical, LaserSafe	Obsolete products not supported by Iomega.	Comet Enterprises, Inc. (801)444-3600 www.gocomet.com	Follow links from www.gocomet.com (some are at Iomega's Web site, others on Comet Enterprises' Web site)

Table 5.7	Sources for "Orphan" Drive Parts, Service, and Media Continued		
Drive	**Status**	**Parts or Repairs**	**Media Drivers**
All SyQuest products (SparQ, EZ-Flyer, others)	SYQT, Inc. purchased product and parts inventory from Iomega after Iomega bought Syquest's intellectual property in 1999.	Parts, repairs, drives, media, and drivers are available from the SYQT, Inc. Web site: www.syqt.com.	

Troubleshooting Removable Media Drives

Table 5.8	Troubleshooting Removable Media Drives	
Drive/Interface	**Problem**	**Solution**
Any parallel-port model	Can't detect drive with install program	Check for IRQ conflicts; IRQ for parallel port must not be used by sound cards or other devices. Verify that install disk has correct drivers. Set parallel port mode to match requirements of drive.
Any SCSI interface model	Drive not available	Check SCSI IDs; each SCSI device must have a unique ID number. Check termination. Verify that correct drivers are installed. ASPI drivers must be installed for both the SCSI interface and each device on the interface.
Iomega Zip— any interface	Drive makes "clicking" sound; can't access files	Drive might have "click of death" problem. Physically examine media for damage. Use Iomega Diagnostics to check media. Download Trouble in Paradise (TIP) from Gibson Research (http://www.grc.com) for more thorough testing.
Any USB interface model	Can't detect drive	Verify that USB ports are enabled and that operating system has USB support (Windows 98/Me/2000/XP are recom- mended). If the drive is bus-powered, attach the drive directly to the USB root hub on the system or to a self-powered external hub. Install drivers for the external hub if used and drive.
Any IEEE-1394 interface model	Can't detect drive	Verify that IEEE-1394 port is working correctly. Verify that the drive works with your operating system. Disconnect and reconnect cable to redetect drive.

| Table 5.8   Troubleshooting Removable Media Drives Continued | | |
Drive/Interface	Problem	Solution
Any drive, any interface	Drive letter interferes with network, CD-ROM, and so on	Under Windows 9x/Me, check drive properties and select an available drive letter not used by the CD-ROM or the network.
		Use Disk Management in Windows 2000/XP or Disk Administrator (NT 4.0) to remap new drives to avoid conflicts with existing drives.

Types of Flash Memory Devices

Several different types of flash memory devices are in common use today and knowing which ones your digital camera is designed to use is important. The major types include the following:

- CompactFlash

- SmartMedia (SSFDC)

- ATA PC Cards (PCMCIA)

- MultiMedia Card (MMC)

- Memory Stick

ATA PC Cards can use flash memory or an actual hard disk. They can be read directly by the Type II or Type III PC Card (PCMCIA) slots found on most notebook computers. CompactFlash is actually a compact version of an ATA PC Card and requires only an inexpensive connector adapter to plug into a standard PC Card slot.

SmartMedia, MultiMedia Card, and Memory Stick flash memory devices require the use of a card reader to interface with notebook or desktop computers; some photo printers include a built-in card reader for instant digital prints. Card readers can attach to any of the following:

- Parallel port

- USB port

- PC Card Type II slot

Most devices that use flash memory storage can be connected via serial ports for direct downloading of images or other data, but this is much slower and is not recommended for heavy-duty use. Most newer devices also support USB connections, which are much faster than serial but are not as fast as a card reader.

Troubleshooting Flash Memory Devices

Normally, flash memory devices are detected automatically and are treated by your system as a removable-media drive. The contents of a flash memory device can be viewed in Windows Explorer and can be copied, moved, or deleted, just as with any other type of read/write media. Table 5.9 lists typical flash memory problems and solutions.

Table 5.9	Troubleshooting Flash Memory Devices	
Symptoms	**Problem**	**Solution**
Compact Flash card not detected when plugged into Lexar JumpShot USB cable	Only Lexar USB-enabled CF cards work with JumpShot USB cable.	Use a regular CF card reader for regular CF cards; use a JumpShot cable only with USB-enabled cards (look for the USB logo on the card).
Flash memory card not detected when plugged into card reader	The card reader might not be detected by the system.	Unplug and reattach the card reader if using USB or IEEE-1394. For other interface types, shut down the system, reattach the card reader, and restart the system; verify that the USB port is enabled and that the system has USB drivers.
Flash memory card not detected when plugged into Type II PC Card adapter	The card or adapter might not be attached securely.	Remove the PC Card from the system. Remove the flash memory card and reattach it to the PC Card adapter. Then reattach the PC Card. Verify that the PC Card slot works with other devices.
Flash memory card works with some devices, but not others	The card might not be compatible with all devices.	Check the device and card vendor's compatibility list.

Because flash memory cards are treated as removable-media disk drives, you can use data-recovery programs such as Norton Unerase and ScanDisk on the media, if necessary. A flash memory card also can be formatted to restore it to proper operation (although all data will be lost).

Tape Backup Drives and Media
Common Tape Backup Standards

Several tape backup standards exist for individual client PC and small server tape backup drives:

- **QIC, QIC-Wide, and Travan**—Three branches of a large and diverse family of low-cost "entry-level" tape backup drives, which can handle data up to 20GB@2:1 compression

- **DAT (Digital Audio Tape)**—A newer technology than QIC and its offshoots, using Digital Data Storage technology to store data up to 40GB@2:1 compression

- **OnStream's ADR (Advanced Digital Recording)**—A recent technology aimed at desktop and small network backup needs, featuring capacity up to 50GB@2:1 compression

- **Ecrix's VXA**—A recent technology that has been approved by the international data-storage standards body ECMA and that provides storage up to 66GB@2:1 compression

Other tape backup standards, such as DLT (Digital Linear Tape) and 8mm, are used primarily with larger network file servers and are beyond the scope of this book.

Travan Tape Drives and Media

Imation created the Travan family of tape drives to provide a standardized development from the crazy-quilt of QIC and QIC-Wide MC (minicartridge) tape drives that stemmed from the original QIC-40 and QIC-80 drives and their DC-2120 cartridges. Note that Travan-1 through Travan NS-8 retain read-only compatibility with the QIC-80 cartridge.

Table 5.10   Travan Family Cartridges and Capacities

Travan Cartridge (previous name)	Capacity/2:1 Compression	Read/Write Compatible with	Read Compatible with
Travan-1 (TR-1)	400MB/800MB	QIC-80, QW5122	QIC-40
Travan-3 (TR-3)	1.6GB/3.2GB	TR-2, QIC-3020, QIC-3010, QW-3020XLW, QW-3010XLW	QIC-80, QW-5122, TR-1
Travan 8GB (Travan 4/ TR-4)	4GB/8GB	QIC-3095	QIC-3020, QIC-3010, QIC-80, QW-5122, TR-3, TR-1
Travan NS-8[1] QIC-80	4GB/8GB		QIC-3020, QIC-3010,
Travan NS-20	10GB/20GB		Travan 8GB, QIC-3095

1. This cartridge can be used in place of the Travan 8GB (TR-4); the same cartridge can be used on either NS8 or TR-4 drives.

Note

Backward compatibility can vary with each drive; consult the manufacturer before purchasing any drive to verify backward-compatibility issues.

Travan and Travan NS

Both Travan and Travan NS drives use the same 8GB or 20GB (2:1 compression) Travan tape cartridges, but their mechanisms, interfaces, and suggested uses vary greatly.

Table 5.11 compares these technologies; Travan NS drives provide faster backup with verification because data is verified during the backup instead of by rewinding the tape, but Travan NS drives require a SCSI interface and are more expensive than Travan drives.

Table 5.11   Travan and Travan NS Compared

	Travan	Travan NS
Single-pass tape verification	No	Yes
Interface types	USB, IDE/ATAPI, SCSI	SCSI
Workstation backup	Yes	Yes
Network backup	No	Yes

Beyond Travan—Larger Tape-Backup Devices

With 30GB and larger hard drives very common on current systems, the 20GB (@2:1) limit of Travan NS20 drives is not sufficient to provide single-tape backup. Several different drive technologies offer reasonable pricing, high performance, and high capacity for use with today's larger hard drives.

Table 5.12 provides an overview of major choices suitable for workstation and small network use (drive prices under $1,200).

Table 5.12   Tape Backup Drives with Capacities Above 20GB (@2:1)—Under $1,200 Retail

Tape Backup Type Vendor Web Site	Technology	Tape Capacities @2:1	Interfaces
OnStream ADR http://www.onstream.com	ADR	30GB	IDE/ATAPI, Parallel, SCSI, USB
Tandberg SLR7 http://www.tandberg.com	SLR	40GB	SCSI
OnStream ADR http://www.onstream.com	ADR	50GB	SCSI
Ecrix VXA-1 http://www.ecrix.com	VXA	66GB	SCSI, IEEE-1394, IDE/ATAPI

Converting Older Tape Backups to Work with a New Drive

NovaStor (http://www.novastor.com) sells its TapeCopy 2.0 program for media conversion. TapeCopy 2.0 converts data between different-format IDE and SCSI-interface tape backup drives, enabling you to use older backup data with your new drive.

Successful Tape Backup and Restore Procedures

A backup tape might be the only thing separating you from a complete loss of data. To ensure that every backup can be restored, follow the guidelines shown in Tables 5.13 and 5.14 when you create a backup or restore one.

Table 5.13 Tape Backup Tips		
Tip	**Benefit**	**Notes**
Perform the confidence test during tape-backup software installation.	Tests the DMA channels in the computer for safe data transfer; sets the default transfer rate for the backup.	Keep a spare blank tape at all times to enable you to perform this test whenever new hardware is installed or before running a new backup for safety.
Select the correct backup type.	A "full" backup backs up the contents of the system, but the operating system must be restored first before restoring the backup. "Disaster recovery" backup creates special boot disks and enables entire system recovery straight from tape to an empty hard drive. Other backup types are designed primarily for data backup.	Make a disaster recovery backup, and test your ability to restore your backup to an empty hard drive. Use other backup types for periodic backups.
Choose speed and safety.	Maximum data compression uses the least amount of tape and is often about as fast as other backup types. Use Compare afterward to ensure readability.	
Don't use multiple tapes for a single backup.	Tape backups are typically rated with 2:1 compression assumed; this ratio is seldom achieved. Using multiple tapes for a single backup can cause a loss of data if the first tape is lost because it contains the tape	Use the actual compression ratio reported during your initial full backup to determine your nominal tape size. If your tape drive is a Travan 3 or smaller, get extra capacity per tape by using Verbatim QIC-EX series tapes (see Table 5.15).

Table 5.13	Tape Backup Tips Continued	
Tip	**Benefit**	**Notes**
	catalog. Back up a large drive with a small tape drive by backing up sections.	
Avoid multitasking during the tape backup.	Let the tape backup run without interruptions due to DMA transfers. Turn off the screensaver and power management. Turn off your monitor.	Don't use floppy drives because floppy DMA 2 is often used during backups.

Table 5.14	Tape Restore Tips
Tip	**Benefit**
Restore full backups to an empty drive, if possible.	Avoids overwriting drive with junk data if your backup has failed.
If your full backup is not a disaster recovery type, install the smallest possible operating system image first.	You'll wait less before you can install your backup software and restore your backup.
Run the confidence test again before you start the restore process.	This verifies that DMA transfers will be successful; it requires a blank tape or one that can be overwritten, so keep one handy.

Tape Drive Troubleshooting

Tape drives can be troublesome to install and operate. Any type of removable media is more susceptible to problems or damage, and tape is no exception. This section lists some common problems and resolutions. After each problem or symptom is a list of troubleshooting steps.

Can't Detect the Drive

For parallel-port drives, use the tape backup as the only device on the drive, and check the IEEE-1284 (EPP or ECP) mode required by the drive against the parallel port configuration.

For USB drives, be sure that you're using Windows 98 or higher *and* that the USB port is enabled in the BIOS; many systems originally shipped with Windows 95 have this port disabled.

For IDE drives, ensure that the master/slave jumpers on both drives are set properly.

For SCSI drives, check termination and device ID numbers.

For external drives of any type, be sure that the drive is turned on a few seconds before starting the system. If not, you might be able to use the Windows 9x/2000/Me/XP Device Manager to "refresh" the list of devices, but if this doesn't work, you'll need to restart the computer.

Backup or Restore Operation Failure

If your tape drive suffers a backup or restore operation failure, follow these steps:

1. Make sure that you are using the correct type of tape cartridge.

2. Remove and replace the cartridge.

3. Restart the system.

4. Retension the tape.

5. Try a new tape.

6. Clean the tape heads.

7. Make sure that all cables are securely connected.

8. Rerun the confidence test that checks data transfer speed with a blank tape (this test overwrites any data already on the tape).

Bad Block or Other Tape Media Errors

To troubleshoot bad block or other types of media errors, follow these steps:

1. Retension the tape.

2. Clean the heads.

3. Try a new tape.

4. Restart the system.

5. Try initializing the tape.

6. Perform a secure erase on the tape (previous data will no longer be retrievable from the tape).

Note that most minicartridge tapes are preformatted and cannot be reformatted by your drive. Do not attempt to bulk-erase preformatted tapes because this will render the tapes unusable.

System Lockup or System Freezing When Running a Tape Backup

If your system locks up or freezes while running a tape backup, follow these steps:

1. Ensure that your system meets at least the minimum requirements for both the tape drive and the backup software.

2. Check for driver or resource (IRQ, DMA, or I/O port address) conflicts with your tape drive controller card or interface; using the floppy drive while making a floppy or parallel-port tape backup is a major cause of DMA conflicts.

3. Set the CD-ROM to master and the tape drive to slave if both are using the same IDE port.

4. Check the BIOS boot sequence; be sure that it is not set to ATAPI (tape/CD-ROM) devices if the tape drive is configured as a master device or as a slave with no master.

5. Make sure that the hard drive has sufficient free space; most backup programs temporarily use hard drive space as a buffer for data transfer.

6. Hard drive problems can cause the backup software to lock up. Check your hard disk for errors with ScanDisk or a comparable utility.

7. Check for viruses.

8. Check for previous tape drive installations; ensure that any drivers from previous installations are removed.

9. Temporarily disable the current VGA driver and test with the standard $640 \times 480 \times 16$ VGA driver supplied by Microsoft. If the problem does not recur, contact your graphics board manufacturer for an updated video driver.

10. Files in some third-party Recycle Bins can cause backup software to lock up. Empty the Recycle Bin before attempting a backup.

11. Disable antivirus programs and Advanced Power Management.

12. Try the tape drive on another computer system and a different operating system, or try swapping the drive, card, and cable with known good, working equipment.

Other Tape Drive Problems

Other issues that might cause problems in general with tape back-ups include the following:

- Corrupted data or ID information on the tape.

- Incorrect BIOS (CMOS) settings.

- Networking problems (outdated network drivers and so on).

- The tape was made by another tape drive. If the other drive can still read the tape, this might indicate a head alignment problem or an incompatible environment.

Tape Retensioning

Retensioning a tape is the process of fast-forwarding and then rewinding the tape to ensure that even tension exists on the tape and rollers throughout the entire tape travel. Retensioning is recommended as a preventive maintenance operation when using a new tape or after an existing tape has been exposed to temperature changes or shock (for example, dropping the tape). Retensioning also restores the proper tension to the media and removes unwanted tight spots that can develop.

Some general rules for retensioning include the following:

- Retension any tapes that have not been used for more than a month or two.

- Retension tapes if you have errors reading them.

- Retension any tapes that have been dropped.

- In some cases, it might be necessary to perform the retension operation several times to achieve the proper effect. Most tape drive or backup software includes a Retension feature as a menu selection.

Chapter 6

Serial and Parallel Ports and Devices

Understanding Serial Ports

The asynchronous serial interface was designed as a system-to-system communications port. *Asynchronous* means that no synchronization or clocking signal is present, so characters can be sent with any arbitrary time spacing.

Each character that is sent over a serial connection is framed by a standard start-and-stop signal. A single 0 bit, called the *start* bit, precedes each character to tell the receiving system that the next 8 bits constitute a byte of data. Then 1 or 2 stop bits follow the character to signal that the character has been sent. At the receiving end of the communication, characters are recognized by the start-and-stop signals instead of by the timing of their arrival.

Serial refers to data that is sent over a single wire, with each bit lining up in a series as the bits are sent. This type of communication is used over the phone system because this system provides one wire for data in each direction. Compared to parallel ports, serial ports are very slow, but their signals can be transmitted a greater distance. The other wires in the serial port are used to control the flow of data to or from the port.

Serial ports also are referred to as COM ports because they are used to communicate between devices.

Serial ports use either 9- or 25-pin male D-connectors, although most devices today use only the 9-pin type. Adapters can convert one type to the other. See Chapter 12, "Connector Quick Reference," for illustrations of the 9-pin (AT-style) serial port, which is standard on most recent systems, and the older 25-pin serial port, the original type used on the original IBM PC and some of its successors. Built-in ports normally are controlled (enabled or disabled) in the BIOS Setup.

Pinouts for Serial Ports

Tables 6.1, 6.2, and 6.3 show the pinouts of the 9-pin (AT-style), 25-pin, and 9-pin-to-25-pin serial connectors.

Table 6.1   9-Pin (AT) Serial Port Connector

Pin	Signal	Description	I/O
1	CD	Carrier detect	In
2	RD	Receive data	In
3	TD	Transmit data	Out
4	DTR	Data terminal ready	Out
5	SG	Signal ground	—
6	DSR	Data set ready	In
7	RTS	Request to send	Out
8	CTS	Clear to send	In
9	RI	Ring indicator	In

Table 6.2   25-Pin (PC, XT, and PS/2) Serial Port Connector

Pin	Signal	Description	I/O
1	—	Chassis ground	—
2	TD	Transmit data	Out
3	RD	Receive data	In
4	RTS	Request to send	Out
5	CTS	Clear to send	In
6	DSR	Data set ready	In
7	SG	Signal ground	—
8	CD	Carrier detect	In
9	—	+Transmit current loop return	Out
11	—	–Transmit current loop data	Out
18	—	+Receive current loop data	In
20	DTR	Data terminal ready	Out
22	RI	Ring indicator	In
25	—	–Receive current loop return	In

Table 6.3   9-Pin-to-25-Pin Serial Cable Adapter Connections

9-Pin	25-Pin	Signal	Description
1	8	CD	Carrier detect
2	3	RD	Receive data
3	2	TD	Transmit data
4	20	DTR	Data terminal ready
5	7	SG	Signal ground
6	6	DSR	Data set ready
7	4	RTS	Request to send

Table 6.3 9-Pin-to-25-Pin Serial Cable Adapter Connections **Continued**			
9-Pin	**25-Pin**	**Signal**	**Description**
8	5	CTS	Clear to send
9	22	RI	Ring indicator

> **Note**
>
> Macintosh systems use a similar serial interface, defined as RS-422. Many external modems in use today can interface with either RS-232 or RS-422, but it is safest to make sure that the external modem you get for your PC is designed for a PC, not a Macintosh.

UARTs

The heart of any serial port is the Universal Asynchronous Receiver/Transmitter (UART) chip (or UART function in a Super I/O chip). The UART completely controls the process of breaking the native parallel data within the PC into serial format and later converting serial data back into the parallel format.

Many low-cost internal modem models lack a true UART and use the resources of the computer and operating system for communications in place of a UART. These so-called *Winmodems* (also called *soft modems* or *controllerless modems*) are less expensive than ordinary modems, but they are slower and, because of lack of driver support, often are not usable with non-Windows operating systems, such as Linux.

UART Types

Most recent systems no longer use a separate UART chip, but have merged the UART's function into the Super I/O chip or South Bridge chips (which are part of the motherboard chipset). However, it's important to know which UART chip (or equivalent) your serial port(s) uses, especially under the following circumstances:

- You want to attach a modem to the serial port.

- You plan to transfer data between machines via the serial port.

- You want to ensure reliable multitasking while using Windows with your modem.

Table 6.4 summarizes the characteristics of the major UART chips (and equivalents) found in PCs. For more information about UARTs, see Chapter 17 of *Upgrading and Repairing PCs, 13th Edition*, from Que.

Table 6.4	Overview of UART Chip Types			
UART Type	**Maximum Speed**	**Buffer**	**Typical System**	**Notes**
8250	Up to 9.6Kbps	No	8088	Original UART; replaced by 8250B
8250A	Up to 9.6Kbps	No	8088	Not recommended because is incompatible with 8250
8250B	Up to 9.6Kbps	No	8088/286	Debugged version of 8250
16450	Up to 19.2Kbps	1-byte	386/486 (19.2Kbps)	Minimum UART for OS/2
16550	Up to 115Kbps	16-byte FIFO	386/486 Pentium	First chip suitable for multi-tasking; can be used as pin-compatible replacement for socketed 16450. Super I/O and South Bridge chips, which contain Super I/O functions emulating the 16550
16650	Up to 230Kbps	32-byte	Specialized I/O cards, internal ISDN terminal adapters	Faster throughput than 16650 series
16750	Up to 460Kbps	64-byte	Specialized I/O cards, ISDN terminal adapters	Faster throughput than 16650, 16650 series
16950	Up to 921.6Kbps	128-byte	Specialized I/O cards, ISDN terminal adapters	Faster throughput than 16550, 16650, and 16750

> **Note**
>
> The previous specifications reflect maximum speeds available
> with standard I/O card designs; some vendors use a clock-
> multiplication feature that can double the effective speed of
> some UARTs in some I/O card applications.

Identifying Your System UART

The minimum desirable UART chip is the 16550 series or above,
but older systems and inexpensive multi–I/O cards might use the
bufferless 8250 or 16450 series UARTs instead. Three methods can
be used to determine which UARTs you have in a system.

MS-DOS Method (Also for Windows NT)

Use a diagnostic program such as Microsoft MSD, CheckIt,
AMIDiag, or others to examine the serial ports. These programs also
list the IRQ and I/O port addresses in use for each serial port.
Because ports are virtualized under Windows, the reports from a
DOS-based utility will not be accurate unless you boot straight to a
DOS prompt and run the diagnostic from there.

OS/2 Method

Use the MODE COMx command from the OS/2 prompt to view serial
port information. Look for an entry called Buffer in the list of serial
port characteristics. If Buffer is set to Auto, the chip is a true
16650A or better. However, if Buffer is set to N/A, it's an older
16450 chip.

Windows 9x/2000/Me/XP Method

Open the Start menu, and then choose Settings, Control Panel.
Locate the Modems icon, double-click it, and then click the
Diagnostics tab. The Diagnostics tab shows a list of all COM ports
in the system, even if they don't have a modem attached to them.
Select the port that you want to check in the list, and click More
Info. Windows communicates with the port to determine the UART
type, and that information is listed in the Port Information portion
of the More Info box. If a modem is attached, additional information about the modem is displayed.

Windows 2000 and XP don't have a diagnostics tab, and the applet
for modem control is called Phone and Modem Options instead.

High-Speed Serial Ports (ESP and Super ESP)

Some manufacturers have introduced Enhanced Serial Ports (ESP) or Super High-Speed Serial Ports. These ports enable a 28.8Kbps or faster modem to communicate with the computer at data rates up to 921.6Kbps. The extra speed on these ports is generated by increasing the buffer size. These ports usually are based on a 16650, 16750, or 16950 UART (see Table 6.4), and some even include more buffer memory on the card.

Lava Computer Mfg. and Byte Runner Technologies are two vendors that offer a complete line of high-speed serial port cards; some models also include parallel ports.

If you use a PCI-based multi–I/O card with Windows 95B or later versions of Windows, IRQ steering will enable you to use the card along with other cards in your system; you will still be able to use your existing serial ports for low-speed devices, if you prefer. However, if you use an ISA-based multi–I/O card, you should disable your system's onboard serial ports to avoid conflicts, and configure the card the same IRQ and I/O port address settings as your system's onboard serial ports.

Serial Port Configuration

Each time a character is received by a serial port, it must get the attention of the computer by raising an *interrupt request line* (IRQ). The 8-bit ISA bus systems have 8 of these lines, and systems with a 16-bit ISA bus have 16 lines. The 8259 interrupt controller chip usually handles these requests for attention. In a standard configuration, COM 1 uses IRQ 4, and COM 2 uses IRQ 3.

When a serial port is installed in a system, it must be configured to use specific I/O addresses (called *ports*) and *interrupts*. The best plan is to follow the existing standards for how these devices should be set up. For configuring serial ports in either Windows or Linux, use the addresses and interrupts indicated in Table 6.5.

Table 6.5   Standard Serial I/O Port Addresses and Interrupts

COM x	I/O Ports	IRQ	Equivalent to Linux[2]
COM 1	3F8–3FFh	IRQ 4	ttys0
COM 2	2F8–2FFh	IRQ 3	ttys1
COM 3	3E8–3EFh	IRQ 4[1]	ttys2
COM 4	2E8–2EFh	IRQ 3[1]	ttys3

1. *Although many serial ports can be set up to share IRQ 3 and 4 with COM 1 and COM 2, it is not recommended. The best recommendation is setting COM 3 to IRQ 10 and COM 4 to IRQ 11 (if available). If ports above COM 3 are required, it is recommended that you purchase a special multiport serial board.*

2. *Linux users must use distributions based on kernel 2.2 or better to enable IRQ sharing. With older distributions, use the* setserial *command (found in the Linux startup) to assign different IRQs to devices using ttys2 (COM3) and ttys3 (COM4); this also requires you to configure the cards to use those IRQs. For more information about* setserial *and serial ports under Linux, refer to the Linux Serial How-To at* http://www.linuxdoc.org/HOWTO/SerialHOWTO.html.

Avoiding Conflicts with Serial Ports

Use Table 6.6 to understand and avoid possible conflicts with serial ports.

Table 6.6   Troubleshooting Serial Port Conflicts

Problem	Reason	Solution
DOS-based program can't find COM 3 or 4 on modem or other device	DOS and PC BIOS support COM 1 and 2 only	Disable COM 2 and set new device to use COM 2; use Windows program instead
Device using COM 3 or 4 conflicts with COM 1 and 2	Shared IRQs don't work for ISA devices	Relocate IRQ for the device to a different port. If the device is external, connect to multiport board (Windows 95/98/NT/2000/XP can handle 128 serial ports). Use PCI-based serial port for COM 3 and above; this permits IRQ sharing with other PCI devices with Windows 95B and above.

Note

For modem troubleshooting, see the section "Modems," later in this chapter.

Troubleshooting I/O Ports in Windows 9*x*/Me/ 2000/XP

Follow these steps to troubleshoot serial ports in these versions of Windows:

1. Open the System properties sheet, select the Hardware tab (if present), and click Device Manager.

2. Click the Ports category and select the specific port (such as COM 1).

3. Click the Properties button and then click the Resources tab to display the current resource settings (IRQ, I/O) for that port.

4. Check the Conflicting Devices List to see whether the port is using resources that conflict with other devices. If the port is in conflict with other devices, click the Change Setting button and then select a configuration that does not cause resource conflicts. You might need to experiment with these settings until you find the right one.

5. If the resource settings cannot be changed, they most likely must be changed via the BIOS Setup. Shut down and restart the system, enter the BIOS setup, and change the port configurations there.

In addition to the COM 1/COM 3 and COM 2/COM 4 IRQ conflicts noted earlier, some video adapters have an automatic address conflict with COM 4's I/O port address.

You also can use the Modems Diagnostic tab (discussed earlier in this chapter) to test a serial port, whether or not a modem is actually present.

Advanced Diagnostics Using Loopback Testing

One of the most useful types of diagnostic tests is the *loopback test*, which can be used to ensure the correct function of the serial port and any attached cables. Loopback tests are basically internal (digital) or external (analog). You can run internal tests by unplugging any cables from the port and executing the test via a diagnostics program.

The external loopback test is more effective. This test requires that a special loopback connector or wrap plug be attached to the port in question. When the test is run, the port is used to send data out to the loopback plug, which routes the data back into the port's receive pins so that the port is transmitting and receiving at the same time. A *loopback* or *wrap plug* is nothing more than a cable that is doubled back on itself.

AMI includes serial and parallel loopback plugs with the AMIDiag suite (http://www.ami.com), and SmithMicro offers loopback plugs as part of its CheckIt Suite diagnostic program (http://www. smithmicro.com). Note that there are several ways to construct a loopback plug, and the correct design differs from program to program. Contact the diagnostic software vendor for pinouts if you want to make your own, or to purchase prebuilt loopback plugs.

Modems

Modems provide a vital communication link between millions of small- to medium-size businesses and homes and the Internet, electronic banking, and other services. The following information will help you get the most out of your modem.

Modems and Serial Ports

External modems connect to existing serial ports and don't contain a UART chip. Most internal modems contain their own serial port and do contain a UART chip.

Any external modem that will be used at speeds of 28Kbps or above must be connected to a 16550A-type UART or better to run at top speeds. For best results with external ISDN terminal adapters, use serial ports equipped with 16750 or 16950 UARTs because they support maximum speeds in excess of 460Kbps.

56Kbps and Older Modem Modulation Standards

Asynchronous modems (also called *analog* modems or *dial-up* modems) frequently are identified by their protocols. Use Table 6.7 to determine the speed and other characteristics of a particular protocol. Most modems support multiple protocols.

Table 6.7 Modem Modulation Standards and Transmission Rates		
Protocol	**Maximum Transmission Rate (bps)**	**Duplex Mode**
Bell 103	300bps	Full
CCITT V.21	300bps	Full
Bell 212A	1200bps	Full
ITU V.22	1200bps	Half
ITU V.22bis	2400bps	Full
ITU V.23	1,200/75bps	Pseudo-Full
ITU V.29	9,600bps	Half
ITU V.32	9,600bps	Full

Table 6.7   Modem Modulation Standards and Transmission Rates Continued

Protocol	Maximum Transmission Rate (bps)	Duplex Mode
ITU V.32bis	14,400bps (14.4Kbps)	Full
ITU V.32fast	28,800bps (28.8Kbps)	Full
ITU V.34	28,800bps (28.8Kbps)	Full
ITU V.34bis	33,600bps (33.6Kbps)	Full
ITU V.90[1]	56,000bps (56Kbps)[2]	Full
ITU V.92[3]	56,000bps (56Kbps)[2]	Full

1. *The maximum upload speed for a V.90 modem (as well as for the X2 and K56flex protocols it replaced) is 33.6Kbps.*

2. *Although ITU V.90 and V.92 (successors to the proprietary 56Kflex and X2 standards) allow for this speed of transmission, the U.S. Federal Communications Commission (FCC) allows only 53,000bps (53Kbps) at this time.*

3. *V.92 is an extension to V.90 and, depending on the ISP's support of these features, can offer the following enhancements: QuickConnect (reduces connection time by learning the line's characteristics), Modem-on-Hold (enables you to take a voice call without losing your connection), and PCM Upstream, which allows uploads as fast as 48Kbps.*

For more information about the V.90 and V.92 56Kbps standards, see *Upgrading and Repairing PC's, 13th Edition,* Chapter 20.

Upgrading from X2 or K56flex to V.90 with Flash Upgrades

The original proprietary 56Kbps standards (X2 and K56flex) have been replaced by V.90. Although V.90 is similar to K56flex, and although some ISPs support both types of modems with the same dial-up number, X2 is quite different and very few ISPs still support 56Kbps connections from X2 modems. If possible, you should upgrade your non–V.90/92 modem to one of these current standards. Many but not all X2 and K56flex modems have flash-upgradeable firmware.

Flash upgrades to V.90 work like a BIOS upgrade for a PC: You download the appropriate software from the modem vendor, run the flash software, and wait a few minutes; then your modem is ready to dial into V.90-based ISPs at top speeds. One major problem is what happens *inside* the modem to the existing firmware:

- **X2 modems to V.90**—X2 and V.90 firmware can coexist in a modem.

- **K56flex to V.90**—Most K56flex modems don't have room for both sets of firmware, so the V.90 firmware *replaces* the K56flex. The lack of a fallback standard has caused problems for some users of V.90 modems that were upgraded from K56flex models. Table 6.8 will help you find a solution if your V.90 connections aren't reliable.

Table 6.8   Troubleshooting the V.90 (ex-K56flex) Modems

Problem	Solution	Method
You can't get a reliable connection with V.90.	Download and install the latest firmware revisions from the vendor's Web site, even if you have a brand-new modem.	If you're having problems making the connection, dial in with your modem on a 33.6Kbps line, or pretend that your modem is an older model by installing it as a 33.6Kbps model from the same vendor.
Your ISP supports both V.90 and K56flex, and you'd like a choice.	If your modem is a so-called "Dualmode" modem, install both K56flex and V.90 firmware. If your modem won't permit both firmware types, download both V.90 and K56flex firmware, try both, and see which one works better.	The modem needs to have a 2MB ROM chip to have sufficient room for both firmware types.
You're not sure that the latest firmware upgrade was really an improvement.	If your vendor has several versions of firmware available for download, try some of the earlier versions as well as the latest version. An earlier version might actually work better for you.	
Your modem is a non–U.S./Canada model.	Download the country-specific upgrade for your modem.	Check the Web site for your country; contact tech support if your country isn't listed.
The firmware upgrade was installed, and the modem works at only 33.6Kbps or less.	Make sure you are using a V.90 dial-up number. Make sure you downloaded updated INF files or other drivers for your operating system.	

> **Note**
>
> The problems with moving from K56flex to V.90 do not apply
> to users who have updated their V.34/V.34bis modems directly
> to the V.90 standard, whether by a downloadable firmware
> update or by a physical modem or chip swap. Even if your
> V.34/V.34bis modem was made by a company that later made
> K56flex modems, you don't need to worry about this unless you
> updated to K56flex before going to V.90. Then the
> troubleshooting advice given earlier applies to you as well.

External Versus Internal Modems

Both external and internal modems are available for desktop systems. Table 6.9 helps you determine which type is better suited to
your needs.

Table 6.9   External Versus Internal Modems

Features	External	Internal
Built-in 16550 UART or higher	No (uses computer's serial port UART or USB port).	Yes, unless it is a Winmodem.
Price comparison	Higher.	Lower.
Extras to buy	May require RS-232 Modem Interface cable or USB cable.	Nothing.
Ease of moving to another computer	Easy—unplug the cables and go! (USB modems require a functioning USB port on the other computer and Windows 98, 2000, Me, or XP.) You must shut down the system before you remove or connect the RS-232 serial modem; USB modems can be hot-swapped.	Difficult—must open the case and remove the card, open the other PC's case, and insert the card.
Power supply	Plugs into wall (brick type) or may be host-powered (USB).	None—powered by host PC.
Reset if modem hangs	Turn modem off and then on again.	Restart computer.
Monitoring operation	Easy—external signal lights.	Difficult—unless your communication software simulates the signal lights.

Table 6.9   External Versus Internal Modems Continued

Features	External	Internal
Interface Type	RS-232 serial or USB port; some models support both types of connections (parallel-port modems were made a few years ago but never proved popular and have been discontinued).	PCI or ISA; PCI is preferred for its extra speed, capability to allow mapping of COM 3 and COM 4 to unique IRQs and support for shared IRQs without conflicts, and capability to work in so-called "legacy-free" systems that no longer include any ISA slots.

1. Although late versions of Windows 95 OSR 2.x have USB support, many USB devices actually require Windows 98 or better. Use Windows 98, 2000, or Me to achieve more reliable support for USB devices.

Modem Troubleshooting

Table 6.10 will help you troubleshoot modem problems and get you back online.

Table 6.10   Modem Troubleshooting (All Types)

Modem Type	Problem	Solution
Any	Modem fails to dial.	Check line and phone jacks on modem. Line jack—modem to telco service.
		Phone jack—modem to telephone receiver.
		If you've reversed these cables, you'll get no dial tone.
		Check the phone cable for cuts or breaks. If the cable looks bad, replace it.
		Make sure that your modem has been properly configured by your OS. See "Identifying Your System UART," earlier in this chapter, to learn how to use Modem Diagnostics.
External	Modem fails to dial.	Make sure that the RS-232 modem cable is running from the modem to a working serial port on your computer and that it is switched on. Signal lights on the front of the modem can be used to determine whether the modem is on and whether it is responding to dialing commands. Make sure that a USB modem is plugged tightly into an active USB port. If it is connected to an external hub, verify that the hub is connected to your system. If the hub is self-powered, make sure that the power-supply cable is plugged into the hub.
PC Card (PCMCIA)	Modem can't dial.	Make sure that it is fully plugged into the PC Card slot. With Windows 9x/Me/2000/XP, you should see a small PCMCIA/PC Card icon on the toolbar. Double-click it to view the cards that currently are connected. If your modem is properly attached, it should be visible. Otherwise, remove it, reinsert it into the PC Card slot, and see if the computer detects it.

Table 6.10	Modem Troubleshooting (All Types) Continued	
Modem Type	**Problem**	**Solution**
		Check dongle used to attach PC Card modems to jack; carry a spare. If your dongle doesn't have a connector to a standard phone line, use a line coupler to attach the short dongle cable to a longer standard RJ-11 cable for easier use. Carry at least a 10-foot RJ-11 phone cable with you for easier use in hotel rooms.
Any	"Couldn't Open Port" error message.	Modem might be in use already, or there might be an IRQ I/O port-address conflict. Use Device Manager to check settings, and reinstall drivers.
	System can't dial from wall jack.	Never use a wall jack unless it is clearly marked as a "data jack" or you check with the hotel staff. A digital phone system's jack looks identical to the safe analog jack that your modem is made for, but its higher voltage will fry your modem. You can get phone-line voltage testers from various sources. If your hotel telephone has a data jack built-in, use it. Some hotels now offer built-in Ethernet in some rooms, so carry your NIC with you as well for faster Web access.
Internal	System locks up when trying to boot up or dial modem.	The modem is trying to share a nonsharable IRQ with another port, probably a mouse. Move a serial mouse that uses the same IRQ as the modem to a different COM port with a different IRQ (from COM 1/IRQ 4 to COM 2/IRQ 3), or use a PS/2 mouse (IRQ 12). If your Pentium-class system lacks a visible PS/2 port, check with your system vendor for the (optional) header cable you need.
		Disable your system's COM 2; set the modem to COM 2 using IRQ 3.
External	Computer can't detect modem.	Check cable type. It must be an RS-232 modem (not null modem or straight-through) cable (see the following pinouts).
		Check power switch and supply.
		COM port might not be working.
		Check BIOS and enable COM port; test port with CheckIt, Windows Modem Diagnostics, or others; use a loopback plug with CheckIt or AMIDiag for the most thorough check.
		Check for IRQ conflicts in the Device Manager or System Information screens.
USB	Computer can't detect modem.	Check USB ports; enable them, if necessary.
		Check USB cables and hubs.

Support for "Brand X" Modems

Many computer users today didn't install their modems or even purchase them as a separate unit. Their modems came "bundled" inside the computer and often have a bare-bones manual that makes no mention of the modem's origin or where to get help. Getting V.90 firmware, drivers, or even jumper settings for OEM modems like this can be difficult.

One of the best Web sites for getting help when you don't know where to start is http://www.windrivers.com, which features a modem identification page with the following features:

- FCC ID. Enter the FCC ID number attached to the modem to determine who made it.

- Lookup by chipset manufacturer.

- Modem throughput tests.

- Links to major modem manufacturers.

Pinouts for External Modem Cable (Nine-Pin at PC)

For most RS-232 (serial) external modems, you need an RS-232 modem cable, which will have a 9-pin female connector on one end and a 25-pin male connector on the other end. Because RS-232 is a flexible standard encompassing many different pinouts for different devices, be sure that the cable is constructed according to Table 6.11, or, purchase a cable marked for serial modem use.

Table 6.11 Serial Modem Cable Pinout		
DB9F Connector (to Nine-Pin PC Serial Port) Pin #	**Signal**	**DB25M Connector (to Serial Modem) Pin #**
3	TX data	2
2	RX data	3
7	RTS	4
8	CTS	5
6	DSR	6
5	SIG GND	7
1	CXR	8
4	DTR	20
9	RI	22

Parallel Port Connectors

Three different types of parallel port connectors are defined by the IEEE-1284 parallel port standard, Type A (DB25F), Type B (Centronics 36), and Type C (high-density 36-pin). Type A connectors are used on PCs, and most parallel printers use Type B. Some HP LaserJets have both Type B and Type C connectors. See Chapter 12 for examples of these connectors.

Parallel Port Performance

Use the following tables to help determine whether your parallel ports are set to the fastest standard supported by your printers or other parallel port devices. On most computers, you adjust these parallel port settings through the CMOS/BIOS configuration screens. If the port is on an expansion card, you might use jumper blocks or a setup program to change the settings.

Table 6.12 summarizes the various types of parallel ports as well as their input and output modes, speed, and hardware settings.

Table 6.12	Parallel Port Types as Defined by IEEE-1284			
Parallel Port Type	Input Mode	Output Mode	Input/ Output Speed	Comments
SPP Standard Parallel Port	Nibble (4 bits)	Compatible	Input: 50KBps Output: 150KBps	4-bit input, 8-bit output
	Compatible (8 bits)	Bidirectional	Input/output: 150KBps	8-bit I/O
EPP (Enhanced Parallel Port)	EPP	EPP	Input/output: 500KBps– 2MBps	8-bit I/O; uses IRQ
ECP (Enhanced Capabilities Port)	ECP	ECP	Input/output: 500KB– 2MB/sec	8-bit I/O; uses IRQ and DMA

EPP Versus ECP Modes

Both EPP and ECP ports are part of the IEEE-1284 bidirectional parallel port standard, but they are not identical. Use Table 6.13 to understand how they differ, and consult your parallel port device manuals to see which mode is best for your system.

Table 6.13	Comparing EPP and ECP Parallel Port Modes			
Port Type	IRQ Usage	DMA Usage	Designed For	Notes
EPP	Yes	No	Tape drives, CD-ROM, LAN adapters	Version 1.7 predates IEEE-1284 standard; IEEE-1284 version often is called EPP 1.9

Table 6.13	Comparing EPP and ECP Parallel Port Modes Continued			
Port Type	IRQ Usage	DMA Usage	Designed For	Notes
ECP	Yes	DMA 3 (standard) DMA 1 (optional; default on some Packard-Bell models)	High-speed printers, scanners	Many systems offer an EPP/ECP port setting for best results with all types of parallel port devices

Some older parallel printers don't recommend either mode and might print erratically if EPP or ECP modes are enabled.

Prerequisites for EPP and ECP Modes

To use these advanced modes, you must do two things:

- Enable the appropriate mode on the parallel port (see the previous section)

- Use a parallel cable rated for IEEE-1284 uses

The IEEE-1284–compatible printer cable transports all signal lines to the printer, is heavily shielded, and produces very reliable printing with old and new printers alike in any parallel port mode. IEEE-1284 cables also can be purchased in a *straight-through* version for use with printer-sharing devices.

Parallel Port Configurations

Table 6.14 lists the standard parallel port settings. Although add-on multi–I/O or parallel port cards can offer additional settings, other settings will work only if software can be configured to use them. Remember that parallel ports set to ECP mode also will use DMA 3 (default) or DMA 1.

Table 6.14	Parallel Interface I/O Port Addresses and Interrupts		
Standard LPTx	Alternate LPTx	I/O Ports	IRQ
LPT1	—	3BC-3BFh	IRQ 7
LPT1	LPT2	378-37Ah	IRQ 7 (LPT1) IRQ 5 (LPT2)
LPT2	LPT3	278h-27Ah	IRQ 5

Testing Parallel Ports

The most reliable way to test printer ports is to use a parallel port–testing program along with the appropriate loopback plug.

This method isolates the port and allows the system to capture output back as input. Parallel port–testing programs are included in major diagnostic programs such as Norton Utilities/System Works, CheckIt, AMIDiag, QA+ family, MicroScope 2000, and many others.

Using a Parallel Loopback Plug

Loopback plugs of different designs are used by diagnostics programs that test parallel ports because of the different testing procedures that they perform. Some testing programs, such as AMIDiag by AMI or SmithMicro's CheckIt Suite, provide loopback plugs for both serial and parallel ports. Otherwise, you should purchase them from the vendor or contact the vendor for the correct pinout if you want to make your own.

Troubleshooting Parallel Ports and Devices

Table 6.15	Resolving Parallel Port Problems	
Symptoms	**Cause(s)**	**Solution**
Device on port not recognized; can't configure printer; printer won't print	Wrong parallel-port setting	Check the device manual; you probably need to change port to EPP, ECP, or EPP/ECP mode.
	Wrong cable	If you're using EPP or ECP, you must use an IEEE-1284 cable.
	Switchbox between device and computer	All cables and the switchbox must be IEEE-1284–compliant; remove the switchbox and connect it directly to the device. If it works, replace noncompliant switchbox or cables.
		The switchbox might need to be switched to the correct port.
	IRQ or I/O port address conflict	EPP and ECP require a nonshared IRQ; use Windows Device Manager to see whether IRQ for the LPT (parallel) port is conflicting with another device; also check the I/O port address and DMA.
		Adjust the settings of the parallel port or other device until the conflict is resolved.
	Device not powered on	Power on the device before starting the computer.
	Port defective	Use loopback and test software to verify that data going out the port is readable.

Printers

Printers can be attached to your computer in a variety of ways.
Major interfaces used for printers include those listed in Table 6.16.

Table 6.16 Printer Interface Standards and Recommended Uses

Interface Type	Benefits	Drawbacks	Operating System Required
Parallel (LPT)	Relatively fast, especially if EPP or ECP modes are used. Supported by virtually any application that can print. No port speed or setup options required in most cases. Standard cable works with virtually any PC and printer combination.	Regular printer cable length restricted to 10 feet due to signal loss. Daisy-chaining with other peripherals doesn't always work. Printer must be last device on daisy-chain.	Works with any operating system.
Serial (RS-232/COM)	Standard cable can reach up to 50 feet; use line drivers and phone cable to reach hundreds of feet. Printer can work with terminals, PCs, or Macintoshes with appropriate cable.	Serial port speed, word length, and stop bits must be set for both printer and application for printing to work. Very slow graphics printing. Different printers require custom cabling.	Works with any operating system, but is obsolete for PC use.

Table 6.16   Printer Interface Standards and Recommended Uses Continued

Interface Type	Benefits	Drawbacks	Operating System Required
USB	Faster than most parallel-port modes. Devices can be daisy-chained through hubs in any order. Hot-swappable; printer can be moved to any system. Many devices are cross-platform–compatible with both PCs and Macs.	Driver problems could cause difficulty for some early USB-based printers.	Requires Windows 98, Windows 2000, Windows Me[1], or Windows XP.
PC Card	Provides power to printer; no electrical cord needed. Allows design of very compact printers for use with notebook computers.	Fragile PC Card can be broken or damaged. Printers with this interface can't work with desktop computers; might need to remove other PC Cards from the notebook computer to enable printing.	Varies with printer.
Network	Enables sharing of a single, high-performance printer among many clients. Fast networks allow printing about as fast as local printing. Can "print" offline to queue and release when printer becomes available.	Requires network cards and configuration. Low-cost, host-based printers can't be networked.	Works with any network operating system. Check printer for limitations.

1. Windows 95 OSR2.1 also includes USB support, but many USB devices will not work with that version. Windows Me can use Windows 98 drivers, but a different driver is required for Windows 2000 or Windows XP.

Printers also can be interfaced by IEEE-1394 and SCSI ports, but these implementations are used primarily by Macintosh systems with high-end inkjet or laser printers in graphic arts environments.

Comparing Host-Based to PDL-Based Printers

Most printers use a page description language (PDL). PDL-based printers receive commands from applications or the operating system that describe the page to the printer, which then renders it before printing. More and more low-cost printers are using a host-based printing system in which the computer renders the page instead of the printer.

Use Table 6.17 to determine which type of printer is suitable for your users.

Table 6.17   PDL Versus Host-Based Printers

Printer Type	Feature	Benefit	Drawback
PDL (includes HP-PCL and compatibles, PostScript)	Page rendered in printer	Printer can be used independent of a PC or particular operating system; MS-DOS support	Higher cost because brains are inside the printer
Host-based	Page rendered by computer	Lower cost because brains are inside the PC, not the printer	Printer must be married to a computer with a compatible operating system and minimum performance requirements; non-Windows support is chancy; often can't be networked

Use Table 6.18 to determine the simplest way to test a printer. Note that host-based printers *must* have their drivers installed before they can print.

Table 6.18   Testing Printers

Printer Type	Test Method
Non-PostScript printer using PDL or escape sequences (HP-PCL, compatibles, dot-matrix, inkjet)	Enter DIR>LPT1 from a command prompt; printer will print directory listing.
PostScript printer	You must send PostScript commands to the printer directly to test it without drivers. You can use PostScript printer test in Microsoft MSD or install correct drivers and use test print. (Windows 9x/NT/ 2000/Me/XP offer a printer test at the end of the driver install process or from the General tab of the printer's properties sheet.

Table 6.18 Testing Printers Continued	
Printer Type	**Test Method**
Host-based printer	Install correct drivers and then use test print, as described earlier.

Printer Hardware Problems

Use Table 6.19 to track down problems and solutions with printers (any interface type).

Symptom	Printer Type	Cause(s)	Solutions
Fuzzy printing	Laser	Damp paper	Use paper stored at proper temperature and humidity.
	Inkjet	Wrong paper type or printer settings	Use inkjet-rated paper; check print setting, and match settings and resolution to paper type; make sure you're using the correct side of the paper (look for a "print this side first" marking on the package).
	Inkjet	Cartridge clogged or not seated correctly	Reseat the cartridge; run a cleaning utility; remove Canon cartridge from unit and clean printhead.
White lines through printed text or graphics	Inkjet	Some nozzles clogged	Use nozzle-cleaning routine on printer or utility program in printer driver to clean; retest afterward.
			On Canon, HP, and other printers with removable printheads, clean printhead with alcohol and foam swab.
			On Epson and other models with fixed printhead, use cleaning sheet to clean printhead.
			On any model, replace printer cartridge if three cleaning cycles and tests don't clear up clogging.
	Impact dot-matrix	Pins in printhead stuck or broken	Remove printhead and clean with alcohol and foam swab; retest.
			If pins are bent or broken, repair or replace printhead.
			Check head gap and adjust to avoid printhead damage; widen head gap for envelopes, labels, and multipart forms; adjust back to regular position for normal paper.
			Change ribbon; discard ribbons with snags or tears.

Table 6.19 Troubleshooting Printer Problems

	Printer		
Symptom	**Type**	**Cause(s)**	**Solutions**
Variable print density	Laser	Toner unevenly distributed in drum or toner cartridge	Remove toner cartridge and shake from side to side; check printer position and ensure that it's level; check for light leaks; replace toner cartridge or refill toner.
Fuzzy white lines on pages	Laser	Dirty corotrons (corona wires)	Clean corotrons per manufacturer recommendation.
Pages print solid black	Laser	Broken charger corotron	Replace toner cartridge if it contains corotron, or repair printer.
Pages print solid white	Laser	Broken transfer corotron	Repair transfer corotron.
Sharp, vertical white lines	Laser	Dirty developer unit	Clean developer, if separate; replace toner cartridge if it contains a developer unit.
Regularly spaced spots	Laser	Spots less than 3 inches apart indicate dirty fusing roller	Clean fusing roller.
		Widely spaced spots, or one per page, indicate scratched or flawed drum	Replace drum and fuser cleaning pad.
Gray print	Laser	Worn out drum	Replace drum (most common with separate drum and toner supply) background.
Loose toner	Laser	Fusing roller not hot enough	Service fusing roller.
Solid vertical black line	Laser	Toner cartridge nearly empty	Shake toner cartridge to redistribute toner.
		Scratched drum	Replace drum or toner cartridge.
Paper jams and misfeeds	Laser and inkjet	Incorrect paper loading; paper too damp; paper wrinkled; paper too heavy/thick for printer	Use paper that is in the proper condition for printing; don't overfill the paper tray; don't dog-ear paper when loading it.

Table 6.19   Troubleshooting Printer Problems Continued

	Printer		
Symptom	**Type**	**Cause(s)**	**Solutions**
Envelope jams	Laser and inkjet	Incorrect paper loading; failure to set laser printer to use rear paper exit tray; printer can't handle envelopes	Check correct envelope-handling procedures; consider using labels to avoid envelopes.
Blank pages between printed pages	Laser and inkjet	Paper stuck together; paper is damp or wrinkled	Riffle paper before loading paper tray; make sure that all paper is the same size.
Blank page between print jobs	Laser and inkjet	Print spooler set to produce a blank divider page	Change print spooler setting.
Error light on printer flashes; printer ejects partial page (might require you to press Page Eject button)	Laser	Memory overflow or printer overrun error	Reduce graphics resolution; simplify a PostScript page; reduce the number of fonts; check that printer memory size is accurately set; run printer self-test to determine the amount of RAM onboard; add RAM to the printer.
Error light blinks; no page ejected or printed	Laser	Various causes	Look up the blink code in printer documentation, and take appropriate action. Error codes vary with printer model; check manufacturer's Web site for a list of codes if the user manual is missing.
LCD panel on printer displays error code or message	Laser	Various causes	Look up the error code or message in manual and take appropriate action. Error codes vary with printer model; check manufacturer's Web site for a list of codes if the user manual is missing. Many less-expensive models use signal lights (see previous).

Table 6.19   Troubleshooting Printer Problems Continued

Printer Connection Problems

Use Table 6.20 to determine the cause and cure for problems with your printer connection.

	Printer Type		
Symptom	**or Port Type**	**Cause(s)**	**Solutions**
Gibberish printing	Any	PDL used for print job doesn't match printer	Make sure that the print job is sent to the correct printer; check the default printer value; check the port used for the printer; check the switchbox for proper printer selection; replace the switchbox with an LPT2 card or with a USB-parallel cable.
	Serial port	Incorrect speed, word length, parity, and stop bits	Both serial ports on the computer and the printer must be set to match.
			Use the DOS MODE or Windows COM Port properties sheet to set the serial port on the computer.
			Printer configuration varies—might involve use of DIP switches, jumper blocks, printer setup panel, or software configuration program; see printer manual.
	Serial port	Incorrect cable pinout	No such thing as a "universal" RS-232 printer cable exists; check pinouts at both the computer and the printer ends; rewire or reorder cable as needed.
	Any	Damaged cable	Look for damaged pins or insulation; use pinouts for each port type to test cable with a loopback plug or with a multimeter with a CONT (continuity) function; retest with a known working cable.
	PostScript laser	PostScript preamble not properly received	Check the cable; check the serial port configuration; reload drivers.
Printer not available	Any	Print job has timed out; computer is using offline mode to spool jobs	Check for paper out, reload paper. Check printer cable or serial port settings. Look for IRQ conflicts and correct them. Set the switchbox to automatic mode, or lock it to the computer that you want to print from.
Printer	USB port	Printer might not be detected by Device Manager	Check Device Manager; remove and reattach printer, and recheck.
			See Chapter 8, "Keyboards, Mice, and Input Devices," for other USB troubleshooting tips.

Table 6.20   Troubleshooting Printer Connections

Table 6.20   Troubleshooting Printer Connections Continued

Symptom	Printer Type or Port Type	Cause(s)	Solutions
Printer doesn't notify Windows of paper out, jams, out of toner or ink, and similar conditions	Laser and inkjet	IEEE-1284 connection not working	Ensure that the port and cable(s) and the switchbox are all IEEE-1284 (EPP or ECP or EPP/ECP). Check the cable connection and CMOS/BIOS configuration. Install an ECP LPT port driver in Windows.
Intermittent or failed communications with printer	Any	Bad switchbox or cables	Use a direct connection to the printer; check cables; replace a rotary-dial manual switchbox with an autosensing switchbox.
	Parallel port	Device daisy-chained with printer	Use printer only. Change the order of the daisy-chain. Avoid using Zip, scanner, and printer on a single LPT port.
	USB port	Hub or driver problems	See Chapter 8 for USB troubleshooting tips.
Port busy; printer goes offline	Laser and inkjet	ECP port prints too fast for the printer	Use Windows 9x/Me Control Panel to load a standard LPT driver in place of an ECP driver; change the setting in BIOS to EPP or bidirectional.

If your USB printer also can be used as a parallel printer, use the parallel (LPT) port if you cannot solve print quality or reliability problems when you use it in USB mode.

Printer Driver and Application Problems

Printers use driver software to communicate with operating systems and applications. Use Table 6.21 to solve problems with drivers and applications.

Table 6.21   Troubleshooting Printer Drivers and Applications

Symptom	Printer Type	Cause(s)	Solutions
Prints okay from command prompt (DIR>LPT1), but not from applications	Any	Printer driver damaged or buggy	Reload printer driver and test. Reinstall printer driver. Switch to compatible new version that can be downloaded.
Form-feed light comes on, but nothing prints	Laser	Incomplete page sent to printer	Normal behavior for Print-Screen or envelope printing. Eject paper manually; otherwise, reinstall the driver.

Table 6.21	Troubleshooting Printer Drivers and Applications Continued		
Symptom	**Printer Type**	**Cause(s)**	**Solutions**
Incorrect fonts print	Laser or inkjet	Printer using internal fonts instead of TrueType	Check the driver setting to determine which fonts will be used.
Incorrect page breaks	Any	Printer changed between document composition and printing	If you change printers or plan to use a fax modem to print your document, select the printer and scroll through your document first to check page breaks due to differences in font rendering and so on; correct as needed.
Page cut off on left, right, and top	Laser or inkjet	Margins set beyond printable area of printer	Reset document margins; use Print to Fit to right, and top scale the page or bottom document to usable paper size; check edges for proper page size set in printer properties.

Chapter 7

USB and IEEE-1394 Ports and Devices

Universal Serial Bus

The *Universal Serial Bus (USB)* port is a high-speed serial connection that enables up to 127 hot-swappable devices of many different types to be connected to a single port, using a single IRQ. On an increasing number of systems, the USB port replaces the traditional serial, parallel, and PS/2 ports (*legacy ports*), and it is becoming the most popular I/O port on systems that still have legacy ports. Use this section to help you detect and configure USB ports effectively.

USB Port Identification

Figure 7.1 helps you identify USB devices and ports. USB ports and cables are pictured in Chapter 12, "Connector Quick Reference."

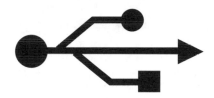

Figure 7.1   This icon is used to identify USB cables, connectors, and peripherals.

Pinout for the USB Connector

Table 7.1 shows the pinout for the USB connector.

Table 7.1	USB Connector Pinout		
Pin	**Signal Name**	**Color**	**Comment**
1	VCC	Red	Cable power
2	– Data	White	
3	+ Data	Green	
4	Ground	Black	Cable ground

Typical USB Port Locations

The location of USB ports varies with the system. On late-model desktop and tower computers using Baby-AT motherboards, you might find one or two USB ports on a card bracket in the rear of the computer. The ports might be mounted on an add-on card or cabled out from motherboard ports.

Most systems using ATX, NLX, or similar motherboards—as well as late-model LPX-based systems—will have one or two USB ports on the rear of the case next to other ports.

Some consumer-oriented, late-model systems have one or more USB ports on the front. These ports are located in the front of the computer for easier connection of digital cameras and card readers for digital image downloading. They are also useful for connecting USB-based keyboards and pointing devices.

Adding USB Ports to Your Computer

If your computer doesn't have USB ports onboard, use one of the following options to add them:

- Purchase USB header cables to extend motherboard USB cable connectors to the outside of the case.

- Purchase and install a USB host adapter card.

Even if your Baby-AT system has connectors for USB header cables, as in Figure 7.2, changes in the USB specification (see the next section) make installing a USB 2.0–compliant host adapter card a better idea for many users.

USB 1.x Versus Hi-Speed USB (USB 2.0)

The original version of USB, USB 1.0, was introduced in January 1996. It was replaced by USB 1.1, which clarified some problems with the 1.0 specification, in September 1998. USB 1.1 is the version of USB supported on all systems with built-in USB ports through most of 2001.

USB 1.1 runs at two speeds, 1.5Mbps and 12Mbps (1.5MBps). High-bandwidth USB devices (drives, scanners, network adapters, and printers) normally run at the higher speed, while pointing devices and keyboards run at the lower speed.

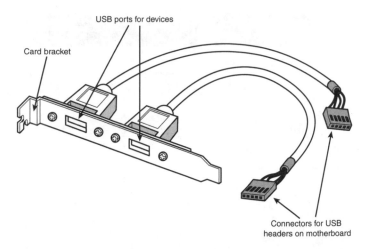

Figure 7.2 A typical USB header cable set; plug it into your Baby-AT or early ATX motherboard to connect devices to the onboard USB ports (if present).

As Table 7.2 shows, USB 1.1, which has been included on virtually all systems since late 1998, is similar in speed to high-speed parallel ports and 10BASE-T Ethernet, but it is much slower than SCSI (see Chapter 4, "SCSI and ATA Hard Drives and Optical Drives") and IEEE-1394/FireWire (mentioned later in this chapter). Thus, although USB devices are easier to move from system to system than SCSI devices, high-capacity removable-media and tape drives are much slower when connected to a USB 1.1–compliant port than they would be if they were connected to SCSI or IEEE-1394 (FireWire) ports.

Table 7.2   USB Data Rates Compared to Other I/O Port Types

Bus Type	Bus Width (Bits)	Bus Speed (MHz)	Data Cycles per Clock	Bandwidth (MBps)
RS-232 Serial	1	0.1152	1/10	0.01152
RS-232 Serial High Speed	1	0.2304	1/10	0.02304
IEEE-1284 Parallel	8	8.33	1/6	1.38
IEEE-1284 EPP/ECP	8	8.33	1/3	2.77
USB 1.1	1	12	1	1.5
USB 2.0	1	480	1	60
IEEE-1394a S100	1	100	1	12.5
IEEE-1394a S200	1	200	1	25

Table 7.2   USB Data Rates Compared to Other I/O Port Types Continued

Bus Type	Bus Width (Bits)	Bus Speed (MHz)	Data Cycles per Clock	Bandwidth (MBps)
IEEE-1394a S400	1	400	1	50
IEEE-1394b S800	1	800	1	100
IEEE-1394b S1600	1	1600	1	200
SCSI	8	5	1	5
SCSI Wide	16	5	1	10
SCSI Fast	8	10	1	10
SCSI Fast/Wide	16	10	1	20
SCSI Ultra	8	20	1	20
SCSI Ultra/Wide	16	20	1	40
SCSI Ultra2	8	40	1	40
SCSI Ultra2/Wide	16	40	1	80
SCSI Ultra3 (Ultra160)	16	40	2	160
SCSI Ultra4 (Ultra320)	16	80	2	320

Table 7.2 also lists a new version of the USB specification, USB 2.0. USB ports built into motherboards through late 2001 were mostly USB 1.1 types. Starting in late 2001 and early 2002, most motherboards switched to incorporating USB 2.0 (Hi-Speed) ports. If your built-in USB ports are the slower 1.1 type, you can purchase a PCI card with USB 2.0 ports on it, thus adding that capability to any system.

How USB 2.0 Improves on USB 1.1

Although both USB 1.1 and USB 2.0 can handle up to 127 devices per root hub, USB 1.1's limited bandwidth (12Mbps) means that putting several devices on a single hub will slow down all devices, especially high-speed devices.

By contrast, USB 2.0 works much better with multiple devices, whether they are USB 1.1–compliant or USB 2.0–compliant. When communicating with an attached USB 2.0 peripheral, the USB 2.0 hub simply repeats the high-speed signals; however, when communicating with USB 1.1 peripherals, a USB 2.0 hub buffers and manages the transition from the high speed of the USB 2.0 host controller (in the PC) to the lower speed of a USB 1.1 device. This feature of USB 2.0 hubs means that USB 1.1 devices can operate along with USB 2.0 devices and not consume any additional bandwidth. In effect, USB 2.0 hubs make USB 1.1 devices work better than USB 1.1 hubs do.

Hi-Speed and Standard USB Icons

Because USB 2.0 products are now entering the market, it's important that you know which products support the different versions of the USB standard. Figure 7.3 compares the standard (USB 1.1) and Hi-Speed (USB 2.0) logos developed by the USB Implementer's Forum (http://www.usb.org) to indicate devices that have passed their certification tests.

Figure 7.3   The new USB-IF USB 1.1–compliant logo (left), compared to the new USB-IF USB 2.0–compliant logo (right).

As you can see from Figure 7.3, USB 1.1 is referred to as simply "USB," and USB 2.0 is referred to as "Hi-Speed USB."

Prerequisites for Using USB Ports and Peripherals

Before you buy or try to install a USB peripheral, make sure that your system meets the requirements shown in Table 7.3. Some adjustments or updates to the system configuration might be necessary.

Table 7.3   Prerequisites for Use of USB Ports/Peripherals

Requirement	Reason	Notes
Windows 98 Windows 2000 Windows Me Windows XP	Has built-in support for USB peripherals	Windows 95B OSR 2.1 and above have USB support, but many peripherals require Win98 or above.
Working USB ports	Many systems are shipped with disabled USB ports.	Check BIOS and enable there, if necessary; some systems might require header cables to bring the USB connector to the rear of the system.

Table 7.3 Prerequisites for Use of USB Ports/Peripherals Continued		
Requirement	Reason	Notes
Device driver support	Many devices might not work with Windows 2000, and some might not work with Windows XP.	Check operating system compliance for any USB device. If a compatible device driver isn't available, the device won't work under that version of Windows.

You can download the free USB Ready utility program at
http://www.usb.org/data/usbready.exe to check your system's
USB readiness at both hardware and software levels.

Verify that the peripheral you are installing is designed for your
operating system. Although USB ports themselves are found on
both PC and Macintosh systems, some USB devices are for use only
on PCs or Macintoshes, not both types of systems. Windows version compatibility is often an issue, especially for Windows 2000 or
Windows XP users.

Using USB Hubs with Legacy (Serial, Parallel, and PS/2) Ports

A number of products on the market enable you to connect various
legacy products to USB ports. The most economical way to connect
serial, parallel, or PS/2-port products is through the use of a multipurpose hub that also features multiple USB ports.

You can also purchase serial-to-USB or parallel-to-USB converter
cables, but these are less flexible and more expensive if you need to
connect multiple legacy devices to a system.

Check the list of supported legacy devices before you buy a converter cable or multipurpose port. USB hubs with PS/2 and serial
ports normally support legacy devices such as modems, keyboards,
and mice; USB hubs with parallel ports normally support printers.
If you use other types of parallel devices, such as drives or scanners,
you will need an actual parallel port to connect them. However,
because daisy-chaining multiple parallel devices can be difficult,
moving the printer to a multipurpose USB hub can free up the LPT
port for use by these other devices.

Online Sources for Additional USB Support

- Linux USB device support and status:

  http://www.qbik.ch/usb/devices

- USB news and troubleshooting sites:

  http://www.usbman.com

  http://www.usbworkshop.com

  http://www.usb.org

Troubleshooting USB Ports

USB ports built into the computer (also called *root hubs*) are becoming the primary external device connection for an increasing number of PCs. Although USB devices are plug-and-play, requiring (and allowing) no configuration, persistent problems with USB devices are common for many users. Use the following tips to help you achieve reliable USB operation:

- Check the prerequisites from Table 7.3.

- If the devices don't work when plugged into an external hub, plug them into the root hub (USB connector on the system). If they work when attached to the root hub, upgrade the external hub's firmware, attach a power supply to it, or replace it. Note that some devices are designed to attach to the root hub only.

- If a new device isn't detected, remove other USB devices, plug in the new device first, and then reattach the other USB devices.

- Check the power usage for the USB bus in the Power dialog box of the operating system.

- Verify that the USB device is drawing no less than 50mA and no more than 500mA. If the device is drawing a large amount of power from a bus-powered hub, it might fail, especially when other USB devices are attached to the same hub. Use a self-powered hub, when possible, for greater reliability.

- Use the Windows Device Manager to verify proper operation of the USB port. Adjust the IRQ settings, if necessary, to avoid conflicts with other devices. Figure 7.4 shows how a typical USB root hub and USB external hub will appear in the Windows 98 Device Manager.

- Install the latest USB device drivers for the device and the operating system. USB devices that work in Windows 98 might not be supported by other versions of Windows.

- If a printer doesn't work properly with the "correct" USB driver, try using a compatible driver for an older model as a workaround.

- Install the latest firmware for the USB device. Bad firmware creates "ghost" versions of devices in the Device Manager when the device is unplugged and reattached.

- Verify that the USB root hub (port) is assigned an IRQ. Normally, IRQ 9 is used, if available. Make sure that IRQ steering is working if all available IRQs are already assigned to other ports.

- Use high-speed (heavily shielded) cabling for high-speed devices, such as printers, scanners, and network connections.

- Separate low-speed from high-speed devices by attaching them to separate USB ports.

- Assign USB controllers to Controller ID 1 if not detected by the game.

- Use the smallest number of hubs possible; some versions of Windows can't use more than five USB hubs (some devices double as hubs).

- Before you purchase a USB device, verify device driver support for your operating system. Windows 2000 supports USB devices, but many vendors are slow about supplying USB drivers for Windows 2000.

- When possible, buy devices that can be connected by either a USB port or a so-called "legacy" port (PS/2 keyboard/mouse port, serial port, parallel port, or SCSI port) to enable you to use the device even if you have problems with your USB ports or peripherals.

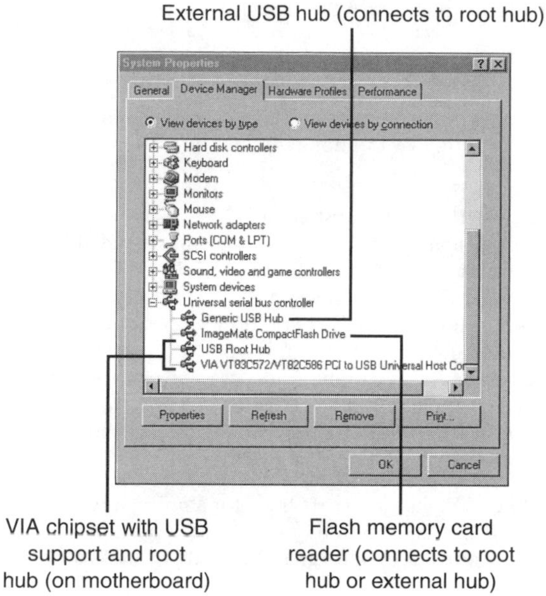

External USB hub (connects to root hub)

VIA chipset with USB
support and root
hub (on motherboard)

Flash memory card
reader (connects to root
hub or external hub)

Figure 7.4   USB devices in a typical system, as shown in the Windows
Device Manager. The chipset on the motherboard provides support for the
USB root hub (1). The external USB hub (2) connects to the root hub and
allows multiple devices such as the CompactFlash card reader (3) to be connected to a single USB port.

IEEE-1394

The so-called *FireWire* or *iLINK* interface pioneered by Apple is also
available for PCs, where it is usually known as *IEEE-1394*. Despite
the fact that IEEE-1394 ports are seldom standard equipment at
present, the performance features that they offer and the increasing
device support suggest that more users will be installing IEEE-1394
ports and devices as time passes. Like USB, IEEE-1394 supports hot-
swapping, making it easy to move devices from one system to
another.

IEEE-1394 is more limited in PC applications than USB, being primarily used for connecting digital video movie cameras for digital
video editing. Other IEEE-1394 peripherals are available, such as
external hard drives, but except for digital video, most other external peripherals use USB instead.

See Chapter 12 for pictures of the IEEE-1394 connector, cable, and socket.

Adding IEEE-1394 Ports to Your Computer

Although most recent systems have USB ports onboard, IEEE-1394 ports are rare among PCs but are more common on Macintosh systems.

A wide variety of IEEE-1394 host adapters are available for purchase. Most host adapters provide two or more six-pin IEEE-1394 ports, provide an adapter cable for four-pin IEEE-1394 devices, and use a single 32-bit PCI slot. Some vendors offer combo add-on products that combine IEEE-1394 and other types of ports, such as USB 2.0. A few IEEE-1394 cards require you to connect a five-pin Molex drive power connector, but most are powered from the standard power levels included in the PCI slot. Some adapters also feature a single port for internal IEEE-1394 devices, although virtually all devices currently on the market are external.

IEEE-1394, like USB, also supports hubs for sharing a single port among multiple devices; up to 63 nodes are supported, with up to 16 devices per node. Each port on an IEEE-1394 card is a node.

Resource Requirements for IEEE-1394 Host Adapters

Regardless of the number of IEEE-1394 ports or devices connected to those ports, an IEEE-1394 host adapter card uses only one IRQ and one I/O port address. The IRQ used by the host adapter should not be shared with other devices. If necessary, take advantage of IRQ steering for PCI cards with Windows 98, 2000, Me and XP to have other PCI cards share an IRQ, to free up an IRQ for the IEEE-1394 host adapter. If your host adapter also has another type of port on board, the other port will also require an IRQ and I/O port address.

The PCI slot that you choose for the IEEE-1394 host adapter must support bus mastering if the host adapter uses this feature. Consult your system or motherboard documentation and your host adapter documentation to see whether this is a requirement for you. You might need to move existing PCI cards around to satisfy this requirement.

Current and Future Versions of IEEE-1394

The current version of IEEE-1394 is technically known as IEEE-1394a, or sometimes as 1394a-2000 because it was adopted in the year 2000. The 1394a version fixed compatibility and interoperability issues with the original IEEE-1394 standard, but it keeps the same connectors and speeds.

The proposed 1394b standard plans to support 1.6Gbps up to 3.2Gbps speeds by using fiber-optic and Category 5 UTP cabling, while retaining compatibility with current 1394a devices.

Comparing IEEE-1394a and USB 1.1/2.0

Because of the similarity in both form and function of USB and 1394a, there has been some confusion about the features of these interface types. Table 7.4 summarizes the differences.

Table 7.4 IEEE-1394a and USB Comparison			
	IEEE-1394a (a.k.a. iLink, FireWire)	USB 1.1	USB 2.0
PC host required	No	Yes	Yes
Max. no. of devices	63	127	127
Hot-swappable?	Yes	Yes	Yes
Max. cable length between devices	4.5 meters	5 meters	5 meters
Transfer rate	200Mbps (25MBps)/ 400Mbps (50MBps)	12Mbps (1.5MBps)	480Mbps (60MBps)
Proposed future transfer rates	800Mbps (100MBps) 1.6Gbps (200MBps) 3.2Gbps (400MBps)	None	None
Typical devices	DV camcorders, High-res digital cameras, HDTV, Set-top boxes, High-speed drives, High-res scanners, Electronic musical instruments	Keyboards, Mice, Joysticks, Low-res digital cameras, Low-speed drives, Modems, Printers, Low-res scanners	All USB 1.1 devices plus: DV camcorders, High-res digital cameras, HDTV, Set-top boxes, High-speed drives, High-res scanners

As Table 7.4 reveals, the main differences are popularity, PC- or non–PC-centricity, and speed. USB is by far the most popular external interface, eclipsing all others by comparison.

Although practically all PCs sold today include USB 1.1 or 2.0 as standard, 1394 is still primarily an aftermarket update; only a small number of current systems and motherboards feature integrated 1394 ports.

USB 1.1 is clearly designed for low-speed peripherals, such as keyboards, mice, modems, and printers, whereas USB 2.0 can be used to connect most high-speed external devices. 1394 is used to connect mostly high-performance digital video electronics products.

Another important benefit of 1394 is that a PC host connection is not required. Thus, 1394 can be used to directly connect a digital video (DV) camcorder and a DV-VCR for dubbing tapes or editing.

Troubleshooting IEEE-1394 Host Adapters and Devices

- **Host adapter is installed but doesn't work**—Make sure that your system has loaded the correct IEEE-1394 driver for the host adapter. Some host adapters don't use the Windows-provided TI chipset driver.

- **Wrong driver is installed for host adapter**—If you have installed the wrong driver, remove the IEEE-1394 host adapter listing from the Windows Device Manager, have the driver CD or disk supplied with the host adapter handy, restart the system, and have the computer search for the best driver. It will find the driver on the disk or CD-ROM and install it.

- **Choppy video during digital editing**—Use UDMA bus-mastering drivers with ATA/IDE hard disks to provide smooth flow of digital video; install and enable as necessary (see Chapter 4).

- **Four-wire devices aren't recognized**—Whereas six-wire devices get power from the IEEE-1394 bus, four-wire devices require their own power supply; ensure that the device is connected and turned on.

- **Device "disappears" from the Windows Device Manager after being connected**—The connected device is probably using power management; after the device's power management is enabled, this is normal. Use the device's power management controls to disable power management while the device is connected to the computer.

- **Device displays a yellow ! in Device Manager or isn't displayed**—Windows 2000 provides support for only host adapters that support OpenHCI (OHCI). Adapters that use non-OHCI drivers must install their own drivers to work. Update the drivers or remove the device and reinstall it, providing the correct drivers to correct the problem.

IEEE-1394 and Linux

Linux has kernel versions 2.2 and above IEEE-1394. To download the support files or for more information about supporting IEEE-1394 devices under Linux, go to linux1394.sourceforge.net/index.html.

Online Sources for Additional IEEE-1394 Support

- IEEE-1394 products:

    http://www.firewire-1394.com

    http://www.askfor1394.com

- IEEE-1394 trade association:

    http://www.1394ta.org

Chapter 8

Keyboards, Mice, and Input Devices

Keyboard Designs

The primary keyboard types are as follows:

- 101-key Enhanced keyboard
- 102-key Enhanced keyboard
- 104-key Windows keyboard
- 83-key PC and XT keyboard (obsolete)
- 84-key AT keyboard (obsolete)

> **Note**
>
> If you need information about the 83-key PC and XT keyboard or the 84-key AT keyboard, see Chapter 7 of *Upgrading and Repairing PCs, 10th Anniversary Edition*—included in PDF format on the 13th Edition CD-ROM.

The basic layout of the 101-, 102-, and 104-key keyboards is virtually identical, with the following differences:

- The 102-key keyboard is designed for use with European languages. It features a smaller left-Shift key and a vertical Enter key to allow room for one additional key. Some symbol keys are also found in different locations.

- The 104-key Windows keyboard adds three keys to the 101-key Enhanced keyboard layout: the left and right Windows keys and the Application key. These three additional keys allow for additional Windows keyboard shortcuts compared to those possible with the 101-key Enhanced keyboard.

Using Windows Keys

Table 8.1 shows a list of all the Windows key combinations (available with Windows NT 4.0, 9*x*, and all later versions) that can be performed with the 104-key Windows keyboard. These keyboard shortcuts can be useful, especially if your mouse stops working or you want to work more quickly with the Windows desktop.

Table 8.1 Windows Key Combinations	
Key Combination	**Resulting Action**
WIN+R	Runs dialog box
WIN+M	Minimizes all
Shift+WIN+M	Undoes minimize all
WIN+F1	Opens Help
WIN+E	Opens Windows Explorer
WIN+F	Finds files or folders
Ctrl+WIN+F	Finds computer
WIN+Tab	Cycles through taskbar buttons
WIN+Break	Displays the System Properties dialog box
Application key	Displays a context menu for the selected item

When a Microsoft 104-key Windows keyboard is used with Microsoft IntelliType Pro Software installed (http://www.microsoft.com/hardware/keyboard/download.asp), the additional key combinations shown in Table 8.2 can be used.

Table 8.2 IntelliType Pro Key Combinations	
Key Combination	**Resulting Action**
WIN+L	Logs off Windows
WIN+P	Opens Print Manager
WIN+C	Opens the Control Panel
WIN+V	Opens the Clipboard
WIN+K	Opens the Keyboard Properties dialog box
WIN+I	Opens the Mouse Properties dialog box
WIN+A	Opens Accessibility Options (if installed)
WIN+Spacebar	Displays the list of IntelliType hotkeys
WIN+S	Toggles the Caps Lock key on and off

Keyboard-Only Commands for Windows 9x/NT4/2000/Me with Any Keyboard

If your mouse stops working, or if you want to work more quickly, use the keys shown in Table 8.3 to perform common Windows actions.

Table 8.3 Keyboard Commands for Windows 9x/NT4/2000/Me	
Key Combination	**Resulting Action**
F1	Starts Windows Help.
F10	Activates menu bar options.
Shift+F10	Opens a context menu (shortcut menu) for the selected item.
Ctrl+Esc	Opens the Start menu. Use the arrow keys to select an item.
Ctrl+Esc, Esc	Selects the Start button. Press Tab to select the taskbar, or press Shift+F10 for a context menu.
Alt+Tab	Switches to another running application. Hold down the Alt key and then press the Tab key to view the task-switching window.
Shift	Press down and hold the Shift key while you insert a CD-ROM to bypass the AutoPlay feature.
Alt+Spacebar	Displays the main window's System menu. From the System menu, you can restore, move, resize, minimize, maximize, or close the window.
Alt+- (Alt+hyphen)	Displays the Multiple Document Interface (MDI) child window's System menu. From the MDI child window's System menu, you can restore, move, resize, minimize, maximize, or close the child window.
Ctrl+Tab	Switches to the next child window of an MDI application.
Alt+<underlined letter in menu>	Opens the corresponding menu.
Alt+F4	Closes the current window.
Ctrl+F4	Closes the current MDI window.
Alt+F6	Switches between multiple windows in the same program. For example, when Notepad's Find dialog box is displayed, Alt+F6 switches between the Find dialog box and the main Notepad window.

Here are the Windows dialog box keyboard commands:

Key Combination	**Resulting Action**
Tab	Moves to the next control in the dialog box.
Shift+Tab	Moves to the previous control in the dialog box.
Spacebar	If the current control is a button, this keyboard command clicks the button. If the current control is a check box, it toggles the check box. If the current control is an option button, it selects the option button.
Enter	Equivalent to clicking the selected button (the button with the outline).
Esc	Equivalent to clicking the Cancel button.

Key Combination	Resulting Action
Alt+<underlined letter in dialog box item>	Moves to the corresponding item.
Ctrl+Tab/ Ctrl+Shift+Tab	Moves through the property tabs.

These are the keyboard combinations for Windows Explorer tree controls:

Key Combination	Resulting Action
Numeric Keypad *	Expands everything under the current selection.
Numeric Keypad +	Expands the current selection.
Numeric Keypad -	Collapses the current selection.
Right arrow	Expands the current selection if it is not expanded; otherwise, goes to the first child.
Left arrow	Collapses the current selection if it is expanded; otherwise, goes to the parent.

Here are the general Windows folder/shortcut controls:

Key Combination	Resulting Action
F4	Selects the Go To a Different Folder box and moves down the entries in the box (if the toolbar is active in Windows Explorer).
F5	Refreshes the current window.
F6	Moves among panes in Windows Explorer.
Ctrl+G	Opens the Go To Folder tool (in Windows 95 Windows Explorer only).
Ctrl+Z	Undoes the last command.
Ctrl+A	Selects all the items in the current window.
Backspace	Switches to the parent folder.
Shift+click	Selects the Close button. (For folders, closes the current folder plus all parent folders.)

These are general folder and Windows Explorer shortcuts for a selected object:

Key Combination	Resulting Action
F2	Renames the object.
F3	Finds all files.
Ctrl+X	Cuts.
Ctrl+C	Copies.

Key Combination	Resulting Action
Ctrl+V	Pastes.
Shift+Del	Deletes the selection immediately, without moving the item to the Recycle Bin.
Alt+Enter	Opens the property sheet for the selected object.
To copy a file	Press down and hold the Ctrl key while you drag the file to another folder.
To create a shortcut	Press down and hold Ctrl+Shift while you drag a file to the desktop or a folder.

Key Switch Types

The most common type of key switch is the mechanical type, available in the following variations:

- Pure mechanical
- Foam element
- Rubber dome
- Membrane

Table 8.4 compares user feel, repair, and servicing issues for these key switch types.

Table 8.4   Mechanical Key Switch Types Compared

Key Switch Type

Feature	Pure Mechanical	Foam	Rubber Dome	Membrane
Tactile feedback	Usually a click	Minimal feedback	Soft click	No click
Durability and serviceability	High: 20-million keystroke rating	Variable: Contacts can corrode; easy to clean	High: Rubber dome protects contacts from corrosion	Extreme: No moving parts, sealed unit for harsh industrial environments

The pure mechanical type of keyboard, often using Alps key switches, is second only to the keyboards using capacitive switches in terms of tactile feedback and durability. Capacitive key switches are rated for up to 25 million keystrokes. Traditionally, the only vendors of capacitive key switch keyboards have been IBM and the inheritors of its keyboard technology, Lexmark and Unicomp (http://www.pckeyboard.com).

Cleaning a Keyboard

You can use the following methods to keep a keyboard clean:

- **Vacuum cleaner**—Vacuum the keyboard at least monthly, and make sure that you use a brush attachment to sweep dirt out of the crevices between the keys.

- **Compressed air**—Turn the keyboard upside down before spraying, to help remove dust and dirt.

Both types of cleaning work best if you remove the keycaps first. The U-shaped chip puller included in most computer repair kits works well for this purpose. To fix a sticky key, spray some compressed air into the space under the cap to dislodge the dirt. Then replace the cap and check the action of the key.

When you remove the keycap on some keyboards, you are actually detaching the entire key from the key switch; be careful during the removal or reassembly of the keyboard, or you'll break the switch. The classic IBM/Lexmark-type keyboards (now made by Unicomp) use a removable keycap that leaves the actual key in place, allowing you to clean under the keycap without the risk of breaking the switches.

If you spill a drink into the keyboard, you might want to disconnect the keyboard from the system, disassemble the keyboard, and flush it out with distilled water.

If the spilled liquid has dried, soak the keyboard in some of the water for a while. When you are sure that the keyboard is clean, pour another gallon or so of *distilled* water (it contains no minerals) over it and through the key switches to wash away any residual dirt. After the unit dries *completely*, it should be perfectly functional.

> **Tip**
>
> If spills or excessive dust or dirt are expected from the environment or conditions the PC is used in, several companies make thin membrane skins that mold over the top of the keyboard, protecting it from liquids, dust, and other contaminants. These skins generally are thin enough that they don't interfere too much with the typing or action of the keys.
>
> One example is CompuCover Inc. (http://www.compucover.com), which provides covers for the latest multimedia keyboards from popular vendors, as well as for traditional desktop, terminal, and notebook computer keyboards.

Adjusting Keyboard Parameters in Windows

To modify the default values for the typematic repeat rate and delay parameters in any version of Windows, open the Keyboard icon in the Control Panel. In Windows 9x/Me/NT/2000/XP, the controls are located on the Speed tab. The Repeat Delay slider controls the number of times that a key must be pressed before the character begins to repeat, and the Repeat Rate slider controls how fast the character repeats after the delay has elapsed. Use the test box to see the effect of the changes that you make before you apply them.

> **Note**
>
> The increments on the Repeat Delay and Repeat Rate sliders in the Keyboard Control Panel correspond to the timings given for the MODE command's RATE and DELAY values. Each mark in the Repeat Delay slider adds about 0.25 seconds to the delay, and the marks in the Repeat Rate slider are worth about one character per second each.

Keyboard Layouts and Scan Codes

Table 8.5 shows each of the three scan code sets for each key in the 101-key and 102-key Enhanced keyboards, in relation to the key number and character. Table 8.6 lists the scan codes for the additional keys on the 104-key Windows keyboard. Scan Code Set 1 is the default; the other two are rarely used. Knowing these scan codes is useful when you are troubleshooting stuck or failed keys on a keyboard. Diagnostics can report the defective key switch by the scan code, which varies from keyboard to keyboard on the character that it represents and its location.

Table 8.5 101-/102-Key (Enhanced) Keyboard Key Numbers and Scan Codes				
Key Number	Key/Character	Scan Code Set 1	Scan Code Set 2	Scan Code Set 3
1	`	29	0E	0E
2	1	2	16	16
3	2	3	1E	1E
4	3	4	26	26
5	4	5	25	25
6	5	6	2E	2E
7	6	7	36	36

Key Number	Key/Character	Scan Code Set 1	Scan Code Set 2	Scan Code Set 3
Table 8.5 101-/102-Key (Enhanced) Keyboard Key Numbers and Scan Codes Continued				
8	7	8	3D	3D
9	8	9	3E	3E
10	9	0A	46	46
11	0	0B	45	45
12	-	0C	4E	4E
13	=	0D	55	55
15	Backspace	0E	66	66
16	Tab	0F	0D	0D
17	Q	10	15	15
18	W	11	1D	1D
19	E	12	24	24
20	R	13	2D	2D
21	T	14	2C	2C
22	Y	15	35	35
23	U	16	3C	3C
24	I	17	43	43
25	O	18	44	44
26	P	19	4D	4D
27	[	1A	54	54
28	]	1B	5B	5B
29	\ (101-key only)	2B	5D	5C
30	Caps Lock	3A	58	14
31	A	1E	1C	1C
32	S	1F	1B	1B
33	D	20	23	23
34	F	21	2B	2B
35	G	22	34	34
36	H	23	33	33
37	J	24	3B	3B
38	K	25	42	42
39	L	26	4B	4B
40	;	27	4C	4C
41	`	28	52	52
42	# (102-key only)	2B	5D	53
43	Enter	1C	5A	5A

Table 8.5   101-/102-Key (Enhanced) Keyboard Key Numbers and Scan Codes Continued

Key Number	Key/Character	Scan Code Set 1	Scan Code Set 2	Scan Code Set 3
44	Left-Shift	2A	12	12
45	\ (102-key only)	56	61	13
46	Z	2C	1A	1A
47	X	2D	22	22
48	C	2E	21	21
49	V	2F	2A	2A
50	B	30	32	32
51	N	31	31	31
52	M	32	3A	3A
53	,	33	41	41
54	.	34	49	49
55	/	35	4A	4A
57	Right-Shift	36	59	59
58	Left-Ctrl	1D	14	11
60	Left-Alt	38	11	19
61	Spacebar	39	29	29
62	Right-Alt	E0, 38	E0, 11	39
64	Right-Ctrl	E0, 1D	E0, 14	58
75	Insert	E0, 52	E0, 70	67
76	Delete	E0, 53	E0, 71	64
79	Left arrow	E0, 4B	E0, 6B	61
80	Home	E0, 47	E0, 6C	6E
81	End	E0, 4F	E0, 69	65
83	Up arrow	E0, 48	E0, 75	63
84	Down arrow	E0, 50	E0, 72	60
85	Page Up	E0, 49	E0, 7D	6F
86	Page Down	E0, 51	E0, 7A	6D
89	Right arrow	E0, 4D	E0, 74	6A
90	Num Lock	45	77	76
91	Keypad 7 (Home)	47	6C	6C
92	Keypad 4 (Left arrow)	4B	6B	6B
93	Keypad 1 (End)	4F	69	69
95	Keypad /	E0, 35	E0, 4A	77
96	Keypad 8 (Up arrow)	48	75	75

Table 8.5   101-/102-Key (Enhanced) Keyboard Key Numbers and Scan Codes Continued

Key Number	Key/Character	Scan Code Set 1	Scan Code Set 2	Scan Code Set 3
97	Keypad 5	4C	73	73
98	Keypad 2 (Down arrow)	50	72	72
99	Keypad 0 (Ins)	52	70	70
100	Keypad *	37	7C	7E
101	Keypad 9 (PgUp)	49	7D	7D
102	Keypad 6 (Left arrow)	4D	74	74
103	Keypad 3 (PgDn)	51	7A	7A
104	Keypad . (Del)	53	71	71
105	Keypad -	4A	7B	84
106	Keypad +	4E	E0, 5A	7C
108	Keypad Enter	E0, 1C	E0, 5A	79
110	Escape	1	76	8
112	F1	3B	5	7
113	F2	3C	6	0F
114	F3	3D	4	17
115	F4	3E	0C	1F
116	F5	3F	3	27
117	F6	40	0B	2F
118	F7	41	83	37
119	F8	42	0A	3F
120	F9	43	1	47
121	F10	44	9	4F
122	F11	57	78	56
123	F12	58	7	5E
124	Print Screen	E0, 2A, E0, 37	E0, 12, E0, 7C	57
125	Scroll Lock	46	7E	5F
126	Pause	E1, 1D, 45, E1, 9D, C5	E1, 14, 77, E1, F0, 14, F0, 77	62

The additional keys on a 104-key Windows keyboard have their own unique scan codes. Table 8.6 shows the scan codes for the new keys.

Table 8.6 104-Key Windows Keyboard New Key Scan Codes			
New Key	Scan Code Set 1	Scan Code Set 2	Scan Code Set 3
Left Windows	E0, 5B	E0, 1F	8B
Right Windows	E0, 5C	E0, 27	8C
Application	E0, 5D	E0, 2F	8D

Many of the latest keyboards feature additional keys for Web browsing, multimedia, or power management. These keys also have scan codes that can be used to detect keyboard errors. For a listing of multimedia and Web browsing–related PS/2 scan codes supported by Windows 2000 and Windows Me, see the Web site http://www.microsoft.com/hwdev/input/w2kbd.htm.

For a listing of scan codes related to power-management keys, see http://www.microsoft.com/hwdev/desinit/ScanCode.htm.

Keyboard Connectors

Although some of the newest systems offer color-coded keyboard connectors and cables, the best way to recognize the keyboard connector is still to know what it looks like. Two common standards exist, and low-cost adapters are available to switch a device using one standard to a connector using the other standard. The keyboard connector standards are as follows:

- **Five-pin DIN connector**—Used on most PC systems with Baby-AT form factor motherboards

- **Six-pin mini-DIN connector**—Used on PS/2 systems and most PCs with LPX, ATX, and NLX motherboards

- **USB connector**—Used on "legacy-free" systems that lack PS/2, serial, or parallel ports

See Chapter 12, "Connector Quick Reference," for examples of these port types.

Table 8.7 shows the physical layout and pinouts of the respective keyboard connector plugs and sockets for the DIN and mini-DIN connector.

Keyboard Connector Signals

Table 8.7 lists the keyboard connector signals for three common keyboard connectors.

Table 8.7 Keyboard Connector Signals			
Signal Name	**5-Pin DIN**	**6-Pin Mini-DIN**	**6-Pin SDL**
Keyboard Data	2	1	B
Ground	4	3	C
+5v	5	4	E
Keyboard Clock	1	5	D
Not Connected	—	2	A
Not Connected	—	6	F
Not Connected	3	—	—

DIN = German Industrial Norm (Deutsche Industrie Norm), a committee that sets German dimensional standards.

SDL = Shielded Data Link, a type of shielded connector created by AMP and used by IBM and others for keyboard cables. It is used inside the keyboard housing to attach the cable to the keyboard's electronics, and the other end of the cable will have the DIN or mini-DIN connector to attach to the computer. Although the SDL design was never standardized, you can use this pinout to trace continuity with a multimeter if you suspect that your keyboard cable is damaged.

USB Keyboard Requirements

Universal Serial Bus (USB) devices have become increasingly popular, and they're well on their way to replacing serial, parallel, keyboard, and mouse port connectors with this single, versatile, sharable port (see Chapter 7, "USB and IEEE-1394 Ports and Devices," for more information about USB).

To use a keyboard connected via the USB port, you must meet three requirements:

- You must have a USB port in the system.

- You must run Microsoft Windows 98, Windows Me, Windows 2000, or Windows XP (all of which include USB keyboard drivers).

- You must have USB Legacy support present and enabled in your system BIOS.

USB Legacy support means that your motherboard ROM BIOS includes drivers to recognize a USB keyboard. Without USB Legacy support in the BIOS, you can't use a USB keyboard when in MS-DOS or when installing Windows on the system for the first time. Also, if the Windows installation fails and requires manipulation outside Windows, the USB keyboard will not function unless it is supported in the BIOS. Virtually all 1998 and newer systems with USB ports include a BIOS with USB Legacy (meaning, USB keyboard) support.

Keyboard Troubleshooting and Repair

Keyboard errors are usually caused by two simple problems. Other more difficult, intermittent problems can arise, but they are much less common. The most frequent problems are as follows:

- Defective cables
- Stuck keys

Use Table 8.8 to help you troubleshoot a defective keyboard.

Table 8.8	Keyboard Troubleshooting	
Problem	**Symptoms**	**Solution**
Defective cable	No keyboard operation; all keys produce errors or wrong characters.	Swap the keyboard with a known, working spare. If the problem isn't repeated, the original keyboard is the problem.
		Replace the cable with a spare (if available—check "scrap" keyboards or vendor spare parts lists), or replace the keyboard.
		Test the cable with a digital multimeter (DMM) with a continuity tester; each wire (see pinouts previously) should make a connection, even when you wiggle the cable. Replace the failed cable or the keyboard.
Stuck key	"Stuck key error" or 3xx error onscreen during POST.	Look up the scancode from table in this chapter to determine which key is stuck. Clean the key switch.
Damaged motherboard keyboard connector	Known working keyboards don't work when plugged in.	For a simple test of the motherboard keyboard connector, you can check voltages on some of the pins. Measure the voltages on various pins of the keyboard connector. To prevent possible damage to the system or the keyboard, turn off the power before disconnecting the keyboard. Then unplug the keyboard and turn the power back on. Make measurements between the ground pin and the other pins, according to Table 8.9.
		Repair or replace the motherboard if voltage fails specifications.

Table 8.8	Keyboard Troubleshooting Continued	
Problem	**Symptoms**	**Solution**
USB keyboard works in Windows configuration, but not in MS-DOS or at startup	USB Legacy mode is not enabled in BIOS/CMOS configuration.	Connect the standard keyboard, start the computer, start BIOS/CMOS configuration, enable USB Legacy mode, save changes, and shut down the computer.
		Reconnect the USB keyboard and retry; the keyboard should now function at all times.

Keyboard Connector Voltage and Signal Specifications

Use Table 8.9 along with a digital multimeter (DMM) to determine whether your keyboard connector is working correctly. See Chapter 7 for voltage values for USB connectors.

Table 8.9	Keyboard Connector Specifications		
DIN Connector Pin	**Mini-DIN Connector Pin**	**Signal**	**Voltage**
1	5	Keyboard clock	+2.0V to +5.5V
2	1	Keyboard data	+4.8V to +5.5V
3	—	Reserved	—
4	3	Ground	—
5	4	+5V power	+2.0V to +5.5V

If your measurements do not match these voltages, the motherboard might be defective. Otherwise, the keyboard cable or keyboard might be defective. If you suspect that the cable is the problem, the easiest thing to do is replace the keyboard with a known good one. If the system still does not work normally, you might have to replace the motherboard.

Keyboard Error Codes

Some BIOSes use the following 3xx-series numbers to report keyboard errors. These error codes will be displayed onscreen during the startup process. Look up the error code and fix the problem.

Table 8.10 lists some standard POST and diagnostics keyboard error codes.

Table 8.10	Keyboard POST Codes
Error Code	**Description**
3xx	Keyboard errors
301	Keyboard reset or stuck-key failure (XX 301; XX = scan code in hex)
302	System unit keylock switch locked
302	User-indicated keyboard test error
303	Keyboard or system-board error; keyboard controller failure
304	Keyboard or system-board error; keyboard clock high
305	Keyboard +5v error; PS/2 keyboard fuse (on motherboard) blown
341	Keyboard error
342	Keyboard cable error
343	Keyboard LED card or cable failure
365	Keyboard LED card or cable failure
366	Keyboard interface cable failure
367	Keyboard LED card or cable failure

Mice and Pointing Devices

Healthy pointing devices are critical to computer operation. Use this section to keep your mouse working properly.

Mouse Motion-Detection Methods

The most common type of mouse mechanism is the optomechanical, used by Logitech and many other vendors. Dirt on the mouse ball or rollers, or fuzz in the light paths will cause skipping and erratic mouse cursor operation. Microsoft and some other vendors use a pure mechanical (roller-type) mechanism for their low-cost mice, which, like the optomechanical design, also can be affected by dirt and dust.

Optical mice, pioneered first by Microsoft and then by Logitech and now offered by many other vendors, use a high-speed CMOS-based optical sensor that is easier to keep clean than the rollerball mechanisms.

Pointing Device Interface Types

The connector used to attach your mouse to the system depends on the type of interface you are using. Mice are most commonly connected to your computer through the following three interfaces:

- Serial port
- Dedicated motherboard mouse port (PS/2 port)
- USB port

Most mice that attach to the USB port also can be adapted to the PS/2 mouse port. Many serial mice are shipped with a PS/2 adapter, too. All of these ports are pictured in Chapter 12.

The PS/2 mouse port is the same mechanical connector as the keyboard six-pin mini-DIN discussed earlier in this chapter, but you cannot interchange the mouse and keyboard.

A fourth connector type, the nine-pin mini-DIN bus-mouse connector, is found on the back of a dedicated bus-mouse interface card or on some old ATI video cards. Bus mice are now considered obsolete, and most cannot be adapted to other types of ports.

> **Note**
>
> Microsoft sometimes calls a bus mouse an *Inport mouse*, which is its proprietary name for a bus mouse connection.

Hybrid Mice

Mice that are designed to work in more than one port type sometimes are referred to as *hybrid mice*. If you have a mouse that has the wrong type of port for your system, how can you tell whether the mouse is a hybrid mouse that can be adapted or whether it is a single-purpose mouse that cannot be adapted?

- Hybrid mice are sold in retail packages that include an adapter made especially for the mouse.

- Single-purpose mice are typically bundled with a system and are designed to use only the system's PS/2 mouse port or USB port, not an adapter.

After-market adapters sold in retail stores work only with hybrid mice, which have the necessary circuitry onboard to work with signals from different port types; they will not work with single-purpose mice.

Wireless Mouse Types

The following are the two methods for interfacing wireless mice:

- Radio control
- Infrared (IR)

Radio-controlled mice are sold by Logitech, Microsoft, Intel, and other companies. The radio receiver plugs into the standard mouse interface(s) listed previously, and the mouse is cordless, using a small battery to power its radio transmitter. Older versions of these mice were very bulky when compared to corded mice, but new wireless mice are about the same size as their corded cousins.

IR mice are rare and sometimes are combined with IR keyboards. The IR receiver plugs into the standard mouse (and keyboard) con-nector and requires a clear line of sight between the mouse and the receiver.

Software Drivers for the Mouse

Depending on your operating system or your operating mode, you might need to manually load a driver or it might be loaded auto-matically for you. Use Table 8.11 to determine what's needed for your mouse.

Table 8.11 Mouse Drive Type and Location by Operating System			
Operating System	**Driver Type**	**Loading Method**	**Notes**
Windows 9*x*, NT, 2000, Me, XP	32-bit .DRV and .VXD	Automatically detected and installed	Most mice with PS/2 ports can use a standard Microsoft driver, although third-party drivers provide support for scroll wheels, third buttons, and so on.
MS-DOS mode under Windows 9*x*/Me	Windows 32-bit driver	Automatically supported in windowed and full-screen modes	In Windows, can use mouse to mark text for the Windows Clipboard.
MS-DOS, including Windows 9*x* command prompt (not MS-DOS mode)	`Mouse.com` or `Device=` `mouse.sys`	Run `MOUSE` from command-line or `Autoexec.bat` or add `device=` `mouse.sys` to Config.sys	Current driver versions from Microsoft and Logitech can load into UMB RAM above 640KB with little conventional memory used.

Mice under Linux are configured through the kernel (for use with standard text-based displays). Xfree86-based graphical user interfaces (*window managers*) require that you specify the device name and mouse protocol used by your mouse or other pointing device. See the manual for your Linux distribution and window manager for details.

Alternative Pointing Devices

Table 8.12 provides an overview of pointing devices used as alternatives to normal mice, including those used with notebook computers.

Table 8.12   Alternative Pointing Devices

Device	Where located	How Operated	Tips and Notes
Glidepoint Developed by Cirque (also called a touchpad)	Flat surface below the Spacebar on notebook PCs; might be a separate device or on the right side of the keyboard on desktop PCs; can be added via an external port.	Move your finger across the surface; use the left and right buttons beneath the Spacebar, or tap/double-tap with your finger in place of clicking/double-clicking.	Most commonly used built-in mouse alternative; also available for desktop PCs. Requires you to move your hand from the keyboard; depends on skin moisture and resistance. Accuracy can be a problem. If you prefer to use a "real" mouse, disable the touchpad in the BIOS because it can still be active on some machines, even when a mouse is installed.
Trackpoint Developed by IBM	Small "eraserhead" pointing stick located in the middle of the keyboard.	Gently press the surface of the "eraser" in the direction you want to go.	Very fast operation because it's on the keyboard. Licensed by Toshiba as "Accupoint" and also found on some IBM/ Lexmark/Unicomp keyboards and on some other notebook computer brands.
Trackball	Rollerball placed below the Spacebar on a notebook computer; also available integrated into desktop keyboards or as separate devices.	Roll the ball with your fingers or thumb to move the mouse pointer in the desired direction.	Popular for some users who have comfort or issues with mice; are available in ergonomic shapes as separate devices.

Keep in mind that many notebook computer users use "real" mice or trackballs when they have room.

Mouse Troubleshooting

If you are experiencing problems with your mouse, you need look in only two places—hardware or software. Because mice are basically simple devices, looking at the hardware takes very little time. Detecting and correcting software problems can take a bit longer, however.

Use Table 8.13 to keep your mouse or pointing device in top condition.

Table 8.13	Troubleshooting Mouse and Pointing Device Problems	
Symptom	**Problem**	**Solution**
Mouse pointer is jerky.	Dirt and dust on rollers and the ball or sensor	Remove the retainer plate on the bottom of the mouse, remove the ball, and clean the ball and rollers with nonabrasive solvents such as contact lens cleaner. Blow dust away from the wheels and sensor. Reassemble and test.
		Remove the trackball ball from the sensor and clean as previously indicated.
		Replace the TrackPoint eraserhead with a new cap.
		Wipe dust from the bottom of the optical mouse.
	Poor choice of mousing surface	For ball-type mice, use a slightly textured surface such as a mouse pad or the 3M Precision Mousing Surface. For optical mice, use any nonmirrored surface (even your tie or your pant leg), but avoid surfaces with a repeating pattern (which can confuse the CMOS motion sensor).
Mouse pointer freezes when another device is used.	IRQ conflict	If the mouse is PS/2, be sure that no other device is using IRQ 12. (modem, and so on) If the mouse is serial, check for a modem on the same IRQ as the mouse. COM 1/3 shares IRQ 4; COM 2/4 share 3 by default. See Chapter 6, "Serial and Parallel Ports and Devices," for information on avoiding mouse/modem conflicts.
		If the mouse is bus, check its IRQ usage and try to find an unused IRQ for bus card.
		Use Windows Device Manager, if available, to find IRQ information.

Table 8.13   Troubleshooting Mouse and Pointing Device Problems Continued

Symptom	Problem	Solution
Mouse won't work at all.	Defective mouse	Replace the original mouse with a known working similar spare. If it works, replace the original mouse for good.
	Defective port	Any mouse plugged into the port won't work. First, check to see whether the port is disabled. If the port is not disabled, use an add-on port card or replace the motherboard.
	Disabled COM, USB, or PS/2 port	Check BIOS or motherboard jumpers, and enable if IRQ used by port isn't already in use.
	Wireless mouse has a dead battery	Check the battery in the mouse; replace it if it's dead or weak.
	Wrong channel set on mouse or transceiver of wireless mouse	The mouse and transceiver must be set to the same channel.
	Infrared mouse can't "see" IR transceiver	Check line-of-sight issues for the IR mouse and transceiver.
	USB mouse drawing too much power for a bus-powered hub (such as those included in some USB keyboard)	Attach the mouse directly to the USB root hub (USB port built into system or USB add-on card), or attach the mouse to a self-powered hub. The problem is most likely to occur with USB optical mice, which require more power than roller or optomechanical mice.
	Mouse setup program configured for the wrong mouse	Rerun the setup program (often available as a tab on the Mouse icon in the Control Panel) and reselect the correct mouse. Remove mice that you no longer use with the system from Device Manager.
	Interference between multiple radio-controlled input devices	Set each input device to a different frequency. Avoid exceeding the minimum distance requirements to minimize interference.
Mouse works as PS/2, but not as serial.	Mouse designed for PS/2 port only	Most "bundled" mice are designed for the PS/2 port only. Retail mice are designed to be used with adapters. Get a mouse built for the serial port.
Mouse locks up when accessed by Microsoft MSD or other diagnostic.	Bad mouse	To verify that the mouse is the problem, run MSD /I to bypass initial detection. Detect computer and other information; then detect the mouse. If the mouse is at fault, you'll lock up your system. Turn off the system, replace the mouse with a known working mouse, and repeat. If the

Table 8.13   Troubleshooting Mouse and Pointing Device Problems Continued

Symptom	Problem	Solution
		replacement mouse works okay, you've solved the problem.
Standard left and right mouse buttons work, but middle or scroll buttons don't work.	Incorrect mouse configuration	A dual-emulation mouse with a PC/MS slider on the bottom must be set to PC (Mouse Systems) mode to activate the middle button. Most Logitech mice can use the Microsoft driver, but Microsoft mice don't support three buttons. Use the correct driver for the mouse.
	Button not programmed	Use the mouse setup program to verify that the middle button is set to work, and check its function.
	Mouse drivers out-of-date	Original scrolling mouse drivers work only in Web browsers and a few other applications. Download and install new drivers from the vendor's Web site.

Chapter 9

Video and Audio

Monitor Resolution

Resolution is the amount of detail that a monitor can render. This quantity is expressed in the number of horizontal and vertical picture elements, or *pixels*, contained in the screen. The greater the number of pixels is, the more detailed the images are. Pixels also are referred to as *pels*, which is short for "picture elements." The resolution required depends on the application. Character-based applications (such as DOS command-line programs) require little resolution, working very well at the standard VGA resolution of 640 × 480 (graphics) or 720 × 400 (text), whereas graphics-intensive applications (such as desktop publishing and Windows software) work best with a resolution of at least 1,024 × 768.

CRTs Versus LCDs

LCD panels, especially all-digital units, provide high-quality displays that are always crisp and perfectly focused. Plus, their dimensions are fully usable and can comfortably display higher resolutions than comparably sized CRTs. Table 9.1 provides common CRT screen sizes and the comparable LCD display panel sizes.

Table 9.1	CRT Versus LCD Usable Screen Size Comparison	
CRT Monitor Size (Also Display Inches)	**CRT Viewing Area (in Inches)**	**Comparable LCD Viewing Area (in Inches)**
14	12.5	12.1
15	13.5	13.3, 13.7
16	14.5	14.1, 14.5
17	15.5	15, 15.1
19	17.5	17, 17.1
20	18.5	18.1

As you can see, the entry-level 15-inch LCD actually provides a usable viewing area similar to a 17-inch CRT.

However, LCD display panels don't perform as well as CRT monitors do when different resolutions must be displayed on the same monitor. The traditional cathode ray tube (CRT, which is the picture tube) monitor is designed to handle a wide range of resolutions, but LCD panels of any type are designed to display a single native resolution (1,024 × 768 with the typical 15-inch LCD display). To change to resolutions other than their native setting, LCD panels must scale the image. Although newer LCD panels provide results at different resolutions that are quite acceptable, older panels often produce inferior results. If you need to change display resolutions frequently (such as for gaming or to preview Web-page designs), you might prefer to use a CRT monitor.

Common Monitor Resolutions

Table 9.2 shows standard resolutions used in PC video adapters, the terms commonly used to describe them, and the recommended monitor size for each resolution.

Table 9.2   Monitor Resolutions and Recommended Monitor Sizes

Resolution	Acronym	Standard Designation	Recommended CRT Size
640 × 480	VGA	Video graphics array	13-inch or larger
800 × 600	SVGA	Super VGA	15-inch or larger
1,024 × 768	XGA	Extended graphics array	17-inch or larger
1,280×1,024	SXGA	VESA 1280	19-inch or larger
1,600×1,280	UXGA	VESA 1600	21-inch or larger

Although Table 9.2 lists acronyms for these resolutions, all but basic VGA are seldom used today. The industry now describes screen resolutions by citing the number of pixels. Nearly all the video adapters sold today support the 640 × 480, 800 × 600, 1,024 × 768 and 1,280 × 1,024 pixel resolutions at several color depths, and most now support 1,600 × 1,280 and even higher resolutions as well.

Note

To understand this issue, you might want to try different resolutions on your system. As you change from 640 × 480 to 800 × 600 and 1,024 × 768, you'll notice several changes to the appearance of your screen.

At 640 × 480, text and onscreen icons are very large. Because the screen elements used for the Windows desktop and software menus are at a fixed pixel width and height, you'll notice that they shrink in size onscreen as you change to the higher resolutions. Some recent versions of Windows, starting with Windows 98, let you select a large icons option in the Display properties sheet. This enables you to use high-resolution selections (which help you see more of your document) and still have large, legible icons.

Monitor Power-Management Modes

One of the first energy-saving standards for monitors was VESA's Display Power Management Signaling (DPMS) spec, which defines the signals that a computer sends to a monitor to indicate idle times. The computer or video card decides when to send these signals.

In Windows 9*x*, you need to enable this feature if you want to use it because it's turned off by default. To enable it, open the Display properties in the Control Panel, switch to the Screen Saver tab, and make sure that the Energy Star low-power setting and Monitor shutdown setting are checked. You can adjust how long the system remains idle before either the monitor picture is blanked or the monitor shuts down completely. Windows 2000/XP/Me default to suspend after 10 minutes, but timings can be adjusted with any of these versions of Windows.

Table 9.3 summarizes the DPMS modes.

Table 9.3	**Display Power Management Signaling**				
State	**Horizontal**	**Vertical**	**Video**	**Power Savings**	**Recovery Time**
On	Pulses	Pulses	Active	None	Not applicable
Standby	No pulses	Pulses	Blanked	Minimal	Short
Suspend	Pulses	No pulses	Blanked	Substantial	Longer
Off	No pulses	No pulses	Blanked	Maximum	System-dependent

Microsoft and Intel developed a more broadly based power-management specification called APM (advanced power management), and Microsoft developed an even more advanced power-management specification called ACPI (advanced configuration and power interface) for use with Windows 98 and beyond. Table 9.4 summarizes the differences between DPMS, APM, and ACPI.

Table 9.4	Power-Management Standards Compared		
Standard	**Devices Controlled**	**How Implemented**	**Notes**
DPMS	Monitor and video card	Drivers for display and video card; must be enabled by operating system such as Windows 9x/2000/Me via Control Panel	DPMS will work alongside APM or ACPI; user defines timer intervals for various modes listed.
APM	Monitor, hard disks, other peripherals	Implemented in BIOS; enabled in BIOS and in operating system (Windows 9x/2000/Me/XP via Control Panel)	User defines timer intervals for various devices in BIOS or operating system.
ACPI	All APM peripherals, plus other PC and consumer devices	Implemented in BIOS; support must be present in BIOS and devices; supports automatic power-up and power-off for PC and consumer devices including printers, stereos, CDs, and others	If ACPI support is present in the BIOS when Windows 98/Me/2000/XP is first installed, Windows ACPI drivers are installed; update BIOS before installing Windows if ACPI support is not present in BIOS.

VGA Video Connector Pinouts

Illustrations of all the following connectors can be seen in Chapter 12, "Connector Quick Reference."

VGA DB-15 Analog Connector Pinout

Virtually all displays in use today are descended from the 1987-vintage IBM VGA display introduced with the IBM PS/2s. The connector pinout is shown in Table 9.5.

Table 9.5	Standard 15-Pin VGA Connector Pinout	
Pin	**Function**	**Direction**
1	Red video	Out
2	Green video	Out
3	Blue video	Out
4	Monitor ID 2	In
5	TTL ground	—_ (monitor self-test)
6	Red analog ground	-_
7	Green analog ground	-_
8	Blue analog ground	-_
9	Key (plugged hole)	-_
10	Sync ground	-_

| Table 9.5 | Standard 15-Pin VGA Connector Pinout Continued | |
Pin	Function	Direction
11	Monitor ID 0	In
12	Monitor ID 1	In
13	Horizontal sync	Out
14	Vertical sync	Out
15	Monitor ID 3	In

On the VGA cable connector that plugs into your video adapter, pin 9 is often pinless. Pin 5 is used only for testing purposes, and pin 15 is rarely used (these are often pinless as well). To identify the type of monitor connected to the system, some manufacturers use the presence or absence of the monitor ID pins in various combinations.

Digital Visual Interface Pinouts

The Digital Visual Interface (DVI) connector is used on an increasing number of LCD display panels as well as some CRT monitors. Many of the newest high-performance video cards feature the DVI-I (digital and analog) version of this connector. DVI can support either high-resolution (dual-link, which is above 1,280 × 1,024 resolution) or low-resolution (single-link, which has a maximum of 1,280 × 1,024 resolution) displays. DVI connectors use three rows of square pins, with pin 14 (power) recessed.

Dual-link displays use all the connectors shown in Table 9.6, whereas single-link displays omit some connectors.

Video cards that have only a DVI-I connector usually come with a special adapter that can connect to either analog VGA or DVI digital display types.

Table 9.6 lists the pin assignments used by both DVI-I and DVI-D connectors.

| Table 9.6 | DVI-I and DVI-D Pinouts | |
Row #	Pin #	How It Is Used
1	1	TMDS data 2-
	2	TMDS data 2+
	3	TMDS data 2/4 shield
	4	TMDS data 4-
	5	TMDS data 4+
	6	DDC clock
	7	DDC data
	8	Analog vertical sync

Table 9.6	DVI-I and DVI-D Pinouts Continued	
Row #	**Pin #**	**How It Is Used**
2	9	TMDS data 1-
	10	TMDS data 1+
	11	TMDS data 1/3 shield
	12	TMDS data 3-
	13	TMDS data 3+
	14	+5V power
	15	Ground (+5, analog H/V sync)
	16	Hot plug detect
	17	TMDS data 0-
	18	TMDS data 0+
3	19	TMDS data 0/5 shield
	20	TMDS data 5-
	21	TMDS data 5+
	22	TMDS clock shield
	23	TMDS clock+
	24	TMDS clock-

DVI-I also has the MicroCross/high-speed pins shown in Table 9.7.

Table 9.7	DVI-I Additional Connectors
C1	Analog red video out
C2	Analog green video out
C3	Analog blue video out
C4	Analog horizontal sync
C5	Analog common ground return (red, green, blue video out)

Video RAM

Video adapters rely on their own onboard memory to store video images while processing them. The amount of memory on the adapter determines the maximum screen resolution and color depth that the device can support in 2D and 3D modes.

Most cards today come with at least 8MB of RAM, and most have 16MB or more. Although adding more memory is not guaranteed to speed up your video adapter, it can increase the speed if it enables a wider bus (from 64 bits wide to 128 bits wide) or provides nondisplay memory as a cache for commonly displayed objects. It also enables the card to support more colors and higher resolutions.

Memory, Resolution, and Color Depth

For maximum realism in such 2D tasks as full-motion video playback, videoconferencing, and photo-editing, a color depth of 24 bits (more than 16 million colors) is desirable at the highest comfortable display resolution possible with your monitor. Use Table 9.8 to determine whether your video card has the memory needed for the color depth and resolution combination you want to use.

Table 9.8   Video Display Adapter Minimum Memory Requirements—2D Operation

Resolution	Color Depth	Number of Colors	RAM on Video Card	Memory Required
640 × 480	8-bit	256	512KB	307,200 bytes
640 × 480	16-bit	65,536	1MB	614,400 bytes
640 × 480	24-bit	16,777,216	1MB	921,600 bytes
800 × 600	8-bit	256	512KB	480,000 bytes
800 × 600	16-bit	65,536	1MB	960,000 bytes
800 × 600	24-bit	16,777,216	2MB	1,440,000 bytes
1,024 × 768	8-bit	256	1MB	786,432 bytes
1,024 × 768	16-bit	65,536	2MB	1,572,864 bytes
1,024 × 768	24-bit	16,777,216	4MB	2,359,296 bytes
1,280 × 1,024	8-bit	256	2MB	1,310,720 bytes
1,280 × 1,024	16-bit	65,536	4MB	2,621,440 bytes
1,280 × 1,024	24-bit	16,777,216	4MB	3,932,160 bytes
1,600 × 1,280	8-bit	256	2MB	2,048,000 bytes
1,600 × 1,280	16-bit	65,536	4MB	4,096,000 bytes
1,600 × 1,280	24-bit	16,777,216	8MB	6,144,000 bytes

From this table, you can see that a video adapter with 4MB can display 65,536 colors in 1,600 × 1,280 resolution mode, but for a true color (16.8M colors) display, you would need to upgrade to a video adapter with 8MB of onboard RAM or reduce resolution to 1,280 × 1,024.

3D video cards require more memory for a given resolution and color depth because the video memory must be used for three different buffers: the front buffer, the back buffer, and the Z-buffer. The amount of video memory required for a particular operation varies according to the settings used for the color depth and the Z-buffer. Triple buffering allocates more memory for 3D textures than double buffering, but it might slow down performance of some games. The buffering mode used by a given 3D video card normally can be adjusted through its properties sheet. Use Table 9.9 to determine the amount of video RAM required for different combinations of 3D modes, resolutions, and color depths.

Table 9.9 Video Display Adapter Memory Requirements—3D Operation			
Resolution	**Color Depth**	**Z-buffer Depth**	**Buffer Mode**
640 × 480	16-bit	16-bit	Double
			Triple
	24-bit	24-bit	Double
			Triple
	32-bit[1]	32-bit	Double
			Triple
800 × 600	16-bit	16-bit	Double
			Triple
	24-bit	24-bit	Double
			Triple
	32-bit[1]	32-bit	Double
			Triple
1,024 × 768	16-bit	16-bit	Double
			Triple
	24-bit	24-bit	Double
			Triple
	32-bit[1]	32-bit	Double
			Triple
1,280 × 1,024	16-bit	16-bit	Double
			Triple
	24-bit	24-bit	Double
			Triple
	32-bit[1]	32-bit	Double
			Triple
1,600 × 1,280	16-bit	16-bit	Double
			Triple
	24-bit	24-bit	Double
			Triple
	32-bit[1]	32-bit	Double
			Triple

1. Although 3D adapters typically operate in a 32-bit mode, this does not mean that they can produce more than the 16,277,216 colors of a 24-bit true color display. Many video processors and video memory buses are optimized to move data in 32-bit words, and they actually display 24-bit color while operating in a 32-bit mode instead of the 4,294,967,296 colors that you would expect from a true 32-bit color depth.

Actual Memory Used	Onboard Video Memory Size Required
1.76MB	2MB
2.34MB	4MB
2.64MB	4MB
3.52MB	4MB
3.52MB	4MB
4.69MB	8MB
2.75MB	4MB
3.66MB	4MB
4.12MB	8MB
5.49MB	8MB
5.49MB	8MB
7.32MB	8MB
4.12MB	8MB
5.49MB	8MB
6.75MB	8MB
9.00MB	16MB
9.00MB	16MB
12.00MB	16MB
7.50MB	8MB
10.00MB	16MB
11.25MB	16MB
15.00MB	16MB
15.00MB	16MB
20.00MB	32MB
10.99MB	16MB
14.65MB	16MB
16.48MB	32MB
21.97MB	32MB
21.97MB	32MB
29.30MB	32MB

Determining the Amount of RAM on Your Display Card

Because the size of video memory is increasingly important to most computer users, it's useful to know how much memory your display card has onboard.

Table 9.10 summarizes some methods that you can use.

Table 9.10 Methods for Determining the Amount of RAM on a Video Card		
Method	**Benefits**	**Cautions**
Use memory/resolution table earlier, and adjust video settings to options requiring 1MB, 2MB, 4MB, and 8MB	If the settings work (a reboot is often required), you have at least that much RAM on your video card.	This method assumes that the videocard is set correctly by the system; it often can't be used to detect memory above 4MB because of driver limitations.
Use third-party system diagnostics such as SiSoft Sandra (http://www.sisoftware.co.uk) to probe the video card	This is a universal solution for organizations with mixed display card standards.	You must use up-to-date diagnostics; shared memory technologies found on low-cost systems might be confusing.
Use diagnostics provided by the video card or video chipset maker to probe the video card.	This is the best source for technical information.	You must use different programs for different chipsets.

Given the low cost and high performance of today's video cards, you should seriously consider replacing any video card with less than 8MB of display memory onboard because even the least powerful cards in use today far outstrip top-end models of just a couple of years ago.

Local-Bus Video Standards

If you are in the market for a new video card, you need to consider your upgrade options. All video cards worth considering use a so-called local-bus technology, which uses a high-speed connection to the CPU that bypasses the slow ISA standard in use for many years. The major current standards are Peripheral Component Interconnect (PCI) and Advanced Graphics Port (AGP). The original local-bus standard, VL-Bus (the VESA Local-Bus), became outdated when the 486 CPU was replaced by Pentium-class CPUs.

PCI and AGP have some important differences, as Table 9.11 shows.

Table 9.11   Local Bus Specifications

Feature	PCI	AGP
Theoretical maximum	132MBps[1]	533MBps throughput (2X) 1.06GBps throughput (4X) 2.12GBps throughput (8X)[2]
Slots	4/5 (typical)	1
Plug and Play support	Yes	Yes
Cost	Slightly higher than PCI	
Ideal use	High-end 486, Pentium	Pentium II, III, 4, Celeron, AMD K6, Athlon, Duron

1. At the 66MHz bus speed and 32 bits, throughput will be higher on the 100MHz system bus.

2. Projected speed per standard; AGP 8X products are not expected until late 2001 or beyond. Obviously, AGP is the more desirable video card standard to use. However, many low-cost systems feature integrated 3D video and lack a separate AGP slot for video upgrades. On these systems, you must use the slower PCI slot if you need to improve your video.

Refresh Rates

The refresh rate (also called the *vertical scan frequency*) is the rate at which the screen display is rewritten. This is measured in hertz (Hz). A refresh rate of 72Hz means that the screen is refreshed 72 times per second. A refresh rate that is too low causes the screen to flicker, contributing to eye strain. A *flicker-free refresh rate* is a refresh rate high enough to prevent you from seeing any flicker; eliminating flicker reduces eye strain. The flicker-free refresh rate varies with the resolution of your monitor setting (higher resolutions require a higher refresh rate) and must be matched by both your monitor and your display card. The speed of the video card's RAMDAC affects the vertical refresh rate options available on the video card, while the monitor's design affects its available refresh rates.

Low-cost monitors often have refresh rates that are too low to achieve flicker-free performance for most users at their highest resolution and thus can lead to eye strain. Also, many low-cost monitors can't focus the picture precisely at their highest resolution, which leads to a fuzzy picture and more eye strain.

RAMDAC

The speed of the RAMDAC (the digital-to-analog converter) is measured in megahertz (MHz); the faster the conversion process is, the higher the adapter's vertical refresh rate will be. Typically, cards with RAMDAC speeds of 300MHz or above will display flicker-free (75Hz or above) at all resolutions up to $1{,}920 \times 1{,}200$. Of course, you must make sure that any resolution you want to use is supported by both your monitor and your video card.

Adjusting the Refresh Rate of the Video Card

The refresh rate of the video card can be adjusted in a couple ways:

- With older cards, a command-line program or separate Windows program often was provided.

- With recent and new cards, the standard display properties sheet offers a selection of refresh rates.

In any case, you need to know the allowable refresh rates for the monitor before you can make an appropriate selection. If your Windows installation uses an unknown, Default Monitor, or Super VGA display type rather than a particular brand and model of monitor, you will be prevented from selecting the higher, flicker-free refresh rates. Install the correct driver for your monitor model to get the highest refresh rates. Note that most recent monitors are configured as Plug-and-Play monitors by Windows because they report their supported refresh rates and resolutions directly to the operating system.

Comparing Video Cards with the Same Chipset

Many manufacturers create a line of video cards to sell at different pricing points. Why not save some dollars and get the cheapest model? Why not say "price is no object" and get the most expensive one? To find the right card for you, look for differences such as those shown in Table 9.12.

Table 9.12 Comparing Video Cards with the Features You Need	
Feature	Effect on You
RAMDAC speed	Less-expensive cards often use a slower RAMDAC. Buy the card with the fastest RAMDAC, especially for use with 17-inch or larger monitors. Faster RAMDACs often are paired with SGRAM or DDR SRAM, which are the fastest types of RAM currently found on video cards.
Amount of RAM	Although AGP video cards can use *AGP memory* (a section of main memory borrowed for texturing), performing as much work as possible on the card's own memory is still faster. PCI cards must perform all functions within their own memory. Less expensive cards in a chipset family often have lower amounts of memory onboard, and most current model cards aren't expandable. Buy a card with enough memory (16MB or more) for your games or applications—today and tomorrow.

Table 9.12 **Comparing Video Cards with the Features You Need Continued**	
Feature	**Effect on You**
Memory type	High-end video cards frequently use the new Synchronous Graphics RAM (SGRAM) or Double-Data-Rate Synchronous DRAM (DDR SRAM), with regular SDRAM as a popular choice for midrange video cards. Choose DDR SRAM, SGRAM, and then SDRAM, in order of preference, when possible.
Memory and core speed	Many suppliers adjust the recommended speed of graphics controllers in an effort to provide users with maximum performance. If you have questions about the rated speed of a controller, check the chip supplier's Web site. Many reputable companies do use overclocked parts, but the best vendors supply large heat sinks or even powered fans to avoid overheating. Memory speed also varies, with many vendors using lower-speed memory on their lower-cost cards.
I/O ports	A DVI-I connector with a VGA adapter enables your video card to work with both CRT and LCD displays, whether analog or video. TV-out enables you to send presentations to video tape or to watch DVD movies on TV. A TV tuner enables you to perform image capture or record TV shows on your system.

Setting Up Multiple Monitor Support in Windows 98/Me/2000/XP

Windows 98 was the first version of Windows to include a video display feature that Macintosh systems have had for years: the capability to use multiple monitors on one system. Windows 98 and Windows Me support up to nine monitors (and video adapters), each of which can provide a different view of the desktop. You can display a separate program on each monitor, use different resolutions and color depths, and enjoy other features. Windows 2000 and Windows XP support up to 10 monitors.

On a multimonitor system, one display is always considered to be the *primary* display. DirectX is supported only on the primary monitor. Additional monitors are called *secondaries* and are much more limited in their hardware support.

Although Microsoft's Web site provides a listing of video cards and chipsets compatible with Windows 98 (use http://search.microsoft.com to locate Knowledge Base article Q182708), it's more difficult to locate specific Microsoft-provided multiple-monitor compatibility information for Windows Me, Windows 2000, and Windows XP.

For this reason, I recommend these third-party Web sites for multiple-monitor support:

> http://www.realtimesoft.com/multimon/
>
> http://www.digitalroom.net/techpub/multimon.html

The RealTimeSoft Web site offers a database of more than 2,000 successful multiple-monitor configurations, listing video card/chipset and motherboard information. You can add your own successful configuration to the database, or you can study it for clues if you're planning to buy an additional video card or if you're having difficulties with your installation.

System Configuration Issues for Multiple-Monitor Support

If the BIOS on your computer does not let you select which device should be the primary VGA display, it decides based on the order of the PCI slots in the machine; AGP slots on some systems have a lower priority than PCI slots. Therefore, you should install the primary adapter in the highest-priority PCI slot. Because many systems do not list the slot priority in their documentation, you might need to experiment by switching the cards around between different PCI expansion slots.

After the hardware is in place, you can configure the display for each monitor from the Display Control Panel's Settings page. The

Table 9.13   Major Multiple-Head Video Cards

Brand	Model	Bus Type(s)	Number of Monitors Supported
Appian Graphics	Jeronimo Pro	PCI	2 or 4
Appian Graphics	Jeronimo 2000	AGP, PCI	2
ATI	Radeon VE	AGP	2
Gainward	CARDEXpert GeForce2 MX Twin View	AGP	2
LeadTek	WinFast GeForce2 MX DH Pro	AGP	2
Matrox	Millennium G450	AGP, PCI	2
Matrox	Millennium G200 MMS	PCI	2 or 4

1. *Optional adapter required.*

primary display is always fixed in the upper-left corner of the virtual desktop, but you can move the secondary displays to view any area of the desktop that you want. You also can set the screen resolution and color depth for each display individually.

In some cases, you might need to disable the secondary adapter before you can run certain programs.

Multiple-Head Video Cards

A card that supports multiple monitors (also called a multiple-head or dual-head card) will save slots inside your system, compared to installing two or more video cards. Also, installing a single video card eliminates the configuration problems inherent in trying to get different video cards and different motherboard/BIOS combinations to work correctly together.

Depending upon the card in question, you can use the multiple-monitor feature in a variety of ways. For example, the ATI Radeon VE features a 15-pin analog VGA connector (for CRTs) and a DVI-I digital/analog connector for digital LCD panels. Thus, you can connect any of the following to the card:

- One analog LCD or CRT display *and* one digital LCD display

- Two analog LCD or CRT displays (when the DVI-I to VGA adapter is used)

Some of the major multiple-head cards on the market are listed in Table 9.13.

Accelerator Chip(s)	Notes
3D Labs Permedia 2 3D (2 or 4)	Supports analog CRTs and LCD displays.
3D Labs Permedia 3 (2)	Supports analog CRTs and LCD displays.
ATI Radeon 3D (1)	Supports analog CRTs and LCD displays. Supports digital flat panel (DVI).
NVidia GeForce2 (1)	Supports analog CRTs and LCD displays. Supports TV-out option.
NVidia GeForce2 (1)	Supports analog CRTs and LCD displays. Supports TV-out option.
Matrox G450 3D (1)	Supports analog CRT and LCD displays. Supports TV-out. Supports digital flat panel (DVI).'
MGA-G200 3D (2 or 4)	Supports analog CRT and digital flat panel (DVI PanelLink). Supports TV-out.

Multimedia Devices

When choosing TV, video-out, or video capture options for your PC, use Table 9.14 to help you decide which solution is best for you.

Table 9.14 Multimedia Device Comparison	
Device Type	**Pros**
Graphics card with built-in TV tuner	Convenience, single-slot solution.
TV-tuner attachment	Allows upgrade to existing graphics cards; might be movable to newer models.
Parallel-port attachment	Universal use on desktop or notebook computer; inexpensive.
USB-port attachment	Easy installation on late-model, USB-equipped computers with Windows 98/Me/2000/XP.
Dedicated PCI interface card	Fast frame rate for realistic video; works with any graphics card.
IEEE-1394 (FireWire, iLINK) connection to digital video	No conversion from analog to digital needed; fast throughput.

Troubleshooting Video Capture Devices

Table 9.15 provides some advice for troubleshooting problems with video capture devices.

Table 9.15 Troubleshooting Video Capture Devices	
Device Type	**Problem**
Parallel-port attachment	Can't detect device, but printers work okay.
TV tuners (built-in graphics card or add-on)	No picture.
All devices	Video capture is jerky.
All devices	Video playback has pauses, dropped frames.
USB devices	Device can't be detected or doesn't work properly.
Interface cards (all types)	Card can't be detected or doesn't work.
IEEE-1394 cards	Card can't be detected or doesn't work.
All devices	Capture or installation problems.

Cons
Upgrading requires card replacement.
Can't be used with all graphics cards.
Frame rate limited by speed of port.
Might not work on Windows 95B OSR 2.x with USB; requires active USB port. Not all devices are compatible with Windows 2000/XP. Low bandwidth, so not suitable for high-resolution or full-motion applications.
High resource requirements (IRQ and so on) on some models; requires internal installation.
Requires IEEE-1394 interface card and IEEE-1394 digital video source; card requires internal installation. Some cards don't include video capture/editing software; verify that separately purchased editing software works with card.

Solution
Check port settings; device might require IEEE-1284 settings (EPP and ECP) or change in BIOS. Make sure that the device is connected directly to the port; avoid daisy-chaining devices unless the device specifically allows it; check Windows Device Manager for IRQ conflicts.
Check cabling; set the signal source correctly in the software.
Frame rate is too low; increasing it might require capturing video in a smaller window. Use the fastest parallel port setting you can; use a faster CPU and increase RAM to improve results.
Hard disk might be pausing for thermal recalibration. Use AV-rated SCSI hard drives or UDMA EIDE drives. Install correct bus-mastering EIDE drivers for the motherboard chipset to improve speed.
Use Windows 98/Me/2000/XP; late versions of Windows 95 have USB drivers, but they often don't work. If you use a USB hub, make sure that it's self-powered.
Check for IRQ conflicts in Windows Device Manager; consider setting the card manually, if possible.
Make sure that the power connector is attached to the card if the card has a four-pin Molex jack; ensure that the correct driver is used for the card.
Use the newest drivers available; check the manufacturer's Web site for updates, FAQs, and so on.

Testing a Monitor with Common Applications

Even without dedicated test and diagnostics software, you can use the software accessories (WordPad, Paint, and so on) that come with Microsoft Windows to test a monitor for picture quality.

One good series of tasks is as follows:

- Draw a perfect circle with a graphics program. If the displayed result is an oval, not a circle, this monitor will not serve you well with graphics or design software.

- Using a word processor, type some words in 8- or 10-point type (1 point equals 1/72 inch). If the words are fuzzy or the black characters are fringed with color, select another monitor.

- Turn the brightness up and down while examining the corner of the screen's image. If the image blooms or swells, it is likely to lose focus at high brightness levels.

- Display a screen with as much whitespace as possible, and look for areas of color variance. This might indicate a problem only with that individual unit or its location, but if you see it on more than one monitor of the same make, it can be indicative of a manufacturing problem, or it could indicate problems with the signal coming from the graphics card. Move the monitor to another system equipped with a different graphics card model, and retry this test to see for certain whether it's the monitor or the video card.

- Load Microsoft Windows to check for uniform focus. Are the corner icons as sharp as the rest of the screen? Are the lines in the title bar curved or wavy? Monitors usually are sharply focused at the center, but seriously blurred corners indicate a poor design. Bowed lines can be the result of a poor video adapter, so don't dismiss a monitor that shows those lines without using another adapter to double-check the effect.

- A good monitor will be calibrated so that rays of red, green, and blue light hit their targets (individual phosphor dots) precisely. If they don't, you have bad convergence. This is apparent when edges of lines appear to illuminate with a specific color. If you have good convergence, the colors will be crisp, clear, and true, provided that there isn't a predominant tint in the phosphor.

- If the monitor has built-in diagnostics (a recommended feature), try them as well to test the display independent of the graphics card and system to which it's attached.

Use Table 9.16 to troubleshoot specified problems.

Table 9.16	Troubleshooting Display Problems	
Symptom	**Cause**	**Solution**
No picture	LED indicates power-saving mode (flashing green or yellow by power switch).	Move the mouse or press Alt+Tab on the keyboard, and wait up to 1 minute to wake up the system if the system is turned on.
	LED indicates normal mode.	Check monitor and video data cables; replace with a known, working spare. Turn off the monitor; reset the mode switch to the correct setting (analog for VGA). Check brightness and contrast control; adjust as necessary.
No picture; no power lights on monitor	No power flowing to monitor.	Cycle the monitor off and on in case power management has kicked in. Check the power cable and replace it. Check the surge protector and replace it. Replace the monitor and retest.
Jittery picture quality	LCD monitors' display not adjusted.	Use display-adjustment software to reduce or eliminate pixel jitter and pixel swim.
	Cables loose.	Check cables for tightness at the video card and the monitor (if removable).
	Defective main or extender cable.	Remove the extender cable and retest with the monitor plugged directly into the video card. If the extended cable is bad, replace it. If the main cable is bad, replace it.
	Jitter is intermittent.	Check for interference; microwave ovens near monitors can cause severe picture distortion when turned on.
	CRT monitor—wrong refresh rate.	Check settings; reduce the refresh rate until acceptable picture quality is achieved.
		Use onscreen picture adjustments until an acceptable picture quality is achieved.
	Intermittent—not due to external interference.	If the problem can be fixed by waiting or gently tapping the side of the monitor, the monitor power supply is probably bad or has loose connections internally; service or replace the monitor.
Picture in DOS or at startup, but not in the Windows GUI	Incorrect or corrupted Windows video driver.	Boot Windows 9x/Me in Safe Mode; boot Windows 2000/XP in Enable VGA Mode. If these display modes work, delete the current video card from Device Manager, and restart the system to redetect the card and reinstall the drivers. If incorrect drivers are selected by Windows, manually choose the correct drivers in Device Manager.

Audio I/O Connectors

Sound cards, or built-in audio chips, provide another significant part of modern PCs' multimedia capabilities. Learning the correct uses for the basic input/output connectors will help you as you set up typical sound-equipped computers. See Chapter 12 for examples of these connectors.

- **Stereo line out or audio out connector**—The line out connector is used to send sound signals from the audio adapter to a device outside the computer, such as stereo speakers, a headphone, or a stereo system. Some adapters provide two jacks for line out: one for the left channel and the other for the right channel.

- **Stereo line or audio in connector**—With the line in connector, you can record or mix sound signals from an external source, such as a stereo system or VCR, to the computer's hard disk.

- **Speaker/headphone connector**—The speaker/headphone connector is provided on most audio adapters, but not necessarily all of them. Some systems use line out instead. When the adapter provides both a speaker/headphone and a line out connector, the speaker/headphone connector provides an amplified signal that can power your headphones or small bookshelf speakers. Most adapters can provide up to 4W of power to drive your speakers. The signals that the adapter sends through the line out connector are not amplified. The line out connector generally provides better sound reproduction because it relies on the external amplifier built into your stereo system or speakers, which is typically more powerful than the small amplifier on the audio adapter.

- **Microphone or mono in connector**—The mono in connector is used to connect a microphone for recording your voice or other sounds to disk. This microphone jack records in mono, not in stereo, and, therefore, is not suitable for high-quality music recordings. Many audio adapter cards use Automatic Gain Control (AGC) to improve recordings. This feature adjusts the recording levels on the fly. A 600-ohm–to–10KB-ohm dynamic or condenser microphone works best with this jack. Some inexpensive audio adapters use the line in connector instead of a separate microphone jack.

- **Joystick connector**—The joystick connector is a 15-pin, D-shape connector that can connect to any standard joystick or game controller. Sometimes the joystick port can accommodate two joysticks if you purchase an optional Y-adapter.

- **MIDI connector**—Audio adapters typically use the same joystick port as their MIDI connector. Two of the pins in the connector are designed to carry signals to and from a MIDI device, such as an electronic keyboard. In most cases, you must purchase a separate MIDI connector from the audio adapter manufacturer that plugs into the joystick port and contains the two round, five-pin DIN connectors used by MIDI devices, plus a connector for a joystick. Because their signals use separate pins, you can connect the joystick and a MIDI device at the same time. You need this connector only if you plan to connect your PC to external MIDI devices. You can still play the MIDI files found on many Web sites by using the audio adapter's internal synthesizer.

- **Internal pin-type connector**—Most audio adapters have an internal pin-type connector that you can use to plug an internal CD-ROM drive directly into the adapter, using a small, round cable. This connection enables you to channel audio signals from the CD-ROM directly to the audio adapter, so you can play the sound through the computer's speakers. This connector does not carry data from the CD-ROM to the system bus; it only provides the CD-ROM drive with direct audio access to the speakers. If your adapter lacks this connector, you can still play CD audio through the computer speakers by connecting the CD-ROM drive's headphone jack to the audio adapter's line in jack with an external cable.

> **Tip**
>
> The line in, line out, and speaker connectors on an audio adapter all use the same 1/8-inch minijack socket. The three jacks usually are labeled, but, when setting up a computer on or under a desk, these labels on the back of the PC can be difficult to read. One of the most common reasons that a PC fails to produce any sound is that the speakers are plugged into the wrong socket.

If your sound card, microphone, and speakers aren't color-coded, do it yourself. See Chapter 2, "System Components and Configuration," for the PC99 standards for color-coding for audio and other ports.

Connectors for Advanced Features

Many of the newest sound cards are designed for advanced gaming, DVD audio playback, and sound production uses, and they have additional connectors:

- **MIDI IN/MIDI OUT**—Some advanced sound cards don't require you to convert the game port (joystick port) to MIDI interfacing by offering these ports on a separate external connector. This permits you to use a joystick and have an external MIDI device connected at the same time. Its typical location is in an external device.

- **SPDIF (also called SP/DIF) IN and SPDIF OUT**—The Sony/Philips Digital Interface Format connector receives digital audio signals directly from compatible devices without converting them to analog format first. Its typical location is in an external device. SPDIF interfaces also are referred to by some vendors as Dolby Digital interfaces.

- **CD SPDIF**—This connects compatible CD-ROM drives with SPDIF interfacing to the digital input of the sound card. Its typical location is on the side of the audio card.

- **TAD IN**—This connects modems with Telephone Answering Device support to the sound card for sound processing of voice messages. Its typical location is on the side of the audio card.

- **Digital DIN OUT**—This supports multispeaker digital speaker systems. Its typical location is in an external device.

- **Aux IN**—This provides input for other sound sources, such as a TV tuner card. Its typical location is on the side of the audio card.

- **I2S IN**—This enables the sound card to accept digital audio input from an external source, such as two-channel decoded AC-3 from DVD decoders and MPEG-2 Zoom Video. Its typical location is on the side of the audio card.

Additional Equipment and Software

Your sound card can be the basis for many different types of recreational and business uses, including gaming, music recording, and digital conversion. Use Table 9.17 to determine what features your sound card needs and what additional products you need for your intended use.

Table 9.17	Sound Card Intended Uses and Feature Comparison		
Intended Use	Features You Need	Additional Hardware	Additional Software
Gaming	Game port 3D sound Audio acceleration	Gaming controller Rear speakers	Games

Table 9.17 Sound Card Intended Uses and Feature Comparison Continued			
Intended Use	**Features You Need**	**Additional Hardware**	**Additional Software**
Playing DVD movies	Dolby 5.1 decoding	Dolby 5.1 speakers compatible with audio adapter	MPEG decoding program
Performing voice dictation and voice command	Audio adapter on program's compatibility list, or equal to SB16 in quality	Voice-recognition microphone	Voice-dictation software
Creating MIDI files	MIDI IN adapter	MIDI-compatible musical keyboard	MIDI composing program
Creating MP3 files	Digital audio extraction	CD-ROM/DVD or CD-RW drive	MP3 ripper
Creating WAV files	Microphone	CD-ROM/DVD or CD-RW drive	Sound-recording program
Creating CD audio files	External sound source	CD-ROM/DVD or CD-RW drive	WAV or MP3-to-CD audio-conversion program

Sound Quality Standards

Many sound card owners never record anything, but if you like the idea of adding sound to a Web site or presentation, you should know the quality and file size impact that typical sound settings will have. The Windows 9x/2000/Me standard sound quality settings are shown in Table 9.18.

Table 9.18 Windows 9x/2000/Me Sound File Resolutions			
Resolution	**Frequency**	**Bandwidth**	**File Size**
Telephone quality	11,025Hz	8-bit mono	11KBps
Radio quality	22,050Hz	8-bit mono	22KBps
CD quality	44,100Hz	16-bit stereo	172KBps

Note that the higher the sound quality is, the larger the file size is. The file sizes are for WAV files saved with the Windows Sound Recorder's default settings. If you want to add sound effects or speech to a Web site, you should get a program such as Real Networks' RealProducer or Windows Producer, both capable of compressing sound as much as 100:1 while still maintaining reasonable quality.

Many new sound cards also support a 48KHz standard designed to match the requirements of DVD audio playback and Dolby AC-3 audio compression technologies. This frequency must be set manually in Sound Recorder if you need to record at this high-frequency level. It creates a file size of 188KBps.

Configuring Sound Cards

Traditionally, sound cards have been one of the toughest single-installation tasks because they use three of the four settings possible for an add-on card: IRQ, DMA, and I/O port addressing. No matter what else you need to install, the rule of thumb is: "The sound card first!"

PCI Versus ISA Sound Cards

PCI cards have become the best choice recently for all types of upgrades, including sound cards. Compared to ISA cards, PCI cards are faster, have a lower CPU utilization rate, and use fewer hardware resources (see Table 9.19). Compare the configuration of the Sound Blaster 16 card with the native configuration for an Ensoniq-chipset PCI sound card.

Table 9.19   Default Resource Assignments for ISA and PCI Sound Card in Native and Emulation Modes

Card Onboard Device	IRQ	I/O	DMA (16-Bit)	DMA (8-Bit)
Sound Blaster 16—ISA Bus				
Audio	5	220h–233h	5	1
MIDI port	—	330h–331h	—	—
FM synthesizer	—	388h–38Bh	—	—
Game port	—	200h–207h	—	—
Ensoniq Audio PCI—PCI Bus Native Mode				
Audio	11	DC80–DCBFh	—	—
Game port	—	200h–207h	—	—
Ensoniq Audio PCI—PCI Bus Legacy (SB Pro) Mode				
Audio	7*	DC80–DCBFh	—	—
MIDI port	—	330h–331h	—	—
FM synthesizer	—	388h–38Bh	—	—
(Ensoniq SoundScape)	—	0530–0537h	—	—
Game Port	—	200h–207h	—	—

*Shared IRQ with printer port; allowed by Ensoniq driver

Although the Ensoniq Audio PCI card uses only one IRQ and one I/O port address in its native mode, if you have software (mostly older Windows and DOS game/educational titles) that requires Sound Blaster Pro compatibility, the Legacy settings also must be used. However, if you are *not* running Sound Blaster–specific software (all your software is native 32-bit Windows, for example), you might be able to disable the Legacy mode for a PCI-based sound card.

Multifunction (Modem and Sound) Cards

Multifunction cards that use digital signal processor (DSP) technology, such as IBM Mwave-based cards, can be very difficult to install in today's IRQ-starved systems. These cards typically combine a modem plus a Sound Blaster–compatible sound card. They also typically require an IRQ and one or more I/O port address ranges for the DSP, as well as the normal settings seen previously and in Chapter 6, "Serial and Parallel Ports and Devices," for the sound card and modem functions.

These cards also might require a very complex software-installation process for the DSP, sound, modem, and soft wavetable sound samples. Because they are resource-hungry, often have limited modem speeds, and are usually ISA-based, I recommend replacing these types of multifunction cards with separate PCI-based sound and modem cards, if possible.

Troubleshooting Audio Hardware
Hardware (Resource) Conflicts

You might notice that your audio adapter doesn't work (no sound effects or music), repeats the same sounds, or causes your PC to freeze. This situation is called a *device*, or *hardware*, conflict centering on IRQ, DMA, and I/O port address settings in your computer (see Chapter 2). Resource conflicts like these are most common with ISA-based sound cards, which cannot share IRQs with other devices and require specific DMA channels.

Detecting Resource Conflicts

Use Table 9.20 to help you determine resource conflicts caused by your sound card.

Table 9.20 Resolving Sound Card Resource Conflicts

Problem	Symptom
Sound card using same IRQ as another device	Skipping, jerky sound or system lockups.
Sound card and another device are using the same DMA channel	No sound at all from sound card.
PCI-slot sound card works okay with Windows, but not MS-DOS apps	Windows software plays. DOS software doesn't play card and can't detect card.
Some DOS and Windows software works, but some can't use card	Error messages about incorrect card settings.
DSP-equipped card, such as IBM Mwave, not installed properly or out of resources	Multifunction sound and modem card doesn't work.
PnP card on a non-PnP system was working but has now stopped working	PnP enumerator program in startup process probably removed or damaged.

How to Detect	Solution
Use Windows Device Manager. For other systems, use IRQ and DMA card, as described in Chapter 2.	For PnP device: Disable automatic configuration for conflicting device and try to set card manually through direct alteration of settings in either the BIOS Setup or Device Manager or by choosing alternative configurations.
	For non-PnP device: Move conflicting device to another setting to allow sound card to use defaults.
Check for Legacy or SB settings in the Windows Device Manager.	If no Legacy support is installed, install it. Follow instructions carefully for using the card with older software. You might need to run a Setup program or TSR before starting the DOS program. You might need a software patch from the game developer. In extreme cases, you might need to use an actual SB Pro/16 card alongside your PCI sound card and use it instead.
Check card or Legacy software settings; alternative settings work okay for some programs, but not others.	The software expects SB default settings; use settings in the preceding table for Sound Blaster 16 (all but DMA 5 apply to SB Pro).
Check Windows Device Manager for DSP host configuration.	Mwave and similar cards require basic SB settings, as in the previous entry, plus serial (COM) port setting resources for the DSP. Reinstall the card with all drivers.
Check CONFIG.SYS or AUTOEXEC.BAT for driver; use REM to create labels before and after driver commands.	Reinstall the software and test; upgrade BIOS to PnP mode, if possible.

Most Common Causes of Hardware Conflicts with ISA Sound Card

The most common causes of system resource conflicts are the following:

- SCSI host adapters

- Network interface cards

- Bus mouse adapter cards

- Serial port adapter cards for COM 3 or COM 4

- Parallel port adapter cards for LPT2

- Internal modems

- Scanner interface cards

All these cards use IRQ, DMA, and I/O port addresses, which, in some cases, can overlap with default or alternative sound card settings.

Other Sound Card Problems

Like the common cold, audio adapter problems have common symptoms. Table 9.21 will help you diagnose sound card problems.

Table 9.21	Diagnosing Sound Card Problems	
Symptom	**Cause**	**Solution**
No sound	Incorrect or missing speaker wires.	Plug speakers into the correct jack (stereo line out/speaker out).
	No power to amplified speakers.	Turn on power. Attach to AC adapter or use fresh batteries.
	Mono speaker attached to stereo plug.	Use stereo speaker or headset.
	Mixer settings too low.	Adjust master volume setting; turn off the mute option.
	Sound card might not be working.	Test with diagnostic software and sounds provided.
	Sound card hardware needs to be reset.	Power down and then on again, or use the reset button to restart the PC.
	Some games play, but others don't.	Check hardware defaults, as previously; verify that the correct version of Windows DirectX or other game API is installed.
	Speaker connector damaged.	Replace audio adapter.
Mono sound	Mono plug in stereo jack.	Use stereo speaker jack.
	Incorrectly wired speakers.	Check color coding.

Table 9.21	Diagnosing Sound Card Problems Continued	
Symptom	Cause	Solution
	Audio card in left channel mono fail-safe mode because of driver problem.	Reload drivers and test stereo sound.
	Speakers with independent volume controls might be set differently.	Adjust volume to match on both.
Low volume	Speakers plugged into headphone jack.	Use higher-powered speaker jack if separate jacks are provided.
	Mixer settings too low.	Boost volume in the mixer.
	Hardware volume control (thumbwheel) on sound card turned too low.	Adjust volume on the card.
	Speakers not powered or require more power.	Power speakers, add amplifier, or replace speakers.
Scratchy sound	Audio card picking up interference from other cards.	Move away from other cards.
	ISA sound card might be dropping signals during hard disk access.	This is a normal problem due to high CPU utilization of the ISA card; use a PCI sound card instead.
	Interference from monitor causing interference.	Move speakers farther away. Put subwoofers on the floor to maximize low-frequency transmission and to keep their big magnets away from the monitor.
	Poor-quality FM-synthesis music from sound card.	Change to a wavetable sound card; check wavetable settings.
Computer won't start after card installation	Card not seated tightly in expansion slot.	Remove the card, reinsert, and restart the PC.
IOS error displayed during Windows 95 startup; system locked up	Sound card software clashes with Windows Input/Output System (IOS).	Check with sound card vendor for an IOS fix program; might be supplied on an install disk. Start Windows 9x in Safe mode to locate and install.
Joystick doesn't work.	Duplicate joystick ports on sound card and another card causing I/O port address conflict.	Disable sound card joystick port.
	Computer too fast for inexpensive joystick port.	Buy a high-speed joystick port. Disable the port on the sound card. Install a replacement joystick port card.
		Slow the computer with a de-turbo button or BIOS routine.
Can't play DVD audio	Hardware resource not enabled on sound card.	Enable the hardware resource or MP3 files, or use SPDIF connections.

Chapter 10

Networking

Client/Server Versus Peer-to-Peer Networking

Table 10.1 compares the features of client/server networking (such as with Novell NetWare, Windows NT Server, and Windows 2000/XP) with peer-to-peer networking (such as with Windows for Workgroups, Windows 9x, Windows Me, and Windows NT Workstation). This table will help you decide which type of network is appropriate for your situation.

Note

Networking is an enormous topic. The following table serves as a reference for field technicians and other professionals. If you need more in-depth information about networking, see *Upgrading and Repairing PCs, 13th Edition*, or pick up a copy of *Upgrading and Repairing Networks, Third Edition*.

Table 10.1 Comparing Client/Server and Peer-to-Peer Networking

Item	Client/Server	Peer-to-Peer
Access control	Via user/group lists of permissions. A single password provides user access to only the resources on that list; users can be given several different levels of access.	Via password lists by resource. Each resource requires a separate password. All-or-nothing access is used. No centralized user list exists.
Security	High, because access is controlled by user or by group identity.	Low, because knowing the password gives anybody access to a shared resource.
Performance	High, because server doesn't waste time or resources handling workstation tasks.	Low, because servers often act as workstations.

Item	Client/Server	Peer-to-Peer
	Table 10.1 Comparing Client/Server and Peer-to-Peer Networking Continued	
Hardware cost	High, because of specialized design of server, high-performance nature of hardware, redundancy features.	Low, because any workstation can become a server by sharing resources.
Software cost	License fees per workstation user are part of the cost of the Network Operating System server software (Windows NT/2000/XP Server, Novell NetWare).	Free; all client software is included with any release of Windows 9x, Windows NT Workstation, Windows 2000 Professional, Windows Me, or Windows XP.
Backup	Centralized when data is stored on server; allows use of high-speed, high-capacity tape backups with advanced cataloging.	Left to user decision; usually mixture of backup devices and practices at each workstation.
Redundancy	Duplicate power supplies, hot-swappable drive arrays, and even redundant servers are common. Network OS normally is capable of using redundant devices automatically.	No true redundancy among either peer "servers" or clients. Failures require manual intervention to correct with high possibility of data loss.

If you choose any form of Ethernet network hardware for your peer-to-peer network, you can upgrade to a client/server network later by adding a server with the appropriate network operating system. Your existing network cards, cables, and other hardware can still be used with the new server.

Choosing Network Hardware and Software

In this section, you'll receive a detailed checklist of the hardware and software that you need to build your network. Although many options are available on the market for network hardware, this discussion assumes that you will be choosing Fast Ethernet hardware that also can work with standard Ethernet networks ("dual-speed" 10/100 cards and hubs). This is the most popular and cost-effective network currently available.

First, start with the number of computers you plan to network together. You need the items discussed in the following section to set up your network.

NIC

One network interface card (NIC) is required for every computer on the network. To simplify technical support, buy the same model of NIC for each computer in a peer-to-peer workgroup network. Today, the best price-performance combination is Fast Ethernet (100BASE-TX) NICs. You should choose dual-speed (10/100) versions of these cards to enable interconnection with standard 10Mbps Ethernet networks.

You should record the brand name and model number of the NIC(s) you are using, as well as the driver version or source. Use Table 10.2 as a guide.

Table 10.2   NIC Location and Information Worksheet

NIC Location and Computer ID	Brand Name	Model #	Cable Type(s)	Speed	Driver Source or Version

USB Connectors As an Alternative to NICs

As an alternative to NICs, you can use USB network adapters. Because USB runs at 12Mbps (slightly faster than 10BASE-T), this is a satisfactory substitute for a 10BASE-T or HomePNA 2.0 network card. However, a USB device will be significantly slower than a NIC on a Fast Ethernet (100Mbps) network.

UTP Cable

Each NIC must be connected by a cable long enough to reach comfortably between the NIC and the hub or switch, which connects multiple computers. Use Table 10.3 as a guide for recording necessary information regarding your cabling. Your cabling should be Category 5 or better.

Table 10.3   UTP Cable Worksheet

Computer ID	Cable Length	Wiring Standard

You need only one hub or switch for the typical workgroup network.

Hubs and Switches

You can use a hub or a switch to connect the different stations of your network. Both hubs and switches feature multiple RJ-45 ports and signal lights that indicate network activity. Both devices require AC power. However, switches have additional features that provide better performance than hubs for your network, as seen in Table 10.4.

Table 10.4	Ethernet Hub and Switch Comparison		
Feature	**Hub**	**Switch**	**Notes**
Bandwidth	Divided by total number of ports in use	Dedicated to each port in use	A 100Mbps hub with four users provides 25Mbps bandwidth per user (100/4). If you use a switch, each user gets full 100Mbps bandwidth.
Data Transmission Type	Broadcast to all connected computers	Direct connection between transmitting and receiving computers	Broadcasting data causes collisions, which slows the network because data must be retransmitted.
Duplex Support	Half duplex only (receive or transmit)	Half or full duplex (receive and transmit) when used with full-duplex NICs; doubles effective bandwidth of the network	If you use a 100Mbps switch that supports full duplex with 100Mbps cards that also support full duplex, you have a network running at 200Mbps.

Desirable Hub and Switch Features

Look for these features to make sure that your hub or switch has growth potential:

- **Dual network card speeds**—This enables you to freely mix and match 10BASE-T and Fast Ethernet or 10/100 NICs and derive full speed from all devices.

- **Additional ports for future expansion**—Because the cost per port drops on larger switches and hubs, it's cheaper to buy excess capacity from the start than to replace your switch/hub or add a switch/hub later.

- **An uplink port, making the switch or hub stackable**—A stackable switch/hub enables you to add an additional device later without replacing the original unit. The additional hub or switch is connected via standard Category 5 UTP cable and can be as far away as the limit for the network type involved. You can connect another switch/hub to a switch/hub that lacks an uplink port only if you use more expensive, harder-to-find crossover cables (or build your own).

- **Full-duplex support (switches only)**—This doubles the effective speed of the network when full-duplex NICs are used.

Use the worksheet shown in Table 10.5 as a guide for recording information about your hub or switch. Dual-speed 10/100 Ethernet/Fast Ethernet hubs will enable you to connect with existing standard Ethernet networks.

Table 10.5   Hub/Switch Worksheet

Hub or Switch	Brand	Model#	# of Ports	Uplink?	Full-Duplex?	Speeds
___	___	___	___	___	___	___
___	___	___	___	___	___	___

Software

Start by using the built-in networking software supplied with your version of Windows. Any recent version of Windows contains network client and simple peer-server software. Your workgroup network can contain any combination of the following:

- Windows for Workgroups 3.11
- Windows 95
- Windows 98
- Windows 2000 Professional
- Windows NT 4.0 Workstation
- Windows Me
- Windows XP

Table 10.6 shows the basic configuration you'll need to complete for any client (accessing services on another PC) and server (sharing services with other PCs) using these versions of Windows.

Table 10.6 Minimum Network Software for Peer-to-Peer Networking		
Item	Client	Server
Windows network client	Yes	No
NetBEUI protocol[1]	Yes	Yes
File and print sharing for Microsoft Networks	No	Yes
NIC installed and bound to previous protocols and services	Yes	Yes
Workgroup identification (same for all PCs in workgroup)	Yes	Yes
Computer name (each PC needs a unique name)	Yes	Yes

1. NetBEUI is no longer supported by Microsoft on Windows XP, but a NetBEUI client is included on the Windows XP CD-ROM for troubleshooting purposes. You can install it manually to enable your Windows XP system to communicate with older Windows computers on a network that uses NetBEUI. Alternatively, you can use the Windows XP Home Networking Wizard to set up your existing Windows network to run with TCP/IP instead of NetBEUI.

Any system that will be used as both a client and a server must have the components from *both* columns installed.

Depending on how you plan to use the computer, one or both of the following might also need to be installed:

- If the computer will access a Novell NetWare client/server network, the IPX/SPX protocol also must be installed and configured.

- If the computer will be used to access the Internet or any other TCP/IP-based network, the TCP/IP protocol also must be installed.

Note that Windows 2000 and Windows Me do *not* install the NetBEUI protocol by default, and Windows XP no longer supports NetBEUI (although it's available on the Windows XP CD-ROM). You must specify it when you set up the network features of either version of Windows if you want to use a Direct Cable Connection or create a simple workgroup network. Windows 2000 and Windows Me use TCP/IP as their default network protocol.

Use the Network icon in the Windows Control Panel to choose your network settings. You'll need the following software to set up the network:

- Operating system CDs, disks, or hard-disk image files
- NIC drivers

Network Protocols

The second most important choice that you must make when you create your network is which network protocol you will use. The network protocol affects which types of computers your network can connect with.

The three major network protocols are TCP/IP, IPX/SPX, and NetBEUI. Unlike data-link protocols, though, network protocols are not tied to particular hardware (NIC or cable) choices. Network protocols are software and can be installed on or removed from any computer on the network at any time, as necessary.

Table 10.7 summarizes the differences among these protocols.

Table 10.7	Overview of Network Protocols and Suites		
Protocol	Included in Protocol Suite	Best Used For	Notes
IP	TCP/IP	Internet and large networks	Also used for dial-up Internet access; native protocol suite of Windows 2000/XP, Windows Me, and Novell NetWare 5.x.
IPX	IPX/SPX	Networks with Novell 4.x and earlier servers	Used by NetWare 5.x for certain special features only.
NetBEUI	—	Windows 9x, Me, 2000, or Windows for Workgroups peer networks	Can't be routed between networks; simplest network protocol. Also used with Direct Cable Connection NIC-less "networking."

All the computers on any given network must use the same network protocol or protocol suite to communicate with each other.

IP and TCP/IP

IP stands for Internet Protocol; it is the network layer of the collection of protocols (or protocol suite) developed for use on the Internet and commonly known as *TCP/IP* (Transmission Control Protocol/Internet Protocol).

Later, the TCP/IP protocols were adopted by the UNIX operating systems, and they have now become the most commonly used protocol suite on PC LANs. Virtually every operating system with networking capabilities supports TCP/IP, and it is well on its way to displacing the other competing protocols. Novell NetWare 5 and Windows 2000/XP use TCP/IP as their native protocol for most services.

Selecting a Network Data-Link Protocol (Specification)

Regardless of the type of network (client/server or peer-to-peer) you select, you can choose from a wide variety of network data-link protocols, also known as *specifications*. The most common ones in use for PCs are listed here. Use Table 10.8 to understand the requirements, limitations, and performance characteristics of the major types of network data-link protocols.

Table 10.8   Network Data-Link Protocols Summary

Network Type	Speed	Max. Number of Stations	Cable Types	Notes
ARCnet	2.5Mbps	255 stations	RG-62 coax UTP[1]/Type 1 STP[2]	Obsolete for new installations; was used to replace IBM 3270 terminals (which used the same coax cable).
HomePNA 1.0	1Mbps	—	RJ-11 phone cable	Easy home-based networking via parallel-port connections or internal ISA, PCI, or PC Card NICs or USB port; replaced by HomePNA 2.0.
HomePNA 2.0	10Mbps	—	RJ-11 phone cable	Easy, faster home-based networking via PCI or PC Card NICs or USB port.
Ethernet	10Mbps	Per segment: 10BASE-T-2 10BASE-2-30 10BASE-5-100 10BASE-FL-2	UTP[1] Cat 3 (10BASE-T), Thicknet (coax; 10BASE-5), Thinnet (RG-58 coax; 10BASE-2), Fiber optic (10BASE-F)	Being replaced by Fast Ethernet; can interconnected with Fast Ethernet by use of dual-speed hubs and switches; use switches and routers to overcome "5-4-3" rule in building very large networks.

Table 10.8	Network Data-Link Protocols Summary Continued			
Network Type	**Speed**	**Max. Number of Stations**	**Cable Types**	**Notes**
Fast Ethernet	100Mbps	Per segment: 2	Cat 5 UTP[1]	Fast Ethernet can be interconnected with standard Ethernet through use of dual-speed hubs, switches, and routers; most common variety is 100BASE-TX; alternative 100BASE-T4 is not widely supported.
Gigabit Ethernet	1000Mbps	Per segment: 2	Cat 5 UTP	Gigabit Ethernet can be interconnected with Fast or standard Ethernet through use of dual-speed hubs, switches and routers.
Token Ring	4Mbps or 16Mbps	72 on UTP[1] 250-260 on type 1 STP[2]	UTP[1], Type 1 STP[2], and Fiber Optic	High price for NICs[3] and MAUs[4] to interconnect clients; primarily used with IBM mid-size and mainframe systems.

1. UTP = Unshielded twisted pair
2. STP = Shielded twisted pair
3. NIC = Network interface card
4. MAU = Multiple access unit

Network Cable Connectors

Several types of network cable connectors are available. Table 10.9 summarizes these and indicates which ones are in current use.

Table 10.9   Network Cable Connectors

Connector Type	Used By	Notes
DB-15	Thick Ethernet	Used a "vampire tap" cable from the connector to attach to the main cable; obsolete.
DB-9	Token Ring	Obsolete.
BNC	RG-62 ARCnet (obsolete) RG-58 Thin Ethernet	Thin Ethernet uses T-connector to enable passthrough to another station or a terminating resistor to indicate end of network segment. Obsolete.
RJ-45	Newer Token Ring 10BASE-T Ethernet, Fast Ethernet, Gigabit Ethernet	Twisted-pair cabling is the overwhelming favorite for most installations.
RJ-11	HomePNA 1.0, 2.0	Telephone-type twisted-pair cabling.

Although virtually all newly installed networks today with conventional cables use twisted-pair cabling, many networks are mixtures of twisted-pair and older cabling types. Token-Ring network interface cards and Ethernet cards with all three of the popular Ethernet connector types remain in wide use. When a network interface card has more than one connector type, you might need to use the card's setup program to select which connector to use.

Wire Pairing for Twisted-Pair Cabling

For large, multioffice installations, network cables usually are built from bulk cable stock and connectors. Because the twisted-pair cabling has eight wires, many pairings are possible. If you are adding cable to an existing installation, you should match the wire pairings already in use. However, the most popular wiring standard is the AT&T 258A/EIA 568B standard detailed in Table 10.10. You can buy prebuilt cabling that matches this standard, or you can build your own.

Table 10.10   RJ-45 Connector Wire Pairing and Placement AT&T 258A/EIA 568B Standard

Wire Pairing	Wire Connected to Pin #	Pair Used For
White/blue and blue	White/blue: #5 Blue: #4	Not used[1]
White/orange and orange	White/orange: #1 Orange: #2	Transmit
White/green and green	White/green: #3 Green: #6	Receive
White/brown and brown	White/brown: #7 Brown: #8	Not used[1]

1. This pair is not used with 10BASE-T or Fast Ethernet 100BASE-TX, but all four pairs are used with Fast Ethernet 100BASE-T4 and with Gigabit Ethernet 1000BASE-TX standards.

Thus, a completed cable that follows the AT&T 258A/EIA 568B standard should look similar to the following when viewed from the flat side of the RJ-45 connector (from left to right):

orange/white, orange, green/white, blue, blue/white, green, brown/white, brown.

Note

You also might encounter the similar EIA 568A standard. It reverses the position of the orange and green pairs listed previously.

Making Your Own UTP Cables

You will need the following tools and supplies to build your own Ethernet cables:

- UTP cable (Category 5 or better)
- RJ-45 connectors
- Wire stripper
- RJ-45 crimping tool

You can buy all the previous tools for a single price from many different network-products vendors. If you are working with a network with a wiring closet, you also will want to add a punchdown tool to your kit.

Before you create a "real" cable of any length, follow these procedures and practice on a short length of cable. RJ-45 connectors and bulk cable are cheap; network failures are not.

Follow these steps for creating your own twisted-pair cables:

1. Determine how long your UTP cable should be. You'll want to allow adequate slack for moving the computer and for avoiding strong interference sources. Keep in mind the maximum distances for TP cables listed later in this chapter.

2. Roll out the appropriate length of cable.

3. Cut the cable cleanly from the box of wire.

4. Use the wire stripper to strip the insulation jacket off the cable to expose the TP wires; you'll need to rotate the wire about 1–1/4 turns to strip away all of the jacket. If you turn it too far, you'll damage the wires inside the cable.

Caution

Don't strip the UTP wires themselves—just the jacket!

---

5. Check the outer jacket and inner TP wires for nicks; adjust the stripper tool and repeat steps 3 and 4 if you see damage.

6. Arrange the wires according to the AT&T 258B/EIA 568B standard listed previously.

7. Trim the wire edges so that the eight wires are even with one another and are slightly less than 1/2 inch past the end of the jacket. If the wires are too long, crosstalk (wire-to-wire interference) can result; if the wires are too short, they can't make a good connection with the RJ-45 plug.

8. With the clip side of the RJ-45 plug facing away from you, push the cable into place. Verify that the wires are arranged according to the EIA/TIA 568B standard *before* you crimp the plug onto the wires. Adjust the connection as necessary.

9. Use the crimping tool to squeeze the RJ-45 plug on to the cable. The end of the cable should be tight enough to resist being removed by hand.

10. Repeat steps 4–9 for the other end of the cable. Recut the end of the cable, if necessary, before stripping it.

11. Label each cable with the following information:

    • Wiring standard

    • Length

- End with crossover (if any)

- _____ (blank) for computer ID

Note

The cables should be labeled at both ends to make matching the cable with the correct computer easy and to facilitate troubleshooting at the hub. Check with your cable supplier for suitable labeling stock or tags that you can attach to each cable.

An excellent online source for this process, complete with illustrations, is http://www.duxcw.com/digest/Howto/network/cable/.

Network Cabling Distance Limitations

Network distance limitations must be kept in mind when creating a network. If you find that some users will be "out of bounds" because of these limitations, you can use repeaters, routers, or switches to reach distant users.

Table 10.11 lists the distance limitations of various kinds of LAN cable.

In addition to the limitations shown in the table, keep in mind that you cannot connect more than 30 computers on a single Thinnet Ethernet segment, more than 100 computers on a Thicknet Ethernet segment, more than 72 computers on a UTP Token Ring cable, and more than 260 computers on an STP Token Ring cable.

Table 10.11 Network Distance Limitations		
Network Standard	**Cable Type**	**Maximum**
Ethernet 10BASE-2	Thin[1]	607 feet
Ethernet 10BASE-5	Thick (drop cable)[1]	164 feet
Ethernet 10BASE-T	Thick (backbone)[1]	1,640 feet
	Category 3 or 5 UTP	328 feet[2]
Fast Ethernet 100BASE-TX/T4	Category 5 UTP	328 feet[2]
Fast Ethernet 100BASE-FX	Fiber optic[3]	1,312 feet[4]

Table 10.11 Network Distance Limitations Continued		
Network Standard	**Cable Type**	**Maximum**
Token Ring	STP	328 feet
	UTP	148 feet
ARCnet[1] (passive hub)		393 feet
ARCnet[1] (active hub)		1,988 feet

1. Indicates obsolete for new installations; can be found in existing installations.

2. Equivalent to 100 meters.

3. 62.5/125 (core/cladding diameter in micrometers) two-strand fiber optic cable.

4. Equivalent to 400 meters.

Thin—RG-58

UTP—Unshielded twisted pair; 10BASE-T and 100BASE-TX use two pairs; 100BASE-TX and Gigabit Ethernet use all four pairs

STP—Shielded twisted pair

ARCnet—RG-62

Properly constructed Fast Ethernet 100BASE-TX Category 5 cable can be certified for Gigabit Ethernet operation. Gigabit Ethernet uses all four-wire pairs.

Specialized Network Options

The following sections cover specialized networks that you might encounter, including the HomePNA networking and wireless networking standards.

Telephone Line Networks

Small-office/home-office (SOHO) users want networks for Internet connection sharing, printer sharing, and file transfer. To avoid the cabling problems and protocol configuration and setup issues of traditional Ethernet networks, the Home Phoneline Network Association (HomePNA) established the HomePNA 1.0 (1Mbps) and faster 2.0 (10Mbps) standards for using existing phone wiring for networking.

The advantages include these:

- Easy setup for technical novices because of the integrated nature of the hardware and software.

- Choice of internal (card-based) or external (parallel port or USB-based) solutions. HomePNA 2.0 supports card and USB-based solutions.

- No rewiring needed; uses the phone lines in the home or home office.

- Simultaneous use of telephone and network (but not dial-up Internet) allowed.

- HomePNA support that can be (and is) incorporated into computers and multipurpose add-on cards (Ethernet or V.90 modems).

- Point-to-point network that requires no hubs or switches.

The disadvantages include these:

- Low speed compared to Fast Ethernet: HomePNA 2.0 is still just 10Mbps.

- Inability to turn a HomePNA-based network into a client/server network later.

- HomePNA interface cards and devices are more expensive than Fast Ethernet, especially for a network of three or more stations.

Wireless Networking Standards

Wireless networking, once considered a narrow "niche" technology hampered by a lack of standards, is now becoming a major network type. This is largely because of the adoption of official standards (IEEE 802.11b, Wi-Fi, and HomeRF) that improve interoperability between brands of devices and lower equipment prices.

Star-Topology Wireless Networks

The following networks use a star topology: Wireless NICs send signals to an access point, which relays the signal to the receiving computer. By using multiple access points in a building or campus environment, users can stay connected as they move from room to room or building to building. The NICs automatically switch to the strongest signal from an access point; thus, this type of wireless network is similar in concept to cellular phone networks. The networks are as follows:

- **IEEE 802.11b**—The leading industry standard is IEEE 802.11b, a wireless Ethernet standard designed to interconnect easily with standard Ethernet 10BASE-T networks. It runs at 11Mbps and uses the same 2.4GHz wavelength used by cellular phones and other communications devices. IEEE 802.11b is supported by a number of leading network hardware vendors, and products from different vendors can be mixed and matched just as conventional "wired" Ethernet products can be. For the best results when mixing and matching products from different vendors, look for Wi-Fi–certified products (see next entry). Some notebook computers from major vendors now integrate IEEE 802.11b NICs and antennas.

- **Wi-Fi**—Wi-Fi is the term used by the Wireless Ethernet Compatibility Alliance (WECA) for IEEE 802.11b hardware that is tested to comply with WECA standards. Wi-Fi–certified hardware of different brands will work together; other non–WECA-certified IEEE 802.11b products might not.

- **RadioLAN Wireless MobiLINK**—The proprietary RadioLAN Wireless MobiLINK uses the 5.8GHz frequency. Thus, it can't connect directly to IEEE 802.11b devices, but it can be connected to standard 10BASE-T Ethernet networks via the Wireless BackboneLINK access point. MobiLINK also works with RadioLAN's Campus BridgeLINK products, which provide building-to-building wireless networking at distances up to 1 mile. MobiLINK runs at 10Mbps, the same as 10BASE-T.

Point-to-Point Wireless Networks

The following standards use a point-to-point topology: Each wireless client sends its signal directly to the receiving client. This is much slower but also much simpler and less expensive than star-topology wireless LANs:

- **HomeRF**—HomeRF is a home-oriented network standard that runs at just 1.6Mbps currently, but future versions will run at 10Mbps. It also can be connected to standard Ethernet networks by means of a wireless bridge. HomeRF products running at 1.6Mbps are available now from a variety of vendors. See the HomeRF Web site for details.

- **Bluetooth**—Bluetooth is a very short-range, slow-speed (400Kbps) standard primarily designed for data interchange between appliance devices, such as pagers, PDAs, and wireless phones, as well as notebook computers. Bluetooth-enabled devices are slowly emerging into the marketplace.

Both HomeRF and Bluetooth use the same 2.4GHz frequency as IEEE 802.11b, so interference between these types of networks is possible. However, developments are under way to develop a method for controlling traffic when both types of wireless devices are present.

Table 10.12 provides an overview of the various wireless network standards currently in use.

Table 10.12	Comparison of Current Wireless Networks			
Network Web Site	Rated Speed	Logical Topology	Connects with 10BASE-T Ethernet Via	Maximum Number of PCs per Access Point
IEEE 802.11b http://www.wifi.org	11Mbps	Logical star (requires access point)	Access point	Varies by brand and model; up to 2048
RadioLAN http://www.radiolan.com	10Mbps[1] (requires access point)	Logical star	Wireless BackboneLINK (access point)	128
HomeRF http://www.homerf.org	1.6Mbps	Point-to-Point	Symphony Cordless Ethernet Bridge or equivalent	10

1. *Actual throughput of RadioLAN compared to average of IEEE 802.11b products is about 25% faster due to higher radio frequency used.*

Wireless Network Configuration and Selection Issues

Wireless NICs require an IRQ and I/O port address range, just as conventional NICs do. Other configuration and product-selection issues include the following:

- **NIC type**—With most wireless networks, you can choose PCI-based NICs for desktop computers and PC Card-based NICs for notebook computers. USB devices are also available. Although the speed of current wireless networks also permits the use of ISA cards, you should avoid these because this 16-bit card design is obsolete.

- **Network security and encryption**—For maximum security, select wireless network products that support either of these features:

  - A seven-digit security code called an ESSID. Wireless devices without this code can't access the network.

  - A list of authorized MAC numbers (each NIC has a unique MAC). A wireless device not on the MAC list can't access the network.

These features must be enabled to be effective. Also, use the strongest data encryption that your network supports. Many of the early versions of IEEE 802.11b network devices supported only the "weak" 40-bit encryption when introduced, but installable updates to "strong" 128-bit encryption should be available for most products. You should switch to strong encryption as soon as possible to provide another layer of network security.

Calculating the Cost per User for Your Wireless Network

The cost per user for a wireless network is affected by several factors, including the following:

- Whether your network requires access points

- How many access points your network needs

- What type(s) of NICs (ISA, PCI, PC Card, or USB) your network needs, and how many you need

- Whether your network needs to interconnect with wired Ethernet networks

Table 10.13 provides a worksheet that you can use to calculate the overall cost of your network and the cost per user. Use it to help determine the best wireless network for your needs and budget.

Table 10.13	Calculating the Cost of Your Wireless Network		
Cost Per Access Point	**Number of Access Points**	**Extended Cost**	**Extended Cost (Add This Column to Determine Total Cost)**
		>>	
Cost per PCI card	Number of PCI cards needed	Extended cost	
		>>	
Cost per PC Card	Number of PC Cards	Extended cost	
		>>	
Cost per USB port device	Number of USB Port devices	Extended cost	
		>>	
Total cost of network hardware (TC)			
Total number of PCI, PC Card, and USB devices (TN)			
Number of computers with built-in wireless network hardware (PCN)			
Add TN + PCN to determine total number of users (USERS)			
Cost per user (divide TC by USERS)			

If you need a separate wireless bridge to a wired network/broadband Internet device or a wireless print server, be sure to add the costs of these devices to the total cost of network hardware (TC) value before calculating the cost per user.

Typically, you can expect the cost per user of even the lowest-cost Wi-Fi LAN to average between $200 and $500 (based on one access point, two PC card adapters, one PCI adapter, and one USB adapter). Thus, the capability to roam with a notebook and to avoid wiring problems must be very critical to make up for the much higher cost of wireless Ethernet networking when compared to basic (and obsolescent) 10BASE-T Ethernet networks (which are comparable in performance to Wi-Fi).

HomeRF networks' cost per user is essentially the average of the costs of the wireless NICs because HomeRF doesn't need an access point. The only additional expenses would be for a wireless bridge (if desired), which is used to connect the HomeRF network to a broadband Internet device or other 10BASE-T–compatible Ethernet network.

TCP/IP Network Protocol Settings

TCP/IP is taking over the computing world, replacing the hodge-podge of competing protocols used earlier in networking (NetBIOS, NetBEUI, and IPX/SPX). TCP/IP is the standard protocol of the World Wide Web, as well as of the latest network operating systems from Novell (NetWare 5) and Microsoft (Windows 2000/XP). Even though it's used by both dial-up (modem) users and LAN worksta-tions, the typical configurations in these situations have virtually nothing in common. Use Table 10.14 as a guide to what must be set, and remember to record the settings that your TCP/IP connec-tions use.

Table 10.14 TCP/IP Properties by Connection Type—Overview			
TCP/IP	**Setting ("Dial-Up Card")**	**Modem Access ("XYZ Network Adapter")**	**LAN Access**
IP address	IP address	Automatically assigned by ISP	Specified (get value from network administrator)
WINS[1] Configuration	Enable/ disable WINS resolution	Disabled	Indicate server or enable DHCP[2] to allow NetBIOS over TCP/IP
Gateway	Add gateway/ list of gateways	None (PPP is used to connect modem to Internet)	IP address of gateway used to connect LAN to Internet

Table 10.14	TCP/IP Properties by Connection Type—Overview		
TCP/IP	**Setting ("Dial-Up Card")**	**Modem Access ("XYZ Network Adapter")**	**LAN Access**
DNS[3] Configuration	Enable/ disable host domain	Usually disabled, unless proxy server used by ISP	Enabled, with host and domain specified (get value from network administrator)

1. WINS = Windows Internet Naming Service; used on NT servers to automatically manage the association of workstation names and locations to IP addresses; used with DHCP (see note 2).

2. DHCP = Domain Host Configuration Protocol; sets up IP addresses for PCs connected to an NT network.

3. DNS = Domain Name System; matches IP addresses to Web site names through the use of name servers.

Configuring the Home Network

The primary purpose for a home network is increasingly the sharing of a single Internet connection, either via Internet Connection Sharing, or via a router connected to a switch or hub. Windows 98, Windows Me, and Windows XP Home Edition all contain Home Networking Wizards that configure home networks for you. Typically, these wizards do two things:

- Set up the computer that has an Internet connection as a Dynamic Host Configuration Protocol (DHCP) server, which can assign IP addresses to other computers on the network

- Set computers that will share the Internet connection to obtain their IP addresses automatically

After the wizards have been run on the home network computers, you can view the TCP/IP and other network settings, as discussed earlier in this chapter. The TCP/IP settings used by the computer that provides Internet access to other computers will be different from the settings used by the other computers.

Routers and TCP/IP

TCP/IP is unique among network protocols because it can be used on small self-contained networks as well as to connect computers (or entire networks) to the Internet, the world's largest network. A *router* makes it possible for TCP/IP traffic to be directed to either the Internet or another computer on a local area network.

When a computer is configured as a gateway (as with Microsoft Internet Connection Sharing, discussed in the section "Internet Connection Sharing (ICS)" of this chapter), that computer also acts as a router. Until recently, self-contained hardware routers were too expensive and too complex to be used on most small-office and home networks for Internet sharing. Now, vendors of small-office/home-office network hardware such as Linksys, D-Link, Netgear and others produce TCP/IP routers, often combined with 10/100 Fast Ethernet switches, which are priced under $200 and provide high-speed Internet sharing.

For more information on low-cost routers, see these vendors' Web sites:

- Linksys: http://www.linksys.com

- D-Link: http://www.dlink.com

- Netgear: http://www.netgear.com

TCP/IP Protocol Worksheet

Use the worksheet shown in Table 10.15 to track TCP/IP settings for either a network card or a dial-up connection. The settings are based on the Networks icon in Windows 9*x*. The first worksheet is blank; the second worksheet lists typical (fictitious) settings for a workstation on a LAN.

Table 10.15   TCP/IP Protocol Settings Worksheet

IP Address					
Address	Subnet	Automatically Assigned			
WINS Configuration					
Enable/ disable	Primary WINS Server	Secondary WINS Server	Scope ID	Use DHCP for WINS resolution	
Gateway (list in order; top = first)					
First	Second	Third	Fourth	Fifth	Sixth
Bindings that will use this protocol (list)					
Advanced (list)					
Use TCP/IP as default					
DNS Configuration					
Disable/ Enable DNS	Host	Domain			
First DNS server	Second DNS server	Third DNS server	Fourth DNS server	Fifth DNS srver	Sixth DNS server
First domain suffix	Second domain suffix	Third domain suffix	Fourth domain suffix	Fifth domain suffix	Sixth domain suffix

Table 10.16 shows how TCP/IP protocols could be set up to enable Internet access via a LAN in an office building. If you use TCP/IP for both Internet and LAN access as your only protocol, your settings will vary. Also, the settings for computers that receive Internet access via a router or some form of Internet Connection Sharing will vary from the settings used by the computer that provides Internet access.

Table 10.16   Completed TCP/IP Protocol Settings Worksheet—LAN Connection

IP Address

Address	Subnet	Automatically Assigned	Notes
192.168.0.241	255.255.255.0	No	If automatically assigned = "Yes", no values are used for either address or subnet

WINS Resolution

Enable/ Disable	Primary WINS Server	Secondary WINS Server	Scope ID	Use DHCP for WINS Resolution	Notes
Disable	(blank)	(blank)	(blank)	(blank)	If "disable", no values for other fields

Gateway (list in order; top=1st)

First	Second	Third	Fourth	Fifth	Sixth
192.168.0.1	192.168.0.2	(blank)	(blank)	(blank)	(blank)

Bindings That Will Use This Protocol (list)

Client for Microsoft Networks enabled	File and print sharing for Microsoft Networks* disabled	Note *This is a very dangerous setting. This might be listed as an option, but do not enable it if you use another protocol for your LAN. Enabling this setting would allow anybody on the Web access to your system.

Advanced (list)

Use TCP/IP as default	Other value(s)	Note *This network also uses NetBEUI for internal LAN communications; if TCP/IP were the only protocol, it would be enabled as the default.
Disabled*	(None)	

DNS Configuration

Disable/ Enable DNS	Host (list)	Domain
Enabled	smithy	Biz-tech.com

First DNS server	Second DNS server	Third DNS server	Fourth DNS server	Fifth DNS server	Sixth DNS server
192.168.0.1	(None)	(None)	(None)	(None)	(None)

Table 10.16   Completed TCP/IP Protocol Settings Worksheet—LAN Connection Continued

First Domain Suffix	Second Domain Suffix	Third Domain Suffix	Fourth Domain Suffix	Fifth Domain Suffix	Sixth Domain Suffix
(None)	(None)	(None)	(None)	(None)	(None)

Troubleshooting Networks

Use Tables 10.17 and 10.18 to help you find solutions to common networking problems.

Troubleshooting Network Software Setup

Table 10.17   Troubleshooting Network Software Setup

Problem	Symptoms	Solution
Duplicate computer IDs	"Duplicate computer name" message at startup	Make sure that every computer on the network has a unique ID (use Control Panel, Network, Identification to view this information). Set the ID before connecting to the network.
Workgroup name doesn't match	Other workstations not visible in Network Neighborhood	Make sure that every computer that's supposed to be working together has the same workgroup name.

Different workgroup names actually create different workgroups, and you'd need to access them by browsing via Entire Network. |
| Shared resources not available | Can't access drives, printers, or other shared items | Make sure that shared resources have been set for any servers on your network (including peer servers).

If you can't share a resource through Windows Explorer on the peer server, make sure that File and Printer Sharing has been installed. |
| Changes to configuration don't show up | Network doesn't work after making changes | Did you reboot? Any change in the Network icon in Windows Control Panel requires the system to be rebooted with Windows 9x/Me.

Did you log in? Network resources can't be accessed unless you log in when prompted. You can use Start, Shutdown, Close All Programs, and log in as a new user to recover quickly from a failure to log in. |

Troubleshooting Networks in Use

Table 10.18	Troubleshooting Networks On-the-Fly	
Problem	**Symptoms**	**Solution**
Connection to network not working for one user	Other users can use shared printers, drives, and so on.	First, have the user use Start, Close All Programs, and log in as a new user. Pressing Cancel or Esc instead of logging in keeps the user off the network.
		Use Network Neighborhood or My Network Places to browse other computers on network. If browsing won't work, make sure that the correct Network name is listed in the properties and that the correct protocols and protocol configurations are present. All computers in a workgroup must use same the workgroup name and protocol(s). If TCP/IP protocol is the only protocol used, either all computers must have an assigned IP address or one system must be configured to provide IP addresses to the other computers. If a router is used, it can be used to provide IP addresses to all computers.
		Next, check cable connections at the server and workstation.
		Check the NIC for proper operation. Use the diagnostics software provided with most cards to test NVRAM, interrupt, loopback, and send/receive signal functions. Use the diagnostics on two NICs on the same network to send and receive signals from each other.
		Use Windows Device Manager and check the NIC's properties. If any resource conflicts are present, the card won't work. Note that IRQ steering on PCI cards with recent chipsets enables multiple devices to share an IRQ without a conflict.
Connection to network not working for multiple users	No one can access the network.	Loose terminators or BNC T-connectors will cause trouble for all workstations on the Thinnet cable segment.
		Hub power or equipment failure will cause trouble for all stations using UTP.

Table 10.18	**Troubleshooting Networks On-the-Fly Continued**	
Problem	**Symptoms**	**Solution**
Have read-only access instead of full access	Files can't be saved to a shared drive.	If you save your passwords in a password cache, entering the read-only password instead of the full-access password will limit your access with peer servers.
		Try unsharing the resource and try to reshare it, or have the user of that peer server set up new full-access and read-only passwords. Or, don't use password caching by unchecking the Save Password box when you log into a shared resource.
		With a client/server network with user lists and rights, check with your network administrator because he will need to change the rights for you.

Troubleshooting TCP/IP

Use Table 10.19, in addition to the TCP/IP information presented earlier, to troubleshoot a TCP/IP connection on either a LAN or a dial-up connection.

Windows 2000 and Windows XP use a single networking wizard to configure both types of network connections. With other versions of Windows, TCP/IP configuration for LANs takes place in the Network icon in Control Panel, whereas modems are configured through the Dial-Up Networking properties sheet for a given dial-up connection.

Web browsers that communicate through proxy servers or gateways with the Internet also might require special configuration options. Use the Internet icon in Control Panel to adjust Microsoft Internet Explorer TCP/IP settings. With Netscape Navigator/Communicator, use Edit, Preferences, Advanced, Proxies to adjust proxy server settings.

Table 10.19   Troubleshooting TCP/IP Connections

Problem	Symptoms	Solution
Incorrect settings in network properties	Can't connect to any TCP/IP resources	Get correct TCP/IP settings from the administrator and enter; restart the PC.
Problem with server type or PPP version	Can't keep connection running in Dial-Up Networking	The wrong version of PPP might be running (classic CompuServe uses CISPPP instead of normal PPP); change the server type in the properties under Dial-Up Networking, not Networks.
Duplicate IP addresses	Error message indicates "the (TCP/IP) interface has been disabled" during startup	Duplicate IP addresses will disable both TCP/IP and NetBEUI networking if NetBEUI is being transported over TCP/IP.
One user to an IP address	Can't share the Web	If you're trying to share your Internet connection, use software such as Windows Internet Connection Sharing, third-party gateway or proxy server programs, or a router.

Windows 98 Second Edition, Windows 2000 Professional, Windows Me and Windows XP all can be configured as a gateway to enable Internet sharing from a cable modem, dial-up modem, ISDN, or DSL modem connection. For details, see "Internet Connection Sharing (ICS)", later in this chapter. |
| | Browser can't display Web pages | To verify that the TCP/IP connection works, open an MS-DOS window and type **PING** *websitename* (replace *web-sitename* with a particular IP address or Web site). If PING indicates that signals are returning, check the proxy settings in the browser. If PING can't connect, recheck your TCP/IP settings for the NIC or modem, and retry after making changes. |

Internet Connection Sharing (ICS)

Windows 98 Second Edition, Windows 2000 Professional, Windows Me, and the new Windows XP all feature a built-in gateway program called *Internet Connection Sharing (ICS)*, which allows users to share a single dial-up, ISDN, cable modem, or DSL connection.

Because ICS is a gateway and clients use TCP/IP networking to use the gateway, only the gateway computer needs to use Win98SE, Windows 2000, Windows Me, or Windows XP. Any computer using TCP/IP with the option to set up a gateway can be used as a client, including computers using older versions of Windows 9*x* and other operating systems.

Requirements for ICS

ICS requires a NIC to be installed in the host computer and a network connection to each guest computer to share the host's Internet connection.

If the Internet connection is made through a NIC (as is the case with DSL or two-way cable modem connections), two NICs are required: one for the Internet connection and one for sharing the connection.

ICS will not work with one-way satellite modems because these devices use a separate connection for downloading and uploading. Special configuration is required if you want to share DirecPC Telephone Return via ICS.

Overview of the Configuration Process

The configuration process has two parts:

- Installing ICS on the gateway computer
- Configuring the clients to use the ICS gateway to reach the Internet

Configuring ICS on the Gateway Computer with Windows 98SE or Windows Me

If ICS was not installed when Windows was installed, install it by choosing Start, Settings, Add/Remove Programs, Windows Setup. Select ICS from the Internet Tools category (Win98 Second Edition) or from the Communications category (WinMe).

Note

Windows Me will start the Home Networking Wizard as soon as you install ICS. The Home Networking Wizard performs the same tasks as ICS in the same sequence as discussed next.

Next, specify whether you are using a dial-up connection (modem or ISDN) or a high-speed connection (LAN, including cable modem or DSL).

If you select dial-up, choose the dial-up connection (which must already be configured) that you'll be sharing, followed by the NIC that connects you with the client PC's that will share the connection.

Windows will create a client configuration floppy and will prompt you to reboot the computer. When you view the Network Configuration in the Control Panel after rebooting, you should see the following:

- Three "adapters" (your actual NIC, the dial-up adapter, and a new one called Internet Connection Sharing)

- Three Internet Connection Sharing protocol entries, listing the previously mentioned adapters

- Three TCP/IP protocol entries, listing the previously mentioned adapters

The TCP/IP protocol entry for Home must point to the NIC that connects the clients to the host PC, the TCP/IP protocol entry called Shared must point to Dial-Up Networking, and the remaining TCP/IP protocol entry must point to Internet Connection Sharing.

Also, check the TCP/IP configuration for Home (the NIC) and verify the IP address; it should be 192.168.0.1. This IP address must be provided to the computers that will share the Internet connection. If the settings aren't correct, remove ICS and start over.

Start an Internet connection on the gateway (host) computer before continuing.

Configuring ICS on the Client Computers with a Windows 9x/Me Host

Although the ICS configuration process on the gateway (host) computer created a disk that can be used for setting up the ICS connection on client computers, most non-Microsoft sources advocate using manual configuration instead. The following steps are required:

1. Install the TCP/IP protocol on each client.

2. Set the Gateway option in the TCP/IP properties for each client's NIC to the IP address of the gateway (ICS) computer: 192.168.0.1 is the usual value (see the previous section of this chapter). Click Add to insert this value after you enter it.

3. Use a Web browser on each guest to verify that the connection is working; Internet Explorer should not have any dial-up settings configured for it and should have no LAN settings enabled. The ICS client for Windows 98 disk selects Use a Proxy Server here, which is not correct. Netscape Navigator/Communicator should be set to Direct Connection to the Internet.

4. Some versions of Netscape Navigator might not work unless you create a dial-up networking "adapter" on the guest and set its gateway, as previously discussed.

Reboot before you test the connection.

Setting Up ICS with a Windows 2000 or Windows XP Host Computer

Windows 2000 and Windows XP have built-in Internet Connection Sharing features. Log in as administrator before starting the following procedure. As with ICS for Windows 9x/Me, a LAN connection to the Internet must be shared by way of a second LAN card.

To share a connection, follow these steps:

1. Open the Network Connections icon in the Control Panel.

2. Right-click the connection that you want to share and select Properties.

3. Select the Internet Connection Sharing tab and enable sharing on your computer.

4. If this is a modem connection, you can select the Enable On-Demand Dialing check box on the same tab as Internet Connection Sharing. Enabling this feature launches the connection whenever other computers connected to this host computer need Internet access.

To connect to a shared connection on a Windows 2000 or Windows XP host, follow these steps:

1. Make sure that you are running Windows 9x, Windows NT, Windows 2000 Professional, or Windows XP on your client.

2. Verify that the NIC that connects your client to the host is set to do the following:

   • Obtain an IP address automatically

   • Use DHCP for WINS resolution

   • Connect to a DNS server automatically

(These settings require changes to the default settings for your NIC's TCP/IP properties.)

3. Adjust the Internet Explorer settings to the following:

- Never dial a connection

- Use a LAN connection

- Automatically detect settings

- Don't use automatic configuration script

- Don't use a proxy server

Note

Useful Web sites that cover this process for all versions of Windows in more detail include `http://www.practicallynetworked.com/sharing/ics/ics.htm` and `http://www.duxcw.com/digest/Howto/network/win98se/`.

The Microsoft Web page `http://support.microsoft.com/support/windows/faq/win98se/w98seics.asp` answers common questions about Win98SE.

If you want the additional benefits of a proxy server, check out products such as WinProxy (`http://www.winproxy.com`), WinGate (`http://www.wingate.deerfield.com`), and Sybergen SyGate (`http://www.sybergen.com`). Many home-oriented networks and modems are bundled with these or similar products, so if you're in the market for a new modem or are building a small network, ask whether a proxy server program for Internet sharing is included with your home or small-office networking kit.

The entire range of broadband Internet connections, including sharing and security issues, is covered in much more detail in *The Complete Idiot's Guide to High-Speed Internet Connections,* by Mark Edward Soper (Alpha Books, 2001).

Direct Cable Connections

By using the direct-connection features built into Windows and an appropriate cable, you can create an "instant network" in just a few minutes without installing any internal network hardware. Use this section to configure and troubleshoot direct connections.

Data-Transfer Cables

You can use four connection types for direct connections between computers:

- Serial ports

- Parallel ports

- USB ports

- IR (infrared) ports

However, with all but IR (which doesn't use a cable but emulates serial or parallel ports), you cannot use the normal cables that you would use for modems, printers, or other devices.

Serial connections require a *null modem cable.* A null modem cable is a special cable that has its circuits crossed so that the transmit data (TD) pin on each serial port connector leads to the receive data (RD) pin on the other. Many of these cables feature both DB-9F and DB-25F connectors for use with both XT-type and AT-type serial ports.

Parallel connections require a *parallel data-transfer cable,* which also crosses the send and receive lines at one end of the cable and has the DB-25M connector on both ends.

USB connections require a *USB direct connect* or file-transfer cable, which uses the same Type A male connectors used by USB devices such as mice and Web cameras. This cable differs from a plain Type A–to–Type A male USB cable by including built-in data-buffering and signal-boosting features to permit reliable data transfer between systems.

Cables such as these are usually available at computer stores that sell cables. They are sometimes called *LapLink* cables, after one of the first software products to introduce the concept of the Direct Cable Connection. The cables supplied with FastLynx and other data-transfer programs for MS-DOS and Windows 3.*x*/9*x*/Me will also work. A good rule of thumb is this: If the cable works for LapLink or the MS-DOS INTERLNK file-transfer utility, you can use it for Direct Cable Connection (known as Direct Serial or Direct Parallel Connections in Windows 2000/XP) as well. We recommend parallel or USB cables because the performance is much higher than with serial cables.

If you plan to use parallel-mode DCC frequently, consider purchasing a high-speed Direct Parallel Universal Fast from Parallel Technologies, creators of the Direct Cable Connection software for Microsoft (http://www.lpt.com). This cable also works with third-party remote-control and file-transfer programs, such as LapLink 2000 and PCAnywhere. This cable boosts performance significantly, especially on systems using ECP or EPP parallel ports; Parallel Technologies also sells high-speed USB file-transfer cables. USB file-transfer cables are available from Belkin (http://www.belkin.com) and Cables to Go (http://www.cablestogo.com) as well.

If you need additional features beyond those available with Direct Cable Connection, LapLink Gold (http://www.laplink.com) provides file-transfer and remote-control features for both direct wired connections and via networks, and it includes serial, parallel, and USB file-transfer cables. LapLink cables are also sold separately.

Direct-Connect Software

After you have the hardware in place, you need the proper software for the two systems to communicate. At one time, you had to purchase a third-party product (such as LapLink) to do this, but the capability is now part of most operating systems, including Windows 9x, Windows Me, Windows NT 4, Windows 2000, and Windows XP. One computer is designated the host, and the other is the guest. The software enables a user, working at the guest machine, to transfer files to and from the host. With Windows, you must specify which folders or drives you will share, and you have the option with Windows 9x, Windows Me and Windows XP Home Edition to specify a password. Windows NT, Windows 2000, and Windows XP Professional require that you add the guest user to your list of authorized users for the host system.

Setting Up Direct Cable Connections

The following sections cover the basic processes for installing direct connections with the most common Windows versions (Windows 9x/Me and Windows 2000/XP).

Setting Up and Using Windows 9x/Me Direct Cable Connection

On Windows 9x/Me, you click the Start menu and then select Programs, Accessories, Direct Cable Connection (on some systems it might be stored in a Communications folder beneath the Accessories folder). Then choose the Host option button. You are prompted to select the COM or LPT port to which you have connected the cable.

On the other computer, you select the same Direct Cable Connection menu item in Windows and choose the Guest option button. Again, you are prompted to choose the correct port, after which the software establishes a connection between the two machines. With the Windows Direct Cable Connection, you can either access the shared drive as a folder or map a drive letter to it with Windows Explorer after the connection is established. Windows 9x and DCC can use parallel, serial, or IR ports. Windows Me also can use a separate IR Link utility for initiating file transfers via the infrared port. You must have the same network protocol (we recommend NetBEUI) installed on both systems.

Setting Up and Using Windows 2000/XPDirect Parallel and Direct Serial Connections

In Windows 2000 and Windows XP, you use the same Network Connection Wizard used for other types of network connections to make the link. Most of the network setup work is already done if you also use modem or LAN networking with the computer. Before you start, ensure that the NetBEUI protocol has been installed. Open the Networks icon in the Control Panel, select your current network connection, and view its properties.

To create a connection, click Start, Settings, Network, and Dial-Up Connections. Open Make New Connection to start the wizard. If you are prompted for telephone information (area code and outside dialing code), fill in the information before continuing. If you don't fill this in, your connection options are limited.

To set up DCC, click Next on the first screen and then select Connect Directly to Another Computer. On the next screen, select Host or Guest. Then, on the following screen, select the parallel or serial port that you want to use (parallel is recommended).

Next, select the user whom you are granting access to from the list of authorized users. If the user to whom you want to grant access isn't listed, add him with the Users option in the Control Panel. Click Next and then Finish to complete the connection setup process. The system waits for you to make the connection.

Windows 9x, Me, NT 4, and 2000 systems can use their versions of DCC to connect to each other as either guest or host.

Windows NT 4 and Direct Cable Connections

Windows NT 4.0 can use only serial-port direct connections, and configuring the direct-connection feature is extremely difficult. The process is covered online at The World of Windows Networking Web site: http://www.helmig.com/j_helmig/dccnt4.htm. You might prefer to use a commercial product such as LapLink Gold to connect with a Windows NT 4–based system.

Using DCC

After a connection has been established, you can use the drive letters or folders representing the host system just as though they
were local resources. You can copy files back and forth using any
standard file-management tool, such as the DOS COPY command or
Windows Explorer. The only difference is that file transfers, of
course, will be slower than local hard drive operations.

DCC is the perfect way to install CD-ROM–based software to older
machines lacking such drives. You can install the DCC Host software on a notebook computer with a CD-ROM drive, install the
DCC Guest software on a desktop computer, cable them together,
and install the software. DCC is also the cheapest network around.

We've also used DCC to run tape backups remotely. We set up the
system that we wanted to back up as the host and logged into it as
guest with the computer containing the tape backup program. After
mapping the remote drive to a drive letter, we were able to back up
the files via a parallel LapLink-style cable.

Some users have set up DCC on machines using the TCP/IP protocol and have used it for game playing. For other advanced tricks,
you can perform with DCC, as well as cable diagrams. If you'd prefer to build your own cable, see the Web site
http://www.tecno.demon.co.uk/dcc/dcc.html.

Troubleshooting Direct Cable Connections

As Table 10.20 and the following checklist indicate, several places
exist where a Direct Cable Connection setup can go wrong. Use
this checklist and Table 10.20 to make this virtually free "network"
work best for you:

- Make sure that the same networking protocols are installed
  on both the host and the guest machines with Windows 9x,
  Me, NT, or 2000. The simplest protocol to install is NetBEUI,
  and that's what Parallel Technologies (creator of DCC) recommends for a basic DCC mininetwork. To configure
  NetBEUI, all you need to supply is the workgroup name
  (same for both guest and host) and a unique computer name
  for guest and for host. With Windows XP, you must install
  NetBEUI manually because this protocol is no longer supported by Microsoft (although it is supplied on the Windows
  XP CD-ROM; see the CD-ROM for details).

- Use the parallel (LPT) or USB ports for DCC when possible;
  although serial (COM) or IR port transfers will work, they are
  unbearably slow. Note that Windows Me refers to IR ports by
  their COM port alias in DCC, not specifically as IR ports.

- Ensure that both host and guest LPT ports are working correctly, with no shared IRQ problems. Use the Windows
  Device Manager to check for IRQ conflicts with the parallel
  port you're using. If you've never used the USB ports, make
  sure that they're working correctly. See Chapter 6, "Serial and
  Parallel Ports and Devices," and Chapter 7, "USB and IEEE-
  1394 Ports and Devices," for LPT and USB port troubleshooting.

- Make sure that the person using the guest computer knows
  the network name of the host computer (set through the
  Network's icon in the Control Panel's Identification tab).
  With a simple protocol such as NetBEUI, it might be necessary to enter the name to log into the host machine.

- If the user you want to connect to your Windows 2000,
  Windows XP, Windows NT host computer isn't on the list of
  authorized users, you'll need to add that user before you set
  up the direct connection.

- Install the Client for Microsoft Networks on the guest computer.

- Don't print to the printer(s) normally connected to the LPT
  port while you're using DCC; the printer will be set for
  offline mode and will require you to manually release the
  print jobs after you re-establish the printer(s). Also, allow any
  print jobs to finish (or hold them or delete them) on any
  port that you want to use for DCC before you set up your
  cables.

- Make sure that the host computer is sharing a drive so that
  the guest computer can copy files from it or move files to it.
  The sharing is accomplished in the same way that peer-to-
  peer network sharing is done on Windows 9x/Me systems;
  on Windows NT/2000/XP, you specify permissions for
  authorized users.

- If you don't want to unplug your printer to use DCC, you
  might want to add a second printer port for DCC use if you
  plan to use this option frequently or use the USB ports.

- Download the Direct Parallel Connection Monitor and troubleshooter from the downloads page at Parallel Technologies'
  Web site: `http://www.lpt.com/Downloads/downloads.htm`.
  This page also features many useful programs and links to
  other file-transfer and sharing products.

Use Table 10.20 to see whether you are ready to connect your computers via DCC.

Table 10.20   Direct Cable Connection-Type Configuration Requirements by Operating System

Operating System	Host Program	Guest Program	Network Components to Install	Port Types Supported
MS-DOS 6.x	INTERSVR.EXE	INERLNK.EXE	None	Serial, parallel
Windows 9x Windows Me	Direct Cable Connection (host and guest)	NetBEUI, MS Network Client	Serial, parallel, IR, USB	No
Windows NT4	Dial-Up Networking (host and guest)	Modem: direct serial connection NT Networking RAS NetBEUI	Serial	Yes
Windows 2000 Windows XP	Direct Parallel or Direct Serial connection (host and guest)	Networking RAS NetBEUI	Serial, parallel, IR, USB	Yes

1. Includes Windows 95, 98, Me, NT 4, 2000, and XP.

Username Required?	Passwords	Drive Mapping and Sharing	Connects with Other OS
No	No	Automatically maps all remote drives	MS-DOS or Windows command-prompt using INTERLNK/INTERSVR
Optional		Host must specify all 32-bit Windows' shares; mapping is optional on guest	
Yes		Host must specify all 32-bit Windows' shares; mapping is optional on guest	
Yes		Host must specify all 32-bit Windows' shares; mapping is optional on guest	

Chapter 11

Tools and Techniques

General Information

Use this chapter as a checklist to help you select the equipment that you need to solve computer problems more quickly and easily. Most of the items in the following lists have been mentioned in other chapters. Use these tools to help you get ready for battle with computer problems—and win!

Hardware Tools and Their Uses

Compare your toolbox's contents to the items listed in Table 11.1; if you are missing some items, sooner or later you'll wish you had them. Add them now. The list is divided into sections, enabling you to customize the toolkit for the types of service tasks you typically perform.

Table 11.1   Basic Hardware Tools Everybody Needs

Item	Purpose	Notes
Phillips-head and flat-blade screwdrivers; use no. 2 size for most jobs	Opening and removing cases and screws	Magnetic tips are okay if you keep them away from magnetic media (Zip, Jaz, Orb, SuperDisk, and backup tapes).
		Discard screwdrivers with worn tips.
		Use no. 1 size screwdrivers for attaching and detaching cables.
Hex-head drivers (assorted sizes)	Opening and removing cases and screws; tightening cable connectors on cards	Use in place of screwdrivers whenever possible.
Needle-nose pliers	Removing and inserting jumper blocks; removing cables; cutting cable ties; straightening bent pins	Most flexible tool in the basic toolbox; often omitted from low-cost "basic" toolkits.
		Buy an assortment of different sizes, offset heads, and so on for flexibility.

Table 11.1	Basic Hardware Tools Everybody Needs *Continued*	
Item	**Purpose**	**Notes**
Three-claw parts retrieval tool	Grabbing small parts such as jumpers and screws from motherboard	It's better than disassembling a PC to find a single screw!
Tweezers	Removing and inserting jumper blocks; picking up parts too large for parts retrieval tool; holding small parts for use	Typical set found in low-cost tool set, normally useless. Replace with one or both of these: eyebrow tweezers from drugstore or hemostat clamps from medical supply store.
Small flashlight	Illuminating dark places in case	Can be combined with magnifier; for bench use, get arm-mounted magnifier with light.
File	Gently trimming edges on drive faceplates or case edges	Get file with a very fine "tooth," and use it sparingly.
Wire cutter or stripper	Fixing damaged power cables or cutting away bad connectors	Check gauges to make sure your stripper can handle the small wires inside a PC. Never cut a wire unless the power is unplugged (not just turned off—because of power-management features in newer systems).
ESD (electrostatic discharge) protection kit	Attach wrist strap to you and cable to ground; unplug system before working inside	Comprises a mat for parts and the wrist strap for you; metal plate on wrist strap must be comfortably tight on your wrist to ground you properly.
Soldering iron	Used on conventionally soldered (not surface-mounted!) chips that have bad solder joints	Practice, practice, practice on "dead" boards before you solder a board that's worth fixing.

Table 11.1	Basic Hardware Tools Everybody Needs Continued	
Item	**Purpose**	**Notes**
Toothpick or thin wire	Probing the depth of screw holes	Helps you avoid damaging a drive by using a mounting screw that's too long.

Tools of the Trade—Drive Installation

Table 11.2 provides a list of tools and parts you'll need to install disk drives.

Table 11.2	Disk Drive Installation Tools and Parts	
Item	**Purpose**	**Notes**
Floppy drive cable	Used as replacement for suspected failures	Some newer Super I/O chips support drive A only.
		Use known, working parts rather than new and unknown parts.
		Use a five-connector cable if you need support for 5.25-inch drives.
IDE hard-drive cable (40-pin)	Used as replacement for suspected failures	Should be no more than 18-inch for use with UDMA drives.
		Check spacing between first and second drive connector if you want to use master and slave on drives in nonadjacent bays.
		Use known, working parts rather than new and unknown parts.
IDE hard drive cable with blue end (40-pin, 80-wire)	Used as replacement for suspected failures	Required for UDMA/ATA-66 and faster UDMA modes; provides higher signal quality for all other drives
		Connect blue end to mother-board.
SCSI ribbon and SCSI external cables	Used as replacement for suspected failures	Use 25-pin, 50-pin, or 68-pin depending on device needs.
		Use known, working parts rather than new and unknown parts.

Table 11.2	Disk Drive Installation Tools and Parts Continued	
Item	**Purpose**	**Notes**
Mounting screws	Attach drives to drive bays	Keep spares from existing or scrapped-out systems.
		Use the shortest screws that work because overlying long screws can destroy a drive.
Y-cable power splitters	Enables a single power connector to run two drives	Examine them carefully. Buy splitters with high-quality construction and wire the same gauge as the power supply.
Mounting frame	Puts 3.5-inch drives in 5.25-inch bay	Standard with most 3.5-inch retail-pack hard drives; save spares.
Digital multimeter (DMM)	Tests power going to drive and cable continuity	Test new and unknown cables before using them.
Spare battery for DMM	Keeps tester working	Keep in original blister packaging so it won't short out.
Jumper blocks	Adjust IDE drive configuration for master, slave	WD drives use the same jumpers as motherboards and add-on cards; some Maxtor and Seagate models use a smaller size.
Rails	Used for mounting 5.25-inch drives to some cases	Check compatibility because rail types vary—two rails per drive.

Tools of the Trade—Motherboard and Expansion Card Installation

Table 11.3 provides a list of helpful tools when installing motherboards and expansion cards.

Table 11.3	Motherboard and Card Installation Parts and Tools	
Item	**Purpose**	**Notes**
Stand-off connectors	Hold motherboard off bottom or side of case	Use existing stand-offs if in good condition. Buy the same size if they must be replaced.
Slot covers	Cover rear of case openings for card slots without cards	System cooling is affected if these are missing.
		Keep spares from scrapped systems or when adding cards.

Table 11.3   Motherboard and Card Installation Parts and Tools Continued

Item	Purpose	Notes
Jumper blocks	Adjust motherboard and add-on card configurations	Buy long-handled jumper blocks for easier configuration changes.
Digital multimeter (DMM)	Tests power going to motherboard and expansion slots	Use power supply case as ground.
Outlet tester	Quick plug-in tester for bad ground, other wiring faults	Finds real cause of "inexplicable" lockups and system failure—bad power.
POST testing card	Used to diagnose bootup problems	Use BIOS POST code tables[1] along with board.
IRQ/DMA testing card	Used to diagnose IRQ and DMA usage and problems	Can be combined with POST features on some models.
Spare Pentium, Pentium II, K6, or other CPUs	Used to test motherboard when no POST codes appear	Salvage low-speed versions from retired "junk" PCs. Be sure you jumper the host system appropriately and rejumper after reinserting original CPU.
Spare memory modules	Used to test motherboard that produces memory errors during POST	Salvage compatible small-size types from retired "junk" PCs. Two 4MB 72-pin SIMMs and one 16MB SDRAM DIMM can test most common PCs.

1. POST codes (also called hex codes) for popular BIOS versions are provided on the CD-ROM supplied with Upgrading and Repairing PCs, 13th Edition, and are also available from the Web sites of BIOS, system, and motherboard vendors.

Tools of the Trade—External Device and Networking Installation

Table 11.4 provides a list of tools and parts you'll need to install external devices and network cables.

Table 11.4   External Devices and Networking

Item	Purpose	Notes
Loopback plug for serial port	Used to test serial (COM) ports and cables	Buy or build to match your favorite diagnostic software. Buy or build a 25-pin version as well as a 9-pin if you want to test modem cables or if your systems have 25-pin serial ports.
Loopback plug for parallel port	Used to test parallel (LPT) ports and cables	Buy or build to match your favorite diagnostic software (see Chapter 6, "Serial and Parallel Ports and Devices"). Can aid in detection of IRQ usage.
IEEE-1284 cable	Known, working spare for all types of parallel printers	Buy 10-foot parallel cable to have extra distance in tricky cabling situations.
"Silver satin" cable	Known, working spare for modems and all-in-one units	Carry 10- to 15- phone foot cable at least (it's small).
RJ-45 network cable, Category 5	Known, working spare for Ethernet, Fast Ethernet, and Token-Ring networks	Use along with hub to test card and port. Use two pieces at 15 feet to 25 feet to make an impromptu network.
Crossover RJ-45 network cable, Category 5	Known, working spare for connections between broadband modems and PCs/routers	Can use this cable without a hub for direct connection between two PCs.
Five-port Ethernet hub 10/100 switch)	Known working connection for RJ-45 cable	Attach spare cable to hub/switch; speed (or check connection with lights.
USB cables and hub	Known, working spares for USB devices	Use powered hub. Have at least one A-to-A extension cable and at least one A-to-"B" device cable.
RS-232 breakout box	Analyzes serial signals for use in cable building and troubleshooting	Allows prototyping of a serial cable.
Device-specific cables	RS-232 modem, SCSI, parallel or serial switchbox, IEEE-1394 or others	Allows isolation of device-specific problems.

Tools of the Trade—Data Transfer

Use Table 11.5 to prepare to pull vital data from systems.

Table 11.5   Data-Transfer Tools, Parts, and Supplies

Item	Purpose	Notes
Parallel data-cable (LapLink or Interlink type)	Used with Interlink, Direct Cable Connection, or LapLink to move files without a network	Parallel transfer is preferred over serial because of speed advantage.
Null-modem serial cable (LapLink or Interlink type)	Used with Interlink, Direct Cable Connection, or LapLink to move files without a network	Parallel version is preferred. Carry this one as a fallback or for use with Windows NT.
USB data transfer cable	Used with Windows versions that Support USB (Windows 98, Me, 2000, XP)	Faster performance than either serial or parallel data-transfer cables; might require special software.
Drives and media		Select from the following, depending on the drive technologies you support: 3.5-Inch floppy 3.5-inch SuperDisk Zip 100 CD-R CD-RW DVD-ROM DVD-RAM SyQuest SparQ And so on.
Tape backup cartridges		You should carry two of each magnetic device and one of each optical device that you support for use as a backup for vital data.

Tools of the Trade—Cleaning and Maintenance

Table 11.6 provides a list of supplies that you should keep on hand for cleaning and maintaining PC hardware.

Table 11.6   Cleaning and Maintenance Supplies

Item	Purpose	Notes
Floppy drive cleaning kit	Removes gunk from read/write heads	Use wet-type cleaner. Not for use on SuperDisk drives!
		Works best when software-driven with a program, such as TestDrive.

Table 11.6	Cleaning and Maintenance Supplies Continued	
Item	Purpose	Notes
SuperDisk cleaning kit	Removes gunk from read/write heads of SuperDisk drives only	Use Imation-brand or Imation-approved kits.
Tape drive cleaning kit	Removes gunk from read/write heads	QIC models also can be used with QIC-wide and Travan. Consult drive manufacturer for service interval and approved cleaning kits.
Endust for Electronics	Effective surface cleaner for monitor cases, monitor glass, keyboards, and other PC parts	Blue and silver can. Never spray directly on object to be cleaned! Spray on lint-free cloth until damp, and then wipe.
Electronic contact cleaner	Stabilant 22a, CAIG ProGold, CAIG CaiLube MCL (contact vendors for product use details)	Great for lubricating and protecting contacts on card slots, disk drive connectors, and so on.
ESD-safe vacuum cleaner	Eliminates dust and gunk instead of blowing it around	Ensure that unit is designed for computer use.
Canned air	Used to clean out dust from power supplies, keyboards, and cases	Hold can at recommended angle; spread newspapers under and behind what you're cleaning to catch the junk you remove.
Foam or chamois cleaning swabs	Used for drive-head and contact cleaning	Use in place of cotton swabs, which shed.
Silicone sprays	Lubricates moving parts	Check label. Spray on swab and apply sparingly to item. Don't spray item directly.

Chapter 12

Connector Quick Reference

Serial Ports and Cables

Pin 1

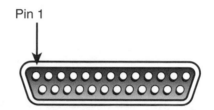

DB-25M 25-pin (XT-type) serial port.

Pin 1

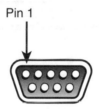

DB-9M nine-pin (AT-type) serial port. Also called a "digital camera port" on some systems.

Pin 1

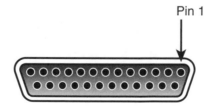

DB-25F 25-pin serial cable.

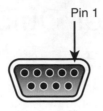

DB-9F nine-pin serial cable.

Parallel Ports

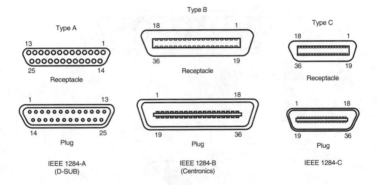

The three different types of IEEE-1284 parallel port connections. The Type A receptacle (DB-25M) is used on computers; The Type B receptacle is used on most printers. Some HP LaserJet printers use both Type B and Type C receptacles.

SCSI Ports

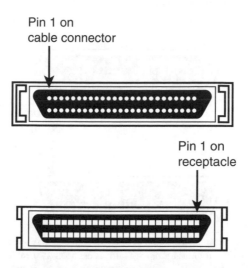

The SCSI HD-50M cable connector (top) and HD-50F receptacle (bottom) are the most common types of external SCSI ports used today; they are compatible with narrow (8-bit) external SCSI devices.

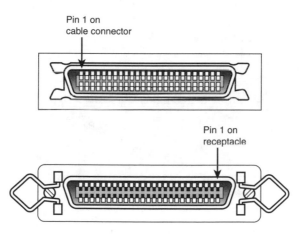

The traditional (Amphenol/Centronics) 50M cable connector (top) and 50F receptacle (bottom) are still widely used for external narrow SCSI devices.

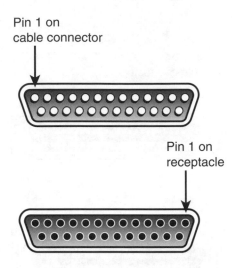

Some low-cost SCSI devices, such as low-cost SCSI adapters bundled with some scanners, and Iomega's Zip SCSI drives use a DB-25M cable connector (top) and receptacle (bottom) that are similar to Type A parallel ports. This cable works with narrow SCSI devices only and is not recommended unless the device cannot use the normal 50-pin cables.

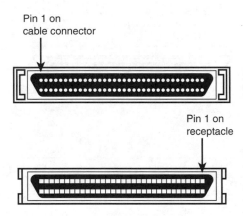

Wide SCSI HD-68M cable connector (top) and HD-68F receptacle (bottom) are used for Wide SCSI external devices.

USB and IEEE-1394 (FireWire)

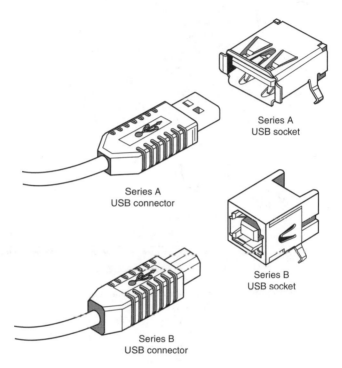

Series A
USB socket

Series A
USB connector

Series B
USB socket

Series B
USB connector

USB Type A and Type B ports and cables. Use a Type A–to–Type B cable to run between USB hubs and most USB devices.

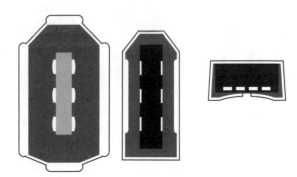

The IEEE-1394 six-wire receptacle (left) and cable (center). The four-wire cable (right) is used by DV camcorders and other devices that don't require power from the cable.

Keyboard and Mouse Ports

Five-pin DIN (top) keyboard connectors are common on Baby-AT mother-boards. Six-pin mini-DIN (middle) keyboard connectors are used on LPX and ATX-based systems, and are also used for a PS/2 mouse. See the markings on the system to determine which port is the mouse port and which is the keyboard port. The SDL connectors (bottom) are used to connect keyboard cables to the logic board inside the keyboard case.

Video Connectors
Video Ports

Video Card Connectors

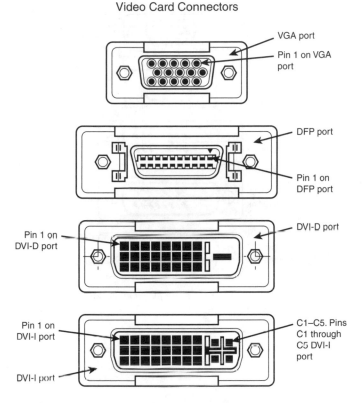

VGA, DFP, DVI-D, and DVI-I video receptacles (top to bottom).

Video Cables

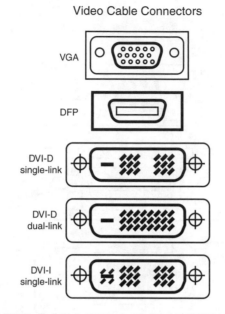

Video Cable Connectors

VGA, DFP, DVI-D single-link, DVI-D dual-link, and DVI-I single-link video cable connectors (top to bottom).

Sound Card Ports
Sound Card Basic External Ports

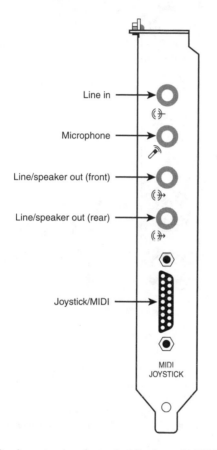

Line in

Microphone

Line/speaker out (front)

Line/speaker out (rear)

Joystick/MIDI

MIDI
JOYSTICK

Speaker out, microphone, dual line in, and MIDI/joystick port (top to bottom) are found on typical sound cards of all types.

DIGITAL DIN OUT
(Dolby Digital 5.1)

SPDIF IN
(digital audio)

SPDIF OUT
(digital audio)

MIDI IN

MIDI OUT

Some or all of these ports—digital DIN, SPDIF in, SPDIF out, MIDI in, and MIDI out (top to bottom)—can be found in various combinations on advanced sound cards. They can be mounted on a daughtercard bracket (shown here), attached to the rear of the sound card itself, or mounted on a box connected to the outside of the computer.

Sound Card Internal Connectors

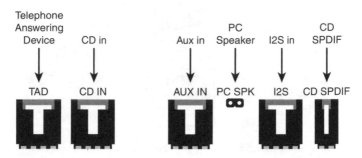

Typical internal sound card ports include, from left to right, a telephone answering device (TAD), for use with modems; CD in, for playing music CDs through the sound card speakers; Aux in, for connecting other devices; PC SPK, for playing PC speaker beeps through the sound card's speakers; I2S in, for playing DVD audio; and CD SPDIF, for playing digital audio from CD-ROM drives with SPDIF output.

Network and Modem Ports and Cables

RJ-45 Port and Cable

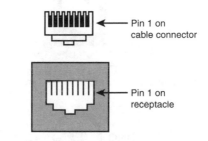

An RJ-45 cable connector (top) and port (bottom), typically used for UTP Ethernet/Fast Ethernet.

RJ-11 Port and Cable Connector

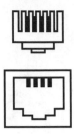

An RJ-11 cable connector (top) and port (bottom), used for modems and other telephone-wire applications such as HomePNA phone-line networks. Ports often are found in pairs, with one connecting to the telephone network and the other acting as a pass-through to a normal telephone.

Older Network Connectors

A DB-15f connector used for Thick Ethernet (10BASE-5) networks, usually found on the rear of a network card along with an RJ-45 or a BNC connector.

The BNC connector, used by Thin Ethernet along with a T-adapter. The adapter is used to connect the cable to the network card.

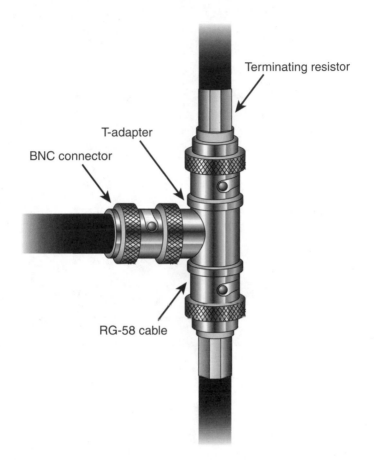

The BNC connector with T-adapter, resistor, and BNC (RG-58 Thin Ethernet) cable.

Index